ON BEING A MOTHER

MARY GEORGINA BOULTON

ON BEING

A Study of Women
with Pre-School Children

A MOTHER

TAVISTOCK PUBLICATIONS
LONDON AND NEW YORK

First published in 1983 by
Tavistock Publications
11 New Fetter Lane, London EC4P 4EE
Published in the USA by
Tavistock Publications
in association with Methuen, Inc.
733 Third Avenue, New York, NY 10017

© 1983 Mary Georgina Boulton

Typeset by Tradespools
Printed in Great Britain by
Richard Clay, The Chaucer Press,
Bungay, Suffolk

British Library Cataloguing in Publication Data

Boulton, Mary Georgina
On being a mother.
1. Mothers
I. Title
306.8'743   HQ759

ISBN 0-422-78540-7
ISBN 0-422-78550-4 Pbk

Library of Congress Cataloging in Publication Data

Boulton, Mary Georgina.
On being a mother.

Bibliography: p.
Includes indexes.
1. Mothers. 2. Mother and child.
3. Family. I. Title.
HQ759.B75   1983   306.8'743   83-9150

ISBN 0-422-78540-7
ISBN 0-422-78550-4 (pbk.)

CONTENTS

PREFACE

This book is a revised and shortened version of my doctoral thesis. In carrying out the research and writing the book I have received help and advice from a number of sources. I am grateful to Professor George W. Brown for his critical interest and guidance throughout the work and to members of the Social Research Unit at Bedford College for their support and encouragement. I would like to extend special thanks to the general practitioners and health visitors who helped me obtain my sample of mothers and to the women themselves who, despite the demands of child care, generously gave their time to what they felt was a worthwhile project. The research for this book was made possible by the financial support of the Commonwealth Scholarship Commission and the Canada Council; the Health Education Council helped with some expenses. Thanks also to Lilian Angell and Susan Hackett who typed drafts of this book with remarkable speed and efficiency. Finally, I am especially grateful to my husband, Ray Fitzpatrick, who has helped me in every way possible. Without his help and inspiration this book would never have seen the light of day.

PART ONE
INTRODUCTION

· 1 ·
PERSPECTIVES ON WOMEN AS MOTHERS

Introduction

One of the major developments that has marked sociology in the 1970s has been the sudden and rapid growth of interest in women's studies. There is now a substantial body of literature on the sociology of women, and the many new journals and publishers' series devoted to women's studies ensure that this will continue to grow. It is, therefore, very surprising to find that even now comparatively little has been written on the experience which dominates a large part of the lives of most women: motherhood and child care.

The importance of looking at this area, however, is clear. Eighty per cent of women become mothers (General Household Survey Unit 1978) and the evidence suggests that maternity is a difficult experience for many of them. The incidence of postnatal depression has been estimated at between 3 per cent and 24 per cent and the incidence of 'normal' Baby Blues is generally accepted to be much higher, at a staggering 50 per cent to 84 per cent (Dalton 1971; Steiner 1979; Oakley 1980). Furthermore, psychological distress associated with maternity is not a transient problem focused on the crisis of childbirth: a number of studies have shown disturbingly high rates of distress among women well beyond the post-partum period. In a study in Camberwell, Brown and his colleagues found that 31 per cent of working-class women with a child under six were clinically psychiatrically disturbed, in contrast to a rate of 15 per cent for the sample as a whole (Brown, Ni Bhrolchain, and Harris 1975; Brown and Harris 1978). Richman (1974, 1976,

1978) also concluded that 30 per cent of the women in her sample of mothers of three-year-olds in Waltham Forest had been 'significantly depressed' over the previous year. Similarly, Moss and Plewis (1977), in a study of mothers of pre-school children in areas of Camden and Paddington, found that in a twelve-month period as many as 52 per cent had suffered from moderate to severe distress at some time. This vulnerability of so many women to severe distress by virtue of their roles as mothers quite clearly suggests the need for research which looks at the social experience of women as mothers, and which throws some light on the problems involved in motherhood as a social role.[1]

Previous research on women's experience as mothers

What do we know already about women's experience as mothers? In a sense, we already know too much. On the one hand, 'everyone knows' that it is 'depressing' to stay at home with young children. On the other hand, 'everyone knows' that children are 'naturally rewarding' to their mothers. It is hardly surprising, then, that the nature of women's experience as mothers is the subject of vociferous debate. The controversies are couched in polemic terms and, particularly in uninformed discussion, people fall into one of two extreme camps: those who see motherhood as 'natural' and those who see it as a 'trap'. Those who see motherhood as natural argue that women are physically, psychologically, and emotionally equipped to bear and raise children and that doing so is experienced as the fulfilment of these inherent needs or tendencies. Those who see it as a trap argue that, because of their biological function of child bearing, women are restricted (by a male-dominated society) to the low-status, menial job of child care and that motherhood is experienced like other low-status, menial jobs as dull, demeaning, and restrictive. While these two positions are clearly vast oversimplifications, they can be traced back to more rigorous theories and research. The concepts used in these theories are much more subtle and the arguments presented much more complicated, but two opposing camps can still be distinguished: one couched in biological terms, the other in social terms.

BIOLOGICALLY BASED THEORIES

The theories which emphasize the biological basis of the mother role start by noting the importance of physical reproduction for the continuation of the species and by stressing the central role in this of the mother's care for her young. For animals whose offspring are born before they are physically able to take care of themselves, the mother's care is too important to be left to chance and so for 'adaptive purposes' a biological basis for it has evolved. This innate predisposition to care for her young is, in turn, the basis for a deep affective tie between mother and child.

There are two main schools which start from this position: the psychoanalytic school and the ethological school.

Psychoanalytic school

Psychoanalysis holds that the desire and capacity to mother is based on an innate, instinctual drive.[2] Alice Balint, for example, states that children are 'born as the realization of the *instinctual wishes* of their mothers. Pregnancy, giving birth, suckling and fondling are *instinctual urges* to a woman and these she satisfies with the help of her baby' (emphasis added) (Balint 1949: 119). Benedeck goes further in stating that the feminine personality is only an expression of this basic 'instinctual tendency to bear children' (Benedeck 1970b:137); Deutsch (1945) equates womanhood with mother-hood; and Winnicott (1975) sees the ability to mother children as 'constitutionally' either present or absent in an individual woman.

Psychoanalytic theory, then, implies that motherliness is a normal characteristic of a mature woman's femininity; that 'motherliness-in-action' is naturally rewarding; and consequently that the experience of dissatisfaction in motherhood is evidence of developmental problems in a woman and poor adjustment to her feminine psychosexual identity. Its approach is essentially an individualistic one, which focuses on the personality of each woman – the inner conflicts, anxieties, fantasies, and resentments which she *brings to* maternity – to account for her experience. It acknowledges features of her current social situation but does not see them as fundamentally important: its emphasis is, instead, on her biography and in particular on her early relationship with her mother and siblings.

(i) The mother-child relationship

The mother's relationship with her child begins during pregnancy, when her changing physical state encourages her to become more interested in herself – a process Winnicott (1956:302) describes as 'primary maternal preoccupation' – and to shift some of her sense of self onto the baby that is growing within her. When the baby is born, the mother's identification with him or her gives rise to *empathy*, the ability to assess delicately the needs and wants of the infant, which is the basis of 'good enough mothering'. The mother experiences the child as an extension of herself, at once part of her and yet separate, and there is a continuity of 'mutuality' of needs and interests between mother and child. Gratification of the needs and interests of one is at the same time gratifying to the other. Alice Balint writes:

> 'Thus, just as the mother is to the child, so is the child to the mother – an object of gratification. And just as the child does not recognize the separate identity of the mother, so the mother looks upon her child as a part of herself whose interests are identical with her own. *The relationship between mother and child* is built upon the *interdependence of the reciprocal instinctual aims . . .* i.e. what is good for one is right for the other also.'
> (Balint 1949:120)

From the psychoanalytic point of view, then, 'good enough mothering' of infants comes easily to normal women, because of their capacity (through maternal preoccupation) for empathy, and is inherently rewarding to them, because of the mutuality of their own and their children's needs.

The infant's first experience of the symbiotic mother-child relationship is the experience of 'primary love': a sense of being cared for without effort or criticism, of being continuous with and indistinguishable from his mother as caretaker. As the infant matures, however, it becomes necessary for him to differentiate himself from his mother and to establish his separateness, in order to develop his own ego. The mother must then be ready to let go of her identification with him and to cease meeting his needs intuitively. Her response to her child during this period is of great importance to the healthy development of his ego: if she does not empathize with him and he does not experience primary love, he will carry with him 'the experience of unthinkable or archaic anxiety' (Winnicott 1970: 255); on the other hand, if she cannot give up her identification with the infant, he will not be able to differentiate himself from her and establish his individuality.

In a normal woman, the intuitive and empathic basis of mothering declines naturally in time with the infant's growth and development and she comes to wait for an indication of need from the child before trying to meet it. She then relates to her child as *external* to herself, as a separate individual who must please her in order to earn her love, and yet also as still *part* of herself, as an individual invested with a great deal of her own ego and idealized ego. At this stage, then:

> 'the mother's relationship to her child, if it finally fulfils the maturational requirements, will have the distinctive characteristic of a freely changeable function . . . of narcissistic and object-libidinal strivings, so the child will always remain part of herself and at the same time always remain an object part of the outside world.'
> (Bibring *et al.* 1961: 71)

That is, the mother relates to the older child as one with whom she strongly identifies and in whom she sees (and loves) her own fantasies and hopes of attaining those ideals which she failed to realize herself:

> 'the child becomes for her the incarnation of the ego ideal modelled after the father which she set up in the past. . . . The narcissistic libido is displaced onto this newly erected ego ideal which becomes the bearer of all those perfections once ascribed to the father. . . . When projected onto the outside world, it *(the introjected object, i.e. the mother's (idealized) image of the child)* retains this character, for it continues to embody the subject's own unattained ideals. This is the psychological path by which, as Freud recognized, women attain from narcissism to full object love.'
> (Deutsch 1950: 174 and 176)

The child, for his part, expresses (through imitative behaviour and the like) his own omnipotent fantasies and his idealization of his mother and so reactivates within her further fantasies – fantasies of omnipotence remaining from her own childhood:

> 'the parent, identifying with the fantasies of the child, accepts the role of omnipotence attributed to him. The normal parent, in spite of his insight into his realistic limitations, embraces the gratifying role of omnipotence. It induces him to identify with his

own parent as he had anticipated being able to do in his childhood fantasies. . . . The parent derives from the process of preoedipal identifications the reassurance that he is a good parent, and even more, the hope that he is or can be better than his parents were.'
(Benedeck 1970a: 128)

From the point of view of psychoanalytic theory, then, the mother's experience of her relationship with her older child is largely the re-experience of fantasies, hopes, dreams, and ideals set up but not attained over the course of her life. It is, again, an inherently rewarding experience – for a time at least – because through the child the mother has new hope of vicariously attaining these ideals and of living out her fantasies.

(ii) Maternity as a developmental phase

Cross-cutting its treatment of the mother-child relationship is the psychoanalytic view of maternity as an integrative stage in the woman's own ego development.

In motherhood, a woman relives the mother-child relationship of her own past. She identifies with both her child (re-experiencing herself as the 'cared-for-child' and sharing with her child the protection of a mother) and her own mother, or the mother she would have liked to have had (caring for her child). This dual identification, however, reactivates all the woman's unresolved conflicts and anxieties developed in relation to her own mother during her childhood. These are re-experienced and expressed in her relationship with her children, to whom she relates in terms of the self-representations, object-representations, and other aspects of her psychic structure developed in the course of her life. She may, for example, act out in her dealings with her child her desire to get back at her own mother for (fantasized) harm done to her as a baby, or her desire to make up for (also fantasized) harm she did to her siblings in childhood. Chodorow notes the different ways in which a woman's psychic structure affects her behaviour and experience as a mother, pointing out that this process changes over the course of the mother-child relationship as new anxieties and conflicts are revived (see also Bowlby 1958a):

'One mother, for instance, may delight in the earliest mothering experience, when she can attend to her infant's earliest needs and

then withdraw and be rejecting when the child becomes more independent. Another may behave in exactly the reverse manner. Both alternatives depend on the associations and (unconscious) memories and feelings related to these issues in each's own infancy.'
(Chodorow 1978: 90)

The main effort of clinical practice has concentrated on the pathologies in the mother-child relationship, which arise from the reactivation of old feelings and conflicts in the mother and result in developmental problems in the child. Psychoanalytic theory, however, holds that for the most part women are able to develop and grow psychologically by re-experiencing and *resolving* in motherhood these unresolved conflicts. As Deutsch elaborates, 'Successful mastering of the past is a prerequisite for women's psychic health; otherwise, new situations provoke new traumas. . . . The reproductive experience gives woman the opportunity to master old anxieties by mastering new ones' (Deutsch 1945: 49–50). Once again, then, psychoanalytic theory sees maternity as an essentially positive experience for women, providing them with the opportunity for final resolution of conflicts and integration of the ego.

In summary, psychoanalytic theory views motherhood as the culmination of a woman's psychosexual development. It represents the fulfilment of instinctual urges and, in the resolution of underlying developmental conflicts, the final stage in maturity. For the majority of women it is an inherently fulfilling experience.[3] For those who do not find fulfilment in motherhood, psychoanalytic theory would look to their personal biography for an explanation and point to unresolved developmental conflicts as the underlying causes. That is, it sees lack of fulfilment essentially as an individual personality problem: a problem of inadequate adjustment by women to their feminine psychosexual identity.[4]

(iii) Discussion

Psychoanalytic theory provides an analytical account of women's experience of motherhood, which concentrates on delineating the psycho-dynamic processes involved. While this focus may highlight and account for psychological aspects of the mother-child relationship, it is only a partial treatment of women's experience as mothers which, as psychoanalysts themselves acknowledge, extends well beyond this. In relation to women's *subjective* experience of motherhood, psychoanalytic theory provides relatively little insight. Much of its analysis is in terms of unconscious feelings and thoughts and even the conscious experiences of women are organized in a way that they would not necessarily recognize themselves. It is also presented on an abstract level, in terms of general themes in a woman's experience and the overall pattern of her relationship with her child, and it gives little idea of the way in which the gratifications it describes are translated from the specific experiences of women's daily lives.

Indeed, because of its approach the question of women's experience as mothers is lost to psychoanalytic theory as a subject of study. In its frame of reference the meaning of children – the fantasies and identification they engender – and the nature of a mother's relationship with them are abstracted from a woman's experience as a mother and are seen as causally related to it. A woman's experience as a mother then becomes merely an empirical indicator of her underlying developmental conflicts and anxieties: it is these conflicts and anxieties that are the real subject matter of psychoanalysis.

Psychoanalytic explanations of women's experience are explanations at the level of the *individual*: personality organization and ego functions (e.g. Breen 1975) and personal biographies (e.g. Chertok 1969) are used to account for differences among women. No attempt is made to go beyond differences between individuals to account for similarities of experience within groups or differences between groups. This is in part because psychoanalytic theory, as a theory of developmental psychology, under-emphasizes current social factors in women's experience. By seeing women's experience of child care as essentially an expression of their personal biography and resulting psychic structure, psychoanalytic theory over-emphasizes the influence of intrapsychic processes on daily experience and ignores the opposite. That is, it stresses that the meaning of an activity and the quality of her relationship with her child inform a woman's daily experience in looking after her child, but it does not suggest that the opposite happens to any significant degree: that the daily experiences of looking after a child in a given social and physical environment inform a woman's relationship with her child and the meaning of child care activities.

For the most part, psychoanalytic theory has developed from clinical experience rather than from systematic investigations (Deutsch 1945; Benedeck 1959, 1970; Winnicott 1975). This clinical work seems to have been primarily with pregnant women and women with infants rather than older pre-school children. Those research studies that have been done tend also to focus on pregnancy and childbirth (Brody 1956; Grimm 1967; Chertok 1969; Breen 1975; Gordon 1978): maternity is seen as the 'culmination' of women's psychosexual development and with their response to childbirth and the care of infants psychoanalysis ends its consideration of women as mothers. The relationship between mothers and their older children is recognized to be problematic, but for the most part psychoanalysis looks at it from the point of view of the child and largely neglects the experience of the mother (Anthony and Benedeck 1970; Dally 1978).

Ethological school

Like psychoanalysis, ethology has been used to argue that a mother's care for her child is 'natural' and 'naturally rewarding'. In addition, the principles and methods of ethology have been used by psychoanalysts and developmental psychologists and this research, too, has contributed to the view of the mother-child relationship as unproblematic for 'normal' women.

Ethology holds that a mother animal's motivation to look after its young derives from the intense tie or *bond* between mother and offspring (Kaufman 1970; Trause, Klaus, and Kennell 1976). Evidence for such a tie comes from observations made in a variety of species of the way mothers behave towards their young (Rheingold 1963): that is, while their offspring are young and dependent, mothers engage in such activities as cradling, holding in ventral-ventral contact, grooming, restraining, and retrieving, and they do so with great intensity and painstaking care. Rejection and punishment gradually replace these maternal activities as the young grow more independent, suggesting that bonds may weaken as maternal care becomes less necessary for the survival of the young. Observations of special recognition and enduring proximity-seeking between mothers and adult females with infants of their own, however, also suggest that they may not disappear entirely (Harlow, Harlow, and Hansen 1963; Hansen 1966).

The *bond* between mother and offspring which ethologists describe has generally been taken by those studying human relationships to equate with the *love* between a woman and her child. Bowlby, for example, makes this connection quite explicitly, saying 'It is common knowledge that affectional bonds and subjective states of strong emotion tend to go together. . . . Thus, in terms of subjective experience the formation of a bond we describe as falling in love, maintaining a bond as loving someone' (Bowlby 1973: 40). The motivation to care for her child is therefore seen to arise from a woman's love for her child, which is also seen as transforming her experience of child care from that of irritation or boredom into that of deep emotional fulfilment. Leach, for example, while arguing that love must be complemented and supported by *interest* appears to agree with those who suggest that this makes child care enjoyable and fulfilling. 'Of course most mothers do love most of their children' she writes; 'of course it is love which makes much of their mothering possible and enjoyable and of course this is why the parallel with any other creative career is far from complete' (Leach 1979: 91). Such a view implies that the bond or love between mother and children makes a woman's experience in looking after them intrinsically rewarding. It also implies that when her experience is not rewarding it is because she has not established adequate bonds with her children: that is, because she does not love them.

In accounting for a woman's experience as a mother, then, ethology and its associated branch of psychology focus on the strength of a woman's bond with her children, which she forms when they are born and which is a constant feature in her relationship with them thereafter. Her current circumstances are recognized as important in interfering with the expression of her bond but the main emphasis in explaining frustration or dissatisfaction is on the early months of motherhood and in particular on the circumstances surrounding an infant's birth which may have led to a failure in bonding.

(i) Bonding

The intense mother-child tie that is the key feature in motherhood, according to ethology, is forged through the process of bonding. Initially, there is a mutual attraction between mother and infant based on biological stimuli: the infant presents 'pleasing' visual, auditory, kenesthetic, or chemical cues that attract the mother and elicit responses from her that are in turn attractive and pleasing to the infant. Thus, mother and infant are initially mutually attractive and satisfying to each other in biological terms.

This biological attraction keeps them in intimate contact for a period immediately after the birth, during which time the close physical contact and the intimate personal experience shared between them give rise to a different sort of bond: the initial biologically based bond becomes elaborated into a social bond 'in which *meanings* rather than the immediate physiological effects of stimuli are functional' (Kaufman 1970: 26).

Bonds are not formed automatically as a mother's instinctive reaction to her child but are established through mutually satisfying interaction in which each responds to the other in ways which are biologically or socially rewarding. Such responses are themselves not automatic or inevitable. While a female is genetically pro-grammed to respond to her offspring, the nature and extent of her response is influenced by a number of other factors, both biological and social. Harlow, Harlow, and Hansen (1963) suggest three sets of factors which affect a mother's responsiveness to her offspring: cues from the infant; experiential variables, especially the mother's own experience with her mother in infancy and her experience with previous offspring; and endocrinological factors relating to preg-nancy, childbirth, lactation, and the resumption of the normal ovulatory cycle. By influencing the way in which a mother responds to her infant, these factors affect the nature of the interaction between them and hence the strength of the bond.

(ii) Psychology and ethology

The research of ethologists proved to be of great interest to a number of psychologists who have adapted the findings and research methods of ethology to their own concerns (Bowlby 1957, 1969; Ainsworth 1969). Most notable of these are John Bowlby and Mary Ainsworth who, along with colleagues at the Tavistock Clinic, have done a great deal of work on the process of bonding or 'attachment' (Bowlby 1958b). While taking the methods of ethol-ogy they have retained a psychoanalytic perspective, using psychoanalytic insights and explanatory theory and reflecting psychoanalytic interests by focusing on the child. A number of other psychologists have also observed mothers and infants but here, too, virtually all work has concentrated on the child and relatively little on the mother. What has been done, however, suggests that the process of bonding in human mothers is similar to that in other species and is influenced by the same sets of factors:

physiological features in the mother; cues from the infant; and the mother's previous experience. These factors influence the strength of the bonds a woman forms with her children and hence the nature of her experience in looking after them.

The literature on the physiological factors influencing maternal responsiveness has been reviewed by Rossi (1977) who concludes that there are endocrinological and genetic features in women which facilitate bonding.[5] For example, in response to her baby's cry a mother produces oxytocin, which stimulates nipple erection and encourages the intimate and mutually satisfying interaction of breastfeeding. Similarly, a mother responds to her infant's alternating attention by 'holding' him with both voice and gaze and this unlearned response again gives rise to rewarding interaction between them (Brazelton, Koslowski, and Main 1974). Although these factors can break down, as when hormonal imbalance follows childbirth, for most women they facilitate rewarding interaction with their infants and so ensure that they form adequate bonds with them.

The second set of factors influencing bonding are cues from the infant. These include the distinct physical appearance of the infant (a large head in proportion to body size; a large and protruding forehead in relation to the rest of the face; large eyes relative to face size; eyes positioned below the horizontal midline of the face; round protruding cheeks) and his expressive behaviour, most particularly his smile and his gaze (Bowlby 1969; Stern 1977). Smiling, gurgling, eye contact, and the like instigate and maintain social interaction between a mother and her child (as distinct from caregiving, instigated by crying, fussing, and the like) which is intrinsically rewarding for her and which enhances bonding (Bell 1974). By engaging his mother's eyes in his gaze, the infant conveys his personal recognition and acknowledgement of her and elicits from her a response of strong identification and commitment; his automatic smile in response to the visual cues of her face conveys interest, preference, and valuation and calls for a response of reciprocal acceptance and responsibility from his mother (Tomkins 1965; Robson 1967; Freedman 1974). When such cues are not forthcoming from the infant, however, (as in the case of blind babies or babies who are excessively fussy or irritable) there is little rewarding social interaction and a mother's attachment may be weak.[6]

The final set of variables affecting responsiveness and bonding is the mother's own experience. For a mother to become attached to her infant and so want to look after him, she must have some sort of basic capacity to relate to others, which is probably developed through forming an attachment to her own mother in childhood. A number of studies of child abuse and neglect suggest that women who do not form an adequate relationship with their children themselves had an inadequate relationship with their mothers (Gil 1973; Kempe and Kempe 1978).

It is clear then, that bonding is not a simple or instinctive response to a child, but a complex process involving the interaction of many factors both biological and social. While under appropriate circumstances bonding occurs smoothly, ethologists and psychologists emphasize that the circumstances surrounding early mother-child interaction are very important. Childbirth is a culturally organized event and the way it is organized in any society can inhibit or distort the development of bonds between mother and child by interfering with the natural sequence of triggers between them (Klaus and Kennell 1976). It is this weak or distorted bond that is seen as responsible for whatever difficulties or dissatisfaction may be experienced in looking after the child in later years.[7]

Even when bonds have been firmly formed, the social and physical circumstances of the mother and child are important influences on the way they are expressed. Ainsworth, Bell, and Stayton (1974) suggest that both the physical environment in which children are brought up and the cultural prescriptions of child rearing interfere with attachment behaviour in children. The implication is that they also distort a mother's behaviour and cause stress in her life and an impoverishment of her relationship with her children. Blurton Jones (1974b) spells this out quite clearly in delineating the difficulties English society, in comparison with Bushman society, puts in the way of mothers: the isolation of English mothers from other adults, their lack of support from older women, the topographical arrangements of the home that physically isolate mother from child, and the close spacing of births creating physical and psychological strains in the mother, all are at odds with the way child care was organized in our 'environment of evolutionary adaptedness' and are likely to affect their experience of motherhood negatively.

In summary, ethology and its associated branch of psychology see bonding, or the formation of an attachment between mother and child, as a natural and normal process. The consequence of bonding is a strong motivation in the mother to look after her children and, the psychologists would add, the experience and expression of love in the act of caring. For a 'normal' woman under 'natural' circumstances, then, her bond with her child ensures that motherhood is not problematic. A number of factors in the mother, child, or social situation, however, can disrupt the natural bonding process and inhibit the establishment of adequate bonds. Further features in the organization of child care can make difficult the 'natural' expression of attachment and so lead to frustration, conflict, and distress in child care. Thus, if there are difficulties in women's experience as mothers, psychologists of this school would suggest that either bonds were never formed or that features in the organization of child care have inhibited their natural expression.

Like the psychoanalytic school, the ethological school sees a woman's experience as a mother largely in terms of characteristics endogenous to the woman: in this case, her attachment to or love for her children. The formation and the expression of this attachment may be substantially influenced by social and physical circumstances but these are secondary factors: the primary factors are, first, the innate predisposition to form a bond and, later, the strength (or absence) of that bond in the mother. These characteristics inherent in the woman herself are the fundamental features shaping her experience as a mother. In contrast to psychoanalysis, this school of psychology emphasizes current social factors throughout her relationship with her children, but like psychoanalysis it takes an essentially individualistic, psychologistic stance in accounting for her experience as a mother.

(iii) Discussion

Ethology provides a descriptive account of maternal care in terms of a theory of 'bonding', but it provides little insight into the subjective experience of women looking after young children: it is *behaviour* rather than *experience* that is of interest to ethologists. Most ethological studies are of rates and changes in rates of behaviour and no attempt is made to draw out the subjective experience of the mother which may be expressed in that behaviour (Blurton Jones 1972; Devore and Konner 1974). This is, of course, 'brought about originally by the futility of trying to empathize with animals' (Blurton Jones 1974a: 285). Ethological studies, then, say nothing about the way the maternal behaviour is *experienced*. The evidence of attachment behaviour, however, is used to postulate the existence of 'affectional bonds' between mother and offspring which in human society are called 'love' (Ainsworth 1969; Bowlby 1973; Klaus and Kennell 1976; Leach 1979). In the view of some developmental psychologists, then, it is the mother's love for her children which motivates her child care activities and it is her love for her children which makes her experience in caring for them intrinsically rewarding.

Since it is on the basis of her behaviour that her love for her children is itself hypothesized, this explanation for her behaviour and experience seems somewhat tautological. The definition of love in terms of maternal behaviour also seems too narrow to be useful: from the mother's point of view, love may be experienced independently of its expression in behaviour towards the child. Furthermore, it seems entirely probable that maternal behaviour – the basis for postulating her love – can be accompanied by feelings of anger, hostility, frustration, irritation, resentment, or indifference. What are the salient feelings here? On the other hand, love may not be expressed in fondling, kissing, and cuddling (Klaus and Kennell 1976), or in retrieval and holding (Bowlby 1969), or in other classic 'maternal behaviours' when cultural norms prohibit them. Does this mean that the women do not love their children?

Virtually all of the research on bonding has focused on the child and the child's attachment to its mother, probably because the observational methods of ethology are particularly well suited to studying children who, like animals, cannot talk about their behaviour or experience. Unfortunately, this seems to have led to a good deal of child-centred thinking being imposed on views about the mother's attachment to her child. A mother's relationship with her child, however, is not simply a mirror image of the child's relationship with her. A young child is totally dependent on its mother. She is the centre of his or her world; the child has not yet incorporated a symbolic meaning system and responses are still closely programmed by genetic make-up. For these reasons, there may be value in seeing the child's attachment behaviour as reflecting its 'love' for its mother. An adult woman, on the other hand, has a life independent of her child and continues to live in a much broader world of her own after it is born. She relates to her children within the context of this wider world and both the demands it makes on her and the meanings she derives from it. Her maternal behaviour – and her experience of motherhood – may well reflect these features of her wider world rather than just her love for her child.

Bonding is important because it is a reliable way of ensuring that mothers care for their defenceless offspring. But its importance should not be overestimated. There are many other ways of ensuring care of the young and in human societies the social forces directed towards this may be more important than the biological forces in bonding. It must also be remembered that the mother-infant bond ensures only a motivation to care for the young: it does not ensure enjoyment, rewards, or emotional gratification in doing so. Indeed, the care which is motivated by the mother-infant bond may be given under social and physical conditions which can make it difficult, stressful, or impossible: in this sense, the bonds could be said to be the basis for intense frustration or anguish.[8]

SOCIALLY BASED THEORIES

In contrast to the biologically based approaches of psychoanalysis and ethology are the social perspectives of sociology and social anthropology. Implicit in these social perspectives is the view that social institutions are of paramount importance in meeting man's needs and shaping his behaviour. Through the products of culture and social organization man can rise above biological limitations and devise new ways of ensuring the care of the young and the continuation of the species. Thus, it is largely society which shapes a woman's relationship with her children and influences her experience as a mother.

Sociology and social anthropology hold that the desire and capacity to look after children are largely socially created. Western industrial society is organized in such a way that it is necessary for the biological mother to look after her own children, or at least to take responsibility for ensuring that her children are looked after. Society therefore engenders in women the desire and capacity to do this. Other societies are organized in such a way that other people, for example the grandmother or the eldest daughter, look after her children, either on their own or with the help of the biological mother (Whiting 1963; Minturn and Lambert 1964; Oakley 1972; Friedl 1975). In these societies the desire and capacity to look after children is engendered in others besides the biological mother. Moyo describes such a system in Matabeleland:

'In kraals the oldest of the sisters in any one family group adopts the title "mama-omdala", vaguely translated as "big mother", "mother-the-big". She is responsible for the bringing up not only of her own children but also those of her younger female siblings and of her daughter's children. . . . Children are breast-fed for about ten to twelve months. But as soon as a child is weaned from the breast it goes to its grandmother. . . .

There is no distinction between a biological mother and her sisters and female cousins who are also "little mothers" to "her" child. The child uses the same term to describe them all, "mama" which means mother. The only distinction is between the "big mother" and the rest, "big mother" being the functional one and all the alternative mothers are just referred to as "little" mothers. . . . It is thought unnatural for the biological mother to show more interest in "her" child than in those of her sisters and cousins.'

(Moyo n.d.: 13–17)

The creation of the wish and ability to look after children – the socialization for motherhood – takes place over the entire course of a woman's life, as messages are given and received on many levels (Hollingworth 1916; Pohlman 1969; Rollin 1970; Bernard 1974; Blake 1974; Franzwa 1974; Oakley 1974b; Peck 1974) and as positive and negative sanctions act to ensure appropriate behaviour.[9] Oakley notes that in our society the message revolves around three connected assumptions which successfully convey the beliefs that 'to be a mother is to be normal and properly feminine' (Oakley 1974b). The result is that women expect and indeed want to look after children in the way society prescribes and that others see as desirable and appropriate for them (Sears, Maccoby, and Levin 1957; Lopata 1971; Busfield and Paddon 1977; Payne 1978).

Social perspectives on motherhood, then, see a woman's experience of motherhood as her experience of a social role, the nature and quality of which depend on the way the role is institutionalized and evaluated in a given society. In accounting for any distress or dissatisfaction a woman may feel in caring for her children social perspectives focus on the structure of society and point to the obligations of the mother role and the social conditions which impinge upon its performance. It is these factors in the social organization of child care, which may vary from one society to another and which may change over time, that they see as crucial to her experience. A woman's personality and past experience are considered important in her identification and orientation within the role but the main emphasis in sociology and social anthropology is on the way the role itself is institutionalized in society and therefore on the social conditions which can make it generally rewarding or distressing.

Early sociological research

While the view of motherhood as a social role implies that a woman's experience as a mother is an open question and a valid topic for research, it is only recently that sociology has addressed itself directly to this subject. Perhaps because of the influence of the biological perspectives just reviewed, during the 1950s and 1960s her experience as a mother was seen as unproblematic for most women. This view, coupled with an interest in developmental issues, meant that virtually all the research on mothers and children focused on the child and looked at a woman's experience as a mother only in passing (Walters and Stinnett 1971). Furthermore, it meant that the findings of this indirect research, which implied that motherhood was often a difficult and distressing experience, were not fully appreciated and that research interest in women's experiences as mothers was not developed. Before going on to consider the more recent sociological work, it is interesting to review this earlier work and to see how the prevailing assumptions about motherhood obscured its findings and inhibited research directly on the question of women's experience as mothers.

(i) Motherhood and marital satisfaction

A major theme in this early research was women's experience of marriage (Hicks and Platt 1970; Laws 1971). Children were seen as a component of marriage and a great deal was written about parenthood from the point of view of its effect on marital satisfaction (Lasch 1977). Blood and Wolfe found that 'marital satisfaction is heightened by the fulfilment of the universal desire to have children' (Blood and Wolfe 1960: 265) but their study is an exception. For the most part, research showed that children had a detrimental effect on marital satisfaction: the birth of the first child was shown to be a 'crisis' for the marriage, either a mild one (Hobbs 1965, 1968; Meyerowitz and Feldman 1966) or severe (LeMasters 1957; Dyer 1963); active child rearing within the family was shown to be correlated with marital dissatisfaction (Hurley and Palonen 1967; Renne 1970); and, in terms of the family lifecycle, marital satisfaction was shown to drop substantially with the birth of the first child and remain low during the active child-rearing years (Burr 1970; Rollins and Feldman 1970; Feldman 1971).

While this research on marital satisfaction might appear to have suggested that parenthood was problematic, such a hypothesis was rarely considered, perhaps because other studies were reporting that children were an important 'source of satisfaction' in marriage (e.g. Luckey and Bain 1970). Such findings seem to have been taken to mean that while children create problems in a marriage, parenthood itself is intrinsically rewarding. Thus, Rollins and Feldman could come to two apparently inconsistent conclusions: first, that the 'experiences of childbearing and childrearing have a rather profound and *negative effect on marital satisfaction* for wives, even in their basic feelings of self-worth in relation to their marriage' (emphasis added); and then that 'both husband and wife rate highly the childbearing and early childrearing phases and are at a low point when launching the children from the home', which they take to be 'an indication of *satisfaction with parenthood*' (emphasis added) (Rollins and Feldman 1970: 383). Conclusions like these both reflected and supported the assumption in the 1950s and 1960s that motherhood was intrinsically rewarding and not problematic; as such they inhibited research into maternal satisfaction despite the obvious implications of the marital satisfaction literature.[10]

(ii) Motherhood and women's employment

A second theme of the early studies was the employment of women with children. Nye and Hoffman point out that interest in this area arose out of reports in the 1950s 'that more than a third of the mothers of school-aged children were employed', reports which 'sharply contradicted the traditional image of the mother' (Nye and Hoffman 1963:6). These reports were not seen as suggesting that full-time motherhood was problematic for women, however, but as 'confront(*ing*) society with the need to consider whether the employment of married women, especially mothers, is compatible with a satisfactory family life and with the healthy physical and psychological development of *children*' (emphasis added) (Thompson and Finlayson 1963: 151).

Effort was directed primarily towards looking at the effects on their children of women working and the women's reasons for working were considered only as part of the background variables for interpreting these effects (Feld 1963; Nye 1963). It was in this context that 'boredom with domesticity' and 'loneliness' were cited as factors in women seeking paid employment despite their maternal responsibilities. Hoffman, for example, pointed out that 'the period when the mother has preschool children may be an extremely frustrating time – a time when she must hold back impulses, defer gratification and above all remain physically at home'. She saw the last child entering school as releasing women from these frustrations and suggested that 'outside employment may be one expression of this release' (Hoffman 1963: 30).

Dissatisfaction with their maternal roles, however, was not an acceptable reason in the 1950s and 1960s for women with young children to look for paid employment. Instead 'economic necessity' was stressed as the underlying reason for women to work outside their homes (Jephcott, Seear, and Smith 1962; Nye and Hoffman 1963; Thompson and Finlayson 1963; Yudkin and Holme 1963; Klein 1965). This explanation for their work tended to underline the integration of paid employment and domestic responsibility, rather than their incompatibility: studies such as the Peak Freen study in Bermondsey stated that 'work was undertaken as a means of helping the family, not as an escape from it' (Fletcher 1962: 152). Furthermore, other studies argued that rewards from 'family inter-relationships' were still the most important satisfactions in life for both employed and non-employed mothers and that these rewards were especially strong among mothers of pre-school children (Weiss and Samelson 1958) who, in turn, had lower employment rates (Cartwright and Jefferys 1958; Jephcott, Seear, and Smith 1962; Klein 1965).

The effect of these studies was to emphasize the continuity between paid work and the mother role and to play down boredom and loneliness as reasons for working. Despite their own observations, they once again reinforced the view of maternity as naturally rewarding and kept the focus of research, as it always had been, on children and their development.

(iii) Motherhood and child rearing

A third focus in the early sociological research was on patterns of child rearing. These studies, too, looked at women's attitudes to motherhood and children, in this case as variables in their childrearing practices. It was in this field, however, that motherhood was most clearly seen as naturally rewarding and research questions were both framed and interpreted in this light. Sears, Maccoby, and Levin, for example, concluded that 'few of the women expressed any real dissatisfaction with their life situation. The majority (86%) expressed few reservations about their acceptance of the mother role' (Sears, Maccoby, and Levin 1957: 47). This conclusion was reached, however, on the basis of naive direct questions and in spite of the evidence of dissatisfaction in a sizeable minority of the sample. The authors ignored their own findings that one-third of the women in their sample were less than pleased when they found out they were pregnant for a second or subsequent time; that 17 per cent were relatively cold towards their children in infancy; and that as many as 27 per cent were relatively cold towards their five-year-olds.

Similarly, Newson and Newson dismissed frustration in motherhood as restricted to the better-than-average education group and went on to say that 'It seems to be generally true that many working-class women find the role of Mam highly satisfying in and of itself' (Newson and Newson 1965: 222). In their subsequent study of four-year-olds (Newson and Newson 1968), they asked only *what* the women enjoyed about their children, a question which presupposed that enjoyment was a fundamental feature of the relationship and which neglected their frustrations and irritations altogether.

Recent sociological research

Interest in the subject of women's experience as mothers has increased in the last decade or so, perhaps as a consequence of the feminist movement questioning the values and assumptions which dominated earlier work on the family. This has generated research which has looked more directly at the question, describing the nature and quality of women's experience as mothers and focusing on the way the mother role is institutionalized, the social conditions that impinge on its performance, and the way children and child care are evaluated in society to account for it.

(i) The evaluation of child care and the position of mothers

Traditionally, motherhood has been seen as a desirable and valued position for women (Sears, Maccoby, and Levin 1957; Newson and Newson 1965), endowing them with full adult status within society (Veroff and Feld 1970) and the moral virtues of social worth and respectability (Rainwater and Weinstein 1974; Lopata 1971). Busfield and Paddon, for example, point out that marriage and motherhood give 'legitimate and acceptable social identities of spouse and parent, identities that not only confer some status in themselves but can be manipulated to enhance one's own status' (Busfield and Paddon 1977: 120).

This view of motherhood, however, merely reflects the obligatory nature of the position for a woman's normality, not any positive value or status attributed to it by society, nor any experience of esteem or prestige by those in it. Indeed, recent analyses of child care point out that it has a *low* status in society (Comer 1974; LeMasters 1974) and that women's self-esteem drops when they leave paid employment for full-time child care (Rossi 1968; Bernard 1974). In a society that values *production*, child bearing and child rearing – that is, *reproduction* – command little concern or respect. The work of child rearing goes unrecognized by society which neither pays wages for it nor gives it due social recognition and respect: a woman who has spent ten years raising three children, for example, is considered to have no qualification for a 'job' and no 'work' experience. Mothers and children are of little account to those in political power who allocate funds away from children's allowances, who cut nursery education budgets, and who plan facilities which oppose or neglect their needs – e.g. no pram parks, no changing facilities in public lavatories, loss of pension benefits for non-employed mothers (Lott 1973; Kamerman 1977; Leach 1979). Motherhood may be necessary for women to establish their femininity, their respectability, and their maturity, but child care is a low-status occupation and women's low self-esteem as mothers reflects this.

(ii) Looking after children

The fundamental obligations attached to the social position of mother are those of *exclusive* responsibility for children and responsibility for them *all the time* (Bernard 1974). The conditions under which these are carried out are those of the isolated nuclear family in its separate households, segregated from the productive sector of society, and cut off from an extended kin network. The main features of the performance of the mother role, then, may be said to be its inevitable exclusion of mothers from people and activities outside the home; its heavy burden of work and responsibility on women in the mother role; and its consequent enforced tie between mother and child.

The effect of the mother role in restricting women's contacts and activities outside the home has been described by a number of researchers. Veroff and Feld (1970), for example, note that role demands of motherhood confine women to the home, curtail 'affiliative contacts', and therefore inhibit 'the affiliation motive'; Oakley (1974a) cites the social isolation of women as a significant aspect of the dissatisfying social context of motherhood; and Kitzinger expands on how the fact that they are 'socially isolated and cut off from the intellectual stimulation they were accustomed to before' leads women to worry 'that they are turning into a "vegetable" ' (Kitzinger 1978: 36). Lopata, too, writes about the restriction on other activities and points out the detrimental effects that this has on a woman's sense of personal identity: 'The care of infants calls for repetitive actions, isolation from interaction and intellectual stimulation and limitations of occasions to display a wide range of personality behaviours in a variety of social contexts which shows the uniqueness of self' (Lopata 1971: 193).

It is the tremendous responsibility entailed in the mother role, however, that has the greatest impact on women's lives. Lopata found that 'awareness of an infant's complete dependence upon the mother is mentioned most frequently as a contrast between this role and outside jobs' (Lopata 1971: 196); Comer that 'it is the totality of the responsibility for a new life which is so overwhelming' (Comer 1974: 191); and Graham and McKee (1980) that uncertainty, a desire to best satisfy the baby's needs, and a sense of responsibility are the basic themes in the experience of motherhood.

Because nuclear families are now relatively small, women have little prior experience of their responsibilities (Kitzinger 1978; Leach 1979) and are psychologically and emotionally unprepared for them (Gavron 1966; Lopata 1971; Bernard 1974; Kitzinger 1978). The isolation of the nuclear family from experienced mothers means, on the one hand, that little practical help is available and child care becomes a series of 'tiring and apparently endless tasks' (Lopata 1971; Comer 1974; Kitzinger 1978; Graham and McKee 1980) and, on the other hand, that no expert is available to reassure the new mother 'that she is doing the right thing, that her baby is normal, or that she has feelings about the child and her relationship with it which other new mothers share' (Kitzinger 1978: 33). At the same time, psychologists and paediatricians stress the mother's terrifying responsibility for her child's eventual personality and achievements, while offering little guidance in dealing with situations which arise. Furthermore, child care is not seen as 'work' but as an aspect of women's caring function and nesting behaviour (Comer 1974). Thus, child care and housework are expected to be performed together despite the fact that, as Oakley (1974a) notes, the activities of each are fundamentally opposed.

The mother's constant and exclusive responsibility for her children, coupled with her isolation from other adults, means that a mother is inevitably tied to her children. Gavron (1966) found that, whatever the women's personal desires to work, most felt psychologically tied to their children and compelled to stay home with them. Lopata found the same situation, but noted that 'not all women feeling tied down after the birth of children express great unhappiness with the arrangement' (Lopata 1971: 194). Oakley (1974a), on the other hand, points out that while closeness to the children was itself highly valued by the women, the physical or psychological tie to the children that it engendered was deeply resented. In contrast, Rainwater, Coleman, and Handel (1959) see the tie between working-class women and their children as the basis for their most important rewards in motherhood. Their emotional absorption in the children distracts the women from the frustrations of their husbands, and the children's constant companionship provides them with a highly valued sense of day-to-day well-being.

In so far as they see rewards in motherhood, sociological studies see them as largely centred on the *emotional relationship* between mother and child that develops as an aspect of the socially based tie. Lopata (1971) found that, in addition to rewards from the social identity ('having children') and role obligations ('bringing up children'), the major satisfactions of motherhood were vicarious ones based on identification with the children ('seeing children happy' and 'knowing children turned out well'). Gavron (1966) implies that for the women in her sample rewards derived from a commitment to their children and their welfare. Oakley looked for the 'emotional rewards children give' (Oakley 1974a: 178); Leach refers to the 'emotional rewards of being an immature and dependent person's completing half' (Leach 1979: 56); and Busfield and Paddon discuss emotional rewards that come from 'doing things for one's children, especially providing them with opportunities that parents have not had for themselves . . . (and) from having a second chance to have or attain what one did not have or get oneself' (Busfield and Paddon 1977: 137).

While these sociological studies largely agree on the sorts of problems and rewards women experience as mothers, and on their foundation in the social organization of child care, they differ dramatically in their views of the end result: the overall quality of women's experience as mothers. The various studies report findings covering the whole range of experience, from fundamentally rewarding for the majority of women at one extreme to fundamentally disagreeable for the majority of women at the other. Taken as a whole, sociological research presents a somewhat disjointed and inconsistent picture of the nature of women's experience as mothers.

At one extreme, Rainwater and his colleagues see motherhood as thoroughly rewarding for most women. It brings a highly valued identity, conferring on working-class women a view of themselves as valuable and worthwhile, and it provides the opportunity both to express and receive love and affection. Only when too many children make too many demands and too much work does child care become frustrating for a woman. (Rainwater, Coleman, and Handel 1959; Rainwater and Weinstein 1960).

Lopata also argues that motherhood is rewarding for the majority of women: the largest proportion of answers (one-third) given to her question 'What are the satisfactions of the housewife role?' pointed directly to the role of mother and another fifth or more referred to the mother role implicitly. She qualifies this positive picture somewhat by stating that women seem to see the changes involved in having children as a set of restrictions put upon them, but she nonetheless concludes that 'the overall impression is of a deeper set of satisfactions than of frustrations' (Lopata 1971: 219).

Likewise, Gavron presents a superficially positive view of women's experience as mothers, though her comments are even more ambiguous than Lopata's. She presents a picture of women in conflict, highlighting the plight of those who have chosen a role they believe in and expect to enjoy, but who suffer from the deprivations the role entails: 'It was not that the majority dislike their roles as mothers. . . . Clearly motherhood was a role that all wished, indeed possibly felt it was their duty, to enjoy and perform well' (Gavron 1966: 119). Despite this, however, she concludes that middle-class women 'were not fully prepared for the responsibilities imposed on them and many were acutely aware of the restrictions it imposed on their lives' while working-class women were 'less prepared for the ties of children and less able to cope with the isolation that follows'. (Gavron 1966: 79 and 89).

Along similar lines, Oakley hints at an inherently contradictory situation: she found that two-thirds of her sample of housewives were satisfied with child care, but adds that 'behind this general concept of "satisfaction" with child-care lie more subtle differences to do with *ambivalent* feelings about children and the demands of the mother role' (Oakley 1974a: 175).

At the other extreme, Comer describes women's experience as mothers in clearly negative terms:

> 'the result of one person taking sole charge of children is that the pleasure of caring for them, watching them grow, protecting them and teaching them is largely outweighed by the day to day frustrations, the restrictions imposed by the outside world and the enormous amount of physical work. . . . The baby's first smile, step or word, its eagerness to discover the world, its unexpected vulnerability . . . these are the occasional *perks* of motherhood – it's like suggesting that a frustrating job in a factory is made worthwhile by the odd fringe benefits, as though the man works all the year round just for the bonus in his Christmas pay packet.'
> (Comer 1974: 180–81)

Only a few others have anything to say on the question of women's experience as mothers. Ginsberg found that 'nearly two-thirds (*of the forty-eight women*) were highly dissatisfied with being in the home full-time as housewives and mothers' (Ginsberg 1976: 77); Wortis also found that 'many of the women who had new infants expressed the same conflicts (*as did Gavron's sample*): boredom, sense of isolation being home alone with the baby, desire to be able to get back to work' (Wortis 1971: 369). After reviewing the literature, Pohlman concludes that 'the decade that follows a woman's first pregnancy is often a dreary, lonely, frustrating one' (Pohlman 1969: 153) and Friedan (1963) describes this in her account of life in suburban America. Prendergast and Prout report that even fifteen-year-old girls, when describing their own observations of what it is like to be a mother at home, give accounts 'dominated by negative aspects – isolation, boredom and depression' (Prendergast and Prout 1979: 3). By contrast, Edgell reports that 'motherhood was experienced as a highly rewarding activity' by the women in his study (Edgell 1980: 92) and Busfield and Paddon that 42 per cent of the wives in their study 'said that there were *no* disadvantages to having children' while 68 per cent said that 'life would be *worse* without children' (Busfield and Paddon 1977: 290 and 140).[11]

In summary, social theory and research present motherhood and child care as a learned social role, the experience of which depends on the way it is institutionalized in a given society. Emotional rewards come from involvement in the dependent child with whom the mother usually develops strong ties, but other problems counter these rewards: the low value placed on reproduction means the experience of low prestige and low self-esteem among many women; the excessive obligations of the mother role frequently mean stress, fatigue, and failure in their work; and the isolation from others often means boredom and loneliness. Sociological theory, then, suggests that the frustration and distress which women in Britain suffer as mothers are normal, expected responses to the social organization of the role. That is, it sees such distress as a social problem and locates its causes in the basic structure of society: in the way society views and values child care, in the way society ensures that children are looked after, and therefore in the organization of society as a whole.

(iii) Discussion

More than either psychoanalysis or ethology, sociology and anthropology address themselves directly to the question of women's experience as mothers. For several reasons, however, the social research which has been done to date is limited in the insights it provides. In most studies, the inadequate conceptualization of the issues involved has meant that a confused and unbalanced picture has been presented. Gavron (1966), for example, describes the women's attitude and behaviour under six arbitrary headings, for which she provides no justification at all. Lopata (1971) is only slightly more sophisticated in conceptualizing the issues in terms of 'satisfactions' and 'problems'. Because the categories they use are essentially arbitrary, the relationship among them is far from clear. It is difficult to know what weight to give to each or to see how they produce an integrated pattern of experience. Taking them together does not necessarily present a complete picture and it certainly does not present a coherent one.

In other studies, the particular concern of the research has meant focusing on only certain aspects of motherhood and so presenting a *partial* picture of it. Rainwater and Weinstein (1974), for example, were interested in restricting births amongst women who were seen as at risk of having too many children; this meant they tried to understand the *positive* meanings that children have for the daily lives of women, which militate against their use of contraception. Their research presents perceptive insights, but inevitably only about the *rewards* of motherhood. In direct contrast to Rainwater and Weinstein is Comer (1974) whose concern is to explode the 'myth of motherhood'. She therefore focuses on the frustration and irritations of motherhood which have been hidden by the myth and demeans the rewards it promises as sentimental trivia. Comer draws on her own experience to present vivid pictures of what motherhood is 'really' like, but her concern with exploding this myth means that the picture she presents is again somewhat one-sided.

Finally, social research has been limited by its need to provide a balance to the view of motherhood as an intrinsically rewarding relationship between mother and child, based on biological ties and natural instincts. In doing this it has taken the traditional sociological perspective of *labour* and applied its concepts to the relationships within the family. These concepts themselves, however, do not embrace the full experience of motherhood but analyse simply the experience of motherhood as *work*: child care. This has meant that a number of studies (e.g. Gavron 1966; Lopata 1971; Oakley 1974a) have reported that the majority of women enjoy motherhood or find it deeply satisfying but, simultaneously, they have concentrated on describing the structural features of the mother role that make it frustrating, irritating, and overwhelming. Oakley (1974a), for example, explicitly conceptualizes the housewife role as a work role (houseworker) and – in so far as she sees the mother role as an aspect of the housewife role – implicitly conceives it, too, as a work role. The experience of the mother role is therefore seen as the experience of child care, influenced by the organization and conditions of the job. Oakley is concerned primarily with documenting 'the conditions of maternity in modern industrial societies' (Oakley 1974a: 177) and the negative feelings they generate. She hints at other aspects of the experience: indeed, she rates 68 per cent of her sample as *satisfied* with child care and 55 per cent as stating they liked or did not mind looking after children. But because of her perspective these other aspects remain unconceptualized and unexplained, and she concludes that:

> 'these interviews document well the dissatisfying social context in which the role of mother is carried out today. Social isolation and constant responsibility bring about discontent. Competition with the demands of housewifery means that to the mother as houseworker the child is sometimes seen as an obstacle to job satisfaction. . . . (*Husband's help with children means*) satisfaction with housework may be increased but only at the expense of satisfaction with child care.'
> (Oakley 1974a: 179–80)

While the domestic labour perspective makes important advances in highlighting these features, it can be taken too far in imposing categories of work satisfaction on women's accounts of their experience and in neglecting those aspects that fall outside these categories.

The sociology of motherhood (and, indeed, of fatherhood) is becoming an important area of research but further development is still needed. Future research needs a sociological perspective that starts from the women's own accounts of their experience and grounds its conceptual categories in these accounts. In addition, it needs to recognize that 'motherhood' refers largely to the years beyond the period immediately following the birth of a baby, certainly beyond the birth of the first baby, and to look at women's experience with older children and with several children. While our knowledge of the strains involved in the transition to motherhood is increasing, 'of the effects of growing children and the changing nature of the maternal role we know very little' (Fransella and Frost 1977: 112).

SUMMARY: BIOLOGICALLY BASED VERSUS SOCIALLY BASED THEORIES

The biologically based theories of maternal care have been used to perpetuate the view that motherhood is naturally rewarding and to support the current institution of child care, which places the responsibility for children on the mother, exclusively and constantly. This arrangement works smoothly and to the satisfaction of both mother and child, it is argued, because it is in line with their biological programming. Any other arrangement is considered unnatural and therefore both harmful to mother and child because it is stressful and doomed to failure because the force of nature will reassert itself (Tiger and Shepher 1977).

Instinctual drives and innate predispositions, however, are shaped and expressed in a social context and both psychoanalysis and ethologically oriented psychology have been criticized for failing to give sufficient recognition to the role of social factors in their accounts of the experience of motherhood. On the one hand, it has frequently been pointed out that the feelings and attitudes which psychoanalysis sees as natural or inevitable are largely the products of the bourgeois Viennese society in which Freud worked (Poster 1978). On the other hand, both historical research (Ariès 1965; Shorter 1975; Stone 1979; Badinter 1981) and anthropological research (Mead 1972; Turnbull 1974; Matthieu 1979) have suggested that it is only when *social* conditions are suitable that mothers form the deep affective ties with their children that ethologists describe.

In contrast to the biologically based theories, social research has been used to challenge the view that motherhood is naturally rewarding and to question the current institution of child care. Empirical research shows that the mother role is often experienced as frustrating and boring because, it is argued, of the restrictive and overburdening way child care is organized in our society. Major changes are therefore called for to relieve women of their exclusive responsibility for children and to reintegrate mothers, children, and child care into society as a whole.

Social research, then, provides a necessary balance to the biologically based theories by analysing the social organization of motherhood and spelling out its negative consequences for women. But the picture that social research presents is fragmented and disjointed: on the one hand, there is the *work* of child care which is stifling and overwhelming; on the other hand, there is the mother-child *relationship* which provides unique emotional rewards. These two elements of motherhood are treated as virtually independent (Lopata 1971; Oakley 1974a). While it is implied that the mother-child relationship is inherently rewarding, only the structure and context of the mother role are actually described and shown to be frustrating.

While the three approaches of psychoanalysis, ethology, and sociology provide many important insights into their experience as mothers, none is concerned with the women's own perspectives on their experience. Each highlights different features in their experience and each points to different issues which influence it, but each in the end fails to capture and convey the subtlety and complexity of the experience as it is actually experienced. In order to understand clearly the nature of women's experience as mothers, it is necessary to take seriously their accounts of their lives and to develop concepts to make sense of those accounts in the way the women themselves do. In this way, it may be possible to present a description of their experience as mothers which will throw some light on the problems involved.

Background, aims, and approaches of this research

The study described in this book was undertaken in the context of a wider programme of work on social factors in the aetiology of depression in women (see Brown and Harris 1978). To complement the social epidemiological investigation of the main study with more detailed and qualitative research, several small-scale studies were carried out on the experience of women in particular social categories. My own interest was in women's experience of motherhood; others looked at such issues as women's attitudes to paid employment (Ginsberg 1976) and their friendship and kinship relationships (O'Connor 1982).

At the time I joined the Social Research Unit an initial analysis of the study of psychiatric disorder among women in Camberwell had shown large differences in rates of depression between working-class and middle-class women (see Brown, Ni Bhrolchain, and Harris 1975). When the 'life stage' of the women was taken into account, these class differences were even more striking; most notably, working-class women with a child under six at home had the highest rate of (recent and chronic) depression of any group (42 per cent), while middle-class women with a child under six at home had the lowest rate of depression (5 per cent). Working-class women with any children at home were also much more likely to develop psychiatric disorder when they experienced a severe life event or difficulty and this higher rate of psychiatric disorder could not be explained fully by their higher rate of events or difficulties. This suggested that other factors intervened to mediate between major events and difficulties and the onset of psychiatric disorder. One such factor was a close, intimate, confiding relationship with husband or boyfriend. Social class differences were again found: working-class women with a child under six were the least likely to have a close, intimate confiding relationship with their husbands – 37 per cent had such a relationship, compared with twice that proportion in the middle-class group.

It was against this background of interest in women with young children, in social class differences in their experience, and in the influence of the marital relationship on their experience that I began my study. My principle aim was to provide a detailed description, from the women's own perspective, of the way they experienced their lives as mothers. Within the context of this general aim, one particular concern was to look at the differences in the experience of working-class and middle-class women. Throughout the book, the two classes are compared and the differences between them considered. A second concern was to look at the practical and emotional support which the women received from their husbands, and the ways in which this influenced their experience as mothers. There is therefore a focus on patterns of support from husbands and on the extent to which they explain variations in the women's experience.

The original plan for the study was to look at women's satisfaction with motherhood from the perspective of domestic labour. The adoption of the labour perspective in looking at women's roles within the family has been fundamental to some of the major advances made by feminist sociologists in the 1970s. It has allowed the use of concepts which have long been the stock-in-trade of sociological analysis and the concept of domestic labour has been particularly valuable in drawing attention to the fact that housework and child care are 'work' and may be experienced as tiring, boring, oppressive, or alienating in the same way that any work may.

During the course of the research, however, it became clear that, while the domestic-labour perspective provided many important insights, it could not deal with the full complexities of women's experience as mothers. First, looking solely at their *satisfaction* with motherhood tended to obfuscate rather than illuminate the nature of their experience. 'Satisfaction' is not a basic response to anything, nor a measure of the quality of experience itself. It is a derivative, comparative reply to a question that depends on other unknown features of an individual's cognitive set which may be any of her values, expectations, or past experiences. While it is of interest as an indicator of a woman's evaluation of her situation, it should not be taken for or confused with the way she experiences that situation.

Second, treating the women's experience of motherhood as the experience of a work role, along the lines of work in the productive sphere of paid employment, did violence to the women's own accounts of their lives. This is not to say that their accounts could have been understood better using the perspective of a biological role or of a gender identity, but simply that the labour perspective ignored or distorted aspects of their experience. While child care is clearly 'work', there are important differences between caring for children in a domestic context and paid employment in an economic context. The basis of the worker's involvement in her work, the relationship between worker and 'worked upon', and the system of beliefs and values surrounding her work, for example, all differ significantly between the world of outside paid employment and that of child care in the home. While the features that they have in common are highlighted and clarified by the labour perspective, those that are unique to motherhood tend to be ignored or distorted when it is viewed in those terms.

Perhaps in order to deal with the shortcomings of an at least implicit labour perspective, previous researchers have added to their discussion of satisfaction with motherhood or child care a discussion of satisfaction with children or the mother-child relationship. Oakley (1980), for example, has looked at 'feelings for the baby' in addition to 'satisfaction with motherhood' and Luxton has discussed 'the *work* of mothering' separately from 'the social relationship between a mother and her children (Luxton 1980: 82). This implicit conceptualization of maternity as a work role (motherhood or child care) *plus* a personal relationship (children) has also enabled both Radl (1974) and Bernard to argue that women may 'love their *children* but not *motherhood* or conversely *motherhood* but not *children*' (Bernard 1974: 30). Along similar lines, Veroff and Feld have suggested that some people 'are perhaps not very involved with their *own roles* as parents even though they might be quite involved with their *children*' (Veroff and Feld 1970: 149).

This way of acknowledging an aspect of women's experience as mothers not recognized by the labour perspective, however, creates as many problems as it solves. While it fills out the work-role analogy, it sets up a false dichotomy in women's experience and panders to a sentimental view of the mother-child relationship. The relationship between a woman and her children is not an abstract one but a relationship of daily interaction structured by the woman's responsibility for her children and lived out under historically specific social and physical conditions. At the same time, the mother role is not an arbitrary set of obligations imposed on a woman, but a socially defined set of guidelines on how to fill an often deeply felt responsibility for dependent children. A woman's experience of child care informs her feelings towards her children and her feelings towards her children inform her experiences of child care: it is inappropriate to try and distinguish between the two. The tendency to do just that, however, has given rise to a good deal of sentimental talk about loving children but not motherhood and to the tautological assessment of negative feelings as dissatisfaction with the mother role and positive feelings as love given and received in the mother-child relationship.

The problems entailed in the domestic-labour perspective when it is applied to the experience of motherhood illustrate the limitations of current sociological concepts for understanding activities in the domestic sphere which Stacey has described in her seminal Two Adams paper (1981). Stacey points out that the historical dominance of men and therefore male concerns in sociology has meant that sociological concepts and theories have been developed exclusively with reference to the *public domain*: industrial production, the market place, and the affairs of the state. These concepts and theories, however, are not necessarily adequate or appropriate for understanding social relations in the *private* or *domestic domain*. Rather, they 'constitute a strait jacket in which we are still imprisoned and within which attempts to understand the total society are severely constrained' (Stacey 1981: 182). Stacey argues for the need to rethink 'what constitutes work, especially in the human services and what the rewards and sanctions, incentives and disincentives are and upon what they are based. These phenomena go well beyond those to be found in the market place' (Stacey 1981: 188).

Although I completed this study long before Stacey clarified the problem so well, I make an attempt here to rethink the concepts for use in the private domain as she advises. Rather than depending on concepts developed for the public domain to make sense of the women's accounts of their experience as mothers, I have developed new concepts grounded in those accounts and reflecting the values, beliefs, rewards, and incentives of the private domain. Two main concepts were defined that reflect the two main themes in the women's accounts. The first theme was the pleasure or irritation and frustration that the women felt in the course of their day-to-day lives looking after their children. The second was the sense that their children gave them a purpose and through this gave their lives meaning and value. This was experienced and conveyed primarily through their feeling of being needed and wanted by their children, which led the women to experience their efforts for the benefit of their children as intrinsically worthwhile and valued. These two themes reflect two different *modes* of experience: the women's *immediate response* to looking after their children and their *sense of meaning and purpose* in doing so. Taken together, they provide a framework for describing women's experience as mothers and for considering the factors which influence it. This, then, gives the book its basic structure.

Part One of the book outlines the issues in women's experience as mothers and previous work relating to them and describes the sample and methods used to look at them in this study. *Part Two* presents a picture of the fifty women's experience as mothers in terms of the two dimensions mentioned above. The chapters in *Part Three* try to account for some of the variation in the nature of the women's experience by looking at features in their family situation. *Part Four* draws together the themes of the study and sets the women's experience in a broader context.

Notes

1. Various studies have suggested that the high rates of both mental disorder and physical illness among women reflect a stress reaction to the strain encountered in the family and gender roles assigned exclusively to them (Bernard 1972; Gove and Tudor 1973; Nathanson 1975; Cooperstock 1978; Cooperstock and Lennard 1978; Gove 1978; Gove and Hughes 1979).
2. This review is based primarily on the 'classic' writers in psychoanalytic theory. Two of the more recent feminist writers within the psychoanalytic school, Chodorow (1978) and Miller (1978), however, disagree with the view of mothering as instinctual or as arising from

women's innate femaleness and stress that the orientation and the ability to mother are *developed* in women in the course of their ego development. However, they still imply that, for 'normal' women, looking after children is 'unproblematic' and 'rewarding' and so they will be treated here alongside the traditional psychoanalytic writers.

3. One point which needs to be emphasized is that psychoanalysis sees maternity as rewarding not primarily in terms of the mother's 'natural', 'feminine' enjoyment of caring for infants but in terms of the meanings and fantasies, the identifications, conflicts, and anxieties that children arouse in her. It is these factors that a woman brings *to* maternity, more than the structural features of the current situation, which psychoanalytic theory stresses as shaping the contours of a woman's experience of motherhood.

4. Benedeck (1970c), for example, suggests that frustration in motherhood arises out of a woman's inability to fulfil her tasks smoothly and intuitively, which itself is because she has introjected a male (i.e. inappropriate) ego ideal.

5. Rossi goes on to conclude that, because these features are specific to women, the bond between a *woman* and child is inevitably potentially stronger than that between a *man* and child. Others, however, have pointed out that infant-elicited behaviour (such as exaggerated facial and vocal expressions) which makes for rewarding interaction and therefore strong attachment is automatic not only in women but in men and boys as well (Stern 1977). They question the biological basis of 'differential behaviour' towards infants and therefore the biological necessity for a stronger bond between a woman, rather than a man, and a child.

6. The problems of bonding have been found to be particularly salient in the case of blind babies who do not present appropriate cues to elicit maternal responses nor to reward their mothers' efforts: 'Instead, the absence of eye contact gives the negative sign of "no interest". The absence of a smile in response to the presentation of the human face has the negative value of "not friendly" ' (Fraiberg 1974: 221).

7. See, for example, Macfarlane, Smith, and Garron (1978), Valman (1980) or Davies (1981). Davies is typical in his statement that: 'Separation of mother and infant after birth increases the risk of bonding failure followed by increased likelihood of post-natal depression, rejection, failure in breast feeding, non-accidental injury and poor family cohesion' (Davies 1981: 293).

8. Most of human evolution took place while man lived under the conditions of the hunter-gatherers, which means that man's biological adaptation is to that physical and social environment. In looking at the social behaviour of hunter-gatherer societies, human ethologists (e.g. Konner 1972; Devore and Konner 1974) can see the function and

adaptive relationship between biological features, physical environment, and social behaviour which is biologically programmed in man. While it may be evident that biological programming is adaptive for the conditions of hunter-gatherers, it is also evident that it is not adaptive for the contrasting conditions of modern industrial society.

9. Veevers's work on voluntarily childless women is particularly interesting in that she suggests that these women, too, initially expect to have children 'as a matter of course' and simply 'put off' having children until they recognize that a decision has been made implicitly (Veevers 1973a, 1973b).

10. While marital satisfaction has remained a popular, if tedious, area of interest in American family sociology, the research carried out has been, on the whole, very poor. Most studies use sophisticated mathematical techniques for sampling and for analysing correlations among variables (e.g. Hudson and Murphy 1980), but this superficial rigour belies appalling sloppiness in both conceptualization and data collection: the very low response rates (around 55 to 60 per cent) make a nonsense of the sampling procedures, and the naive operational definitions and measures (e.g. Chadwick, Albrecht, and Kunz 1976) make a nonsense of the complex correlations. The most popular measure of marital satisfaction is the Locke (1959) Marital Adjustment Scale (e.g. Russell 1974; Spanier, Lewis, and Cole 1975) which has been shown to be highly contaminated by 'social desirability' (Edmonds 1967; Edmonds, Withers, and Dibatista 1972; Miller 1975), a point which those using the scale usually fail to mention. The results of these studies are therefore highly suspect. They are also highly contradictory. For example, Hobbs and his disciples (Russell 1974; Hobbs and Cole 1976) have continued to produce findings which suggest that the birth of the first child is only slightly disruptive of the marital relationship and that marital satisfaction five months after the birth is higher than it was before conception. The general thrust of research on marital satisfaction over the family lifecycle, on the other hand, has consistently pointed to a substantial *drop* in marital satisfaction in the period following the birth of the first child (Ryder 1973; Rollins and Cannon 1974; Glenn and Weaver 1978; Houseknecht 1979; Schram 1979). Contrary to this is the research which has suggested that the care of young children is one of the main sources of satisfaction for women in *marriage* (Chadwick, Albrecht, and Kunz 1976) which is itself challenged by Russell (1974) who reported that women find that the gratifications children bring are *personal* ones, including feelings of 'fulfilment' and 'a purpose for living', rather than ones which benefited the marital relationship. Finally, the demographic data on the relationship between children and marital instability or divorce have been used to support opposing

positions (Bacon 1974; Thornton 1977; Gibson 1980). This diversity and obvious inconsistency in the research findings on children and marital satisfaction have never been confronted directly.

11. Busfield's and Paddon's work (1977) is interesting because it highlights the fact that having children means more than just taking on the identity and activity of the mother role in our society: having children means creating a family and experiencing life within and through that group.

METHODS

The study on which this book is based was designed to obtain from a sample of women extended accounts of their lives as mothers, so far as possible in their own terms. Since the intention was to explore patterns and themes in women's accounts, it seemed necessary to rely upon a relatively small number of respondents. Practical considerations also suggested that a small-scale intensive study was most appropriate for a single investigator and a sample of fifty was therefore decided upon. Such small samples have proved to be invaluable in 'mapping out an area, describing a field and connecting events, processes or characteristics which appear to go together' (Oakley 1974a: 33). There is now a notable tradition of small-scale studies which have produced valuable insights into family processes precisely because their small sample enabled a sensitive and flexible handling of the data. This includes Bott's study of networks (1957), Oakley's study of housework (1974a, 1974b), Hart's study of divorce (1976), and Leonard's study of courtship (1980). It is within this tradition that this study stands.

Sample

In specifying the criteria for choosing the sample, I was guided first by the wish to obtain a relatively homogeneous sample of women who enjoyed what are generally considered 'good' social conditions. Because I was limited to looking at a small sample, I wanted a group of women who were similar in age, marital status, number and age of children, and employment status. Each of these factors could influence a woman's experience in different ways and so could obscure the relationship between her experience and the variables of husband's help and support that I intended to look at. In addition, I wanted to exclude those living in serious social difficulties because others have already shown that such difficulties create distress for mothers. I was not particularly interested in showing this again, partly because these findings are often taken to imply that more money or better housing alone, without more fundamental social change, could solve the 'problem' of maternal distress. I was more interested in looking at women living in good social conditions – conditions which are seen as appropriate and advantageous for raising children – and documenting their experience. Any frustration which emerged from their accounts could not be put down to poverty in general but would need to be traced back to other features in the way the care of children is organized in our society. I therefore used the following criteria for choosing the sample: (i) married women living with their husbands who were (ii) between the ages of 21 and 35, (iii) not engaged in full-time, paid employment, (iv) having two, three, or four children (v) at least one of whom was under five years of age, and (vi) living in one of two outer London suburbs.

A second consideration in selecting the sample was that of social class. At the time I began the study, there was a good deal of evidence to suggest both that the experience of working-class women with young children differed in important ways from the experience of their middle-class counterparts and that social class had an important influence on women's experience as mothers. The work by Brown and his colleagues referred to in Chapter 1 pointed to considerable differences in the rates of psychiatric disorder among working-class and middle-class women with children at home, and suggested that this was associated with differences in the quality of their marriages. Other studies highlighted differences in values, attitudes, and patterns of behaviour between working-class and middle-class women which might have been expected to have a direct influence on their experience as mothers. Komarovsky (1962: 57), for example, suggested that there were important class differences in orientation to and satisfaction in domestic roles. In contrast to the discontent prevalent among middle-class women, for the working-class women she studied 'housewifery is not only positively evaluated in principle but is in fact a source of satisfaction'. Both the Newsons (1965) and Gavron (1966: 81) elaborated on this contrast, reporting that 'the working-class wife . . . expects to find her main source of satisfaction in her family and thus to become a mother is to achieve one of the things she wants, whereas the middle-class wife expects to be an independent person in her own right and thus finds that the presence of young children frustrates her from fulfilling what she considers to be her rightful role'. In the same way, Oakley (1974a: 188) described differences in orientations to housework between working-class and middle-class women in which 'working-class women (were) much more closely involved with the housewife role and with domestic interests and activities generally'. Social class differences in values, attitudes and patterns of child-rearing were also well documented (von Mering 1955; Kohn 1959, 1963; Newson and Newson 1965, 1968) as were social class differences in attitudes to children and the mother-child relationship (Rainwater, Coleman, and Handel 1959; J. Klein 1965). Finally, patterns of conjugal role relationships had been shown to differ between the social classes, with working-class couples more likely to have a segregated role relationship and middle-class couples a joint role relationship (Bott 1957; Young and Willmott 1962; Oakley 1974a).

As this review has indicated, the emphasis in the research literature at the time was on the *differences* in the experience of women associated with their different positions in the class structure (rather than on the *similarities* in their experience associated with their common position in a gender stratified society) and the focus in describing and accounting for these differences was on *values, attitudes, and behaviour*. Both of these preoccupations influenced my approach to my own study. That is, in the context of the prevailing research trends it seemed appropriate to structure my own study by selecting two groups of women – one working-class and one middle-class – and to explore the nature and influence of their different values, attitudes, and behaviour as mothers. I therefore selected twenty-five working-class and twenty-five middle-class women for my main research sample, using the conventional indicator of social class, husband's occupation. Throughout this book, the data describing the nature of the women's attitudes and experience will be presented separately for these two sub-samples in order to facilitate the exploration of social class differences.

In recent years, there has been growing criticism of this approach to selecting and analysing samples, particularly with regard to studies of women. Social class is a problematic concept, with a variety of meanings relating to different views of the nature of social structure (see Giddens 1973; Parkin 1979), and a variety of measurement complications (see Oakley 1981b). The way in which social class is taken to influence experience is also complex and controversial. In the area of health, for example, Townsend and Davidson (1982: 112–23) outline four contrasting approaches to the explanation of social class relationships: artefactural explanations; theories of natural or social selection; materialist or structuralist explanations; and cultural/behavioural explanations. The first approach suggests that social class is an artificial variable 'thrown up by attempts to measure social phenomena' (p. 113) and that social class relationships are artefactual and of little causal significance. The second approach casts social class as a dependent variable, the consequence of selection on the basis of other variables such as strength or intelligence. In Townsend's and Davidson's view, however, the more important approaches for explaining social class differences are the last two. The materialist or structuralist approach emphasizes the direct or indirect effects of material conditions such as income, housing amenities, degree of security and stability of employment, and levels of job satisfaction or stress on the experience of those in different social class groups. The cultural/behavioural approach focuses on the autonomous and independent role of ideas, attitudes, and behaviour that may be 'illustrative of socially distinguishable styles of life, associated with and reinforced by, social class' (p. 118).

As their outline suggests, there are potentially a variety of ways in which social class can operate to influence experience. A major shortcoming in analyses by social class is that the observation of a class relationship in itself provides no indication of the way in which class is operating, or the aspects of social class membership that are important in that particular instance. Social class is a crude measure, with little explanatory power in its own right. A statistical relationship between social class and another variable is useful in establishing that there are issues worth investigating. Once this is done, however, it is necessary to look at more precise components of class experience to try to specify what is going on. Brown and Harris (1978), for example, eventually isolated precise provoking agents (severe events and difficulties) and vulnerability factors (lack of a confiding relationship, loss of mother before the age of eleven, three or more children under fourteen at home, and lack of employment) to specify the way in which social class operated in the onset of psychiatric disorder: the social class differences in rates of depression could be seen entirely as the effect of the unequal distribution of these provoking agents and vulnerability factors between the classes.

For a study of women's experience as mothers, it might have proved more profitable to have looked at specific components of their material and cultural circumstances such as housing conditions and amenities, amount and security of income, access to community facilities (e.g. nurseries and playgroups, education, employment attitudes and ambitions), and identification with domestic roles. It is likely to be the effects of variables such as these that observed social class differences reflect. This more precise approach to assessing the effects of variations in social circumstances is perhaps particularly relevant for studies of the experience of women 'between whom occupational social class differentiates much less than in the case of men and for whom the tradition of categorization by husband rather than by self can be seen as participation in the cultural typification of women that relegates them to a second-hand status' (Oakley 1980: 102). Social class distinctions developed with reference to the situation of men may not always reflect meaningful distinctions among women. Dividing women along the lines of husband's occupation may therefore act to confuse rather than to clarify our understanding of their experience and to draw attention away from more useful lines of division among them. However, this sample was chosen, and the analysis completed, before such arguments were articulated. It is therefore with a class-stratified sample and analysis that I have worked.

The women's social class was assessed on the basis of their husband's occupation, which was classified according to the simplification of the Registrar General's classification of occupations that draws the distinction between manual and non-manual occupations. The non-manual or middle-class group consisted of women whose husbands were professional, managerial, white collar, or skilled workers who were foremen in their trade (I, II, IIInm) and the manual or working-class group consisted of women whose husbands were skilled manual, semi-skilled manual, and unskilled manual workers (IIIm, IV, V). In the light of current criticism of this method of assessing social class for women (Acker 1973; Eichler 1980; Graham and McKee 1980; Delphy 1981; Oakley 1981b; Murgatroyd 1982), some explanation of its use in this study seems necessary.

The fundamental problems in using the husband's occupation to assess a married woman's social class are the unjust and questionable assumptions on which it is based: the assumptions that the family is the unit of stratification and that inferences can be drawn about all members of a family on the basis of the husband's position in the occupational structure. These assumptions deny that a married woman has any relationship to the social structure independent of her family and her ties to her husband and impose on her a class position which is not her own but one mediated by her husband. In criticizing these assumptions, a number of feminist sociologists have argued that *gender* is a factor that needs to be taken into account in models of stratification and class systems. Gender is an enduring social characteristic which affects the valuation put on people and positions and which is the basis for structured social inequalities. A woman's relationship to social structure is therefore different from a man's and, to explain the social position of women, a new model of class and stratification which takes account of these differences is needed.

One such model describes a system of stratification by gender which cross-cuts or overrides the system of stratification by occupation. In this model, women are seen as constituting a separate caste (Acker 1973) or social class (Eichler 1980) within the gender-based stratification system. Looking at women in these terms highlights the many restrictions and inequities to which they are subject by virtue of their gender and the many interests and life patterns they also share in common. Most women become mothers, for example, and as mothers they share common concerns (for a safe and healthy environment for their children, for educational facilities, and so on) and are subject to the same fundamental constraints (sole and final responsibility for their children).

In so far as they do enjoy similar social circumstances which differ significantly from those of men, the case for regarding women as a social class is a good one. It might therefore be argued that to use conventional measures of social class such as the Registrar General's is misleading and inappropriate in this study. The evidence reviewed above, however, suggests that there are wide differences in social experience among women who are identified by this conventional classification by husband's occupation. Since the further exploration of these differences was one of the aims of this research, it seemed sensible to classify the women in the same way. In addition, a second aim of the research was to describe the involvement of men in child care and to look at the way that socially derived differences in their attitudes and behaviour influenced the women's experience as mothers. For investigating this influence, the Registrar General's classification of husband's occupation seemed an appropriate method of assessing social class.

By contrast, the other methods of assessing a woman's social class – by her own current occupation, by her occupation prior to having children, or by her father's occupation – were of limited value for the purposes I had in this research. First, it was not feasible to classify the women according to their own occupations since none had full-time jobs and only nineteen had part-time jobs. If motherhood was taken as their primary occupation, all the women could be classified but doing so would not produce the variability in the sample that it was specifically intended to explore. Second, it was not useful to classify the women according to their occupations prior to having children because this again tended to hide the variability in their social experience.[1] The limited educational and occupational opportunities available to them act to concentrate women from a variety of different circumstances into a narrow range of traditionally female occupations. In this study, only eight women had had manual occupations before their children were born while forty-two had had non-manual occupations. The occupational classification which the women in this latter category share therefore tends to obscure the differences among them in their current social experience in other dimensions of their lives. Since these differences in current social experience were a focus of the research, this method had little to recommend itself for this study. Third, it was not appropriate to classify women according to their father's occupation. Had the influence of early circumstances been a main focus of the research, there might have been a case for doing so. In practice, it would have produced different results in only two cases, where women whose fathers had had manual occupations married men who had non-manual occupations. There were no grounds for assuming that her social background was the most significant influence on a woman's experience. Despite its many problems, therefore, in the context of the particular aims of this study husband's occupation seemed the most useful method for classifying the women. It produced the variability in women's experience which was a focus of the research; it allowed comparisons with other studies; and it facilitated the exploration of socially based patterns of men's involvement in children and child care and their effect on the women's experience as mothers.

The sample of fifty women was chosen from the lists of health visitors attached to two general practices in different parts of London. Initially, thirty women from each area were chosen to allow for refusals and women who could not be contacted. In the event, only one woman declined to be interviewed, which meant a very high response rate of 98 per cent. Two practices in markedly different parts of London were used in order to ensure a wide variation in the background and current circumstances of the women in the sample. The first area was a predominantly working-class suburb in south London, about nine miles from Charing Cross. It was a grey area with narrow streets of tiny two- or three-bedroomed Victorian terraced houses broken by two small modern developments, one private and one council. The community centred on a lively high street which provided a cinema, a Wimpy Bar, and a supermarket as well as a number of small specialty shops. There was no Underground service for the area, but a good rail and bus service provided transport to central London and, perhaps more importantly, to the shopping centres of Croydon. Only one park was within walking distance but the open countryside of Surrey and the resorts of the south coast were accessible to those who had cars.

The second area was a predominantly middle-class suburb in north London, again about nine miles from Charing Cross. In sharp contrast to the first area, this was the epitome of the leafy suburbs. Long streets of large, inter-war semi-detached houses meandered according to the planners' designs through open fields and park-land. The whole area stood on the edge of the Hertfordshire green belt. The size of the houses and the gardens surrounding them meant that the area itself was quite large and most houses were a good mile from the main road and the string of shops that served as a high street. There was no public transport within the area itself but once onto the main road there was very good transport to central London by bus or Underground.

The women in the sample ranged in age from twenty-two to thirty-four and had been married between three and thirteen years. They had children ranging in age from eleven months to twelve years (*Table 2(1)*); thirty-nine had two children, eight had three children, and three had four children (*see Table 2(2)*). Nineteen had had part-time paid employment within the previous three months, six of whom worked at home (*see Table 2(2)*). Forty of the fifty women lived in houses and only ten in flats; nine were council tenants, one a private tenant, and forty owner-occupiers.

Table 2(1) *Age of children*

| Age (to nearest half year) | Social class | | |
	working class no.	middle class no.	total no.
under 1	3	3	6
1–2	9	18	27
2–3½	16	12	28
3½–5	14	13	27
5–6½	8	6	14
6½–8	2	4	6
8+	4	2	6
total	56	58	114

Table 2(2) *Number of children in the family*

| Number of children in the family | Social class | | |
	working class no.	middle class no.	total no.
2	20	19	39
3	4	4	8
4	1	2	3
total	25	25	50

Table 2(3) *Employment status of women in last three months and social class*

| Employment status | Social class | | |
	working class no. (%)	middle class no. (%)	total no. (%)
not employed	16 (64)	15 (60)	31 (62)
domestic work (for others)	2 (8)	0	2 (4)
childminding ⎫ at	3 (12)	0	3 (6)
homework ⎬ home	1 (4)	0	1 (2)
typing ⎭	0	2 (8)	2 (4)
outside paid employment	3 (12)	8 (32)	11 (22)
total	25 (100)	25 (100)	50 (100)

Methods of data collection

Each of the women in the study was interviewed on at least two occasions, usually a week apart; each interview session lasted about two hours, making a total, on average, of four hours interview for each woman. (The range was from three to five and a half hours.) The interviews were tape-recorded and then transcribed by the interviewer. In analysing the women's accounts, both the transcripts and the audio recordings were used.

In order to overcome some of the problems widely considered to be inherent in simple questionnaire surveys, the approach I used in interviewing the women was that of the 'non-schedule standardized interview' described by Richardson, Dohrenwend, and Klim (1965) and developed further by Brown and Rutter (Brown and Rutter 1966; Rutter and Brown 1966). There are several limitations, especially in this field, of traditional methods of questionnaire research which made the non-schedule standardized interview a more fruitful means of obtaining information. In the first place, the meaning of responses to standardized questions may be unclear to the extent that it is uncertain how the respondent has interpreted the question. Brown's and Rutter's approach encourages the interviewer to clarify such ambiguities wherever possible. In the second place, questionnaires normally depend on pre-coded answers into which the respondent is forced to fit. Again, the meaning attached to the choices selected is left unexplored. These problems are especially salient in areas of life which have strong emotional or moral significance and in which questionnaire responses may easily be biased towards the socially acceptable (Edmonds 1967).

The interview schedule was designed with two particular aims in mind. First, it was intended to obtain detailed descriptions, in the women's own terms, of specific events and circumstances in their lives as mothers. (It proved useful to focus on the previous day for such accounts.) With detailed questioning, the women were encouraged to build up a train of associations about the areas under question, both to aid their memory of them and to establish good rapport and participation in the interview. At the same time, the descriptions given by the women encouraged or facilitated important spontaneous expressions of views and feelings that proved of great importance in the interpretation of the recorded interviews. Often, as Brown and Rutter argue, it is as much the tone or emotional quality of responses to this style of interviewing as the actual content that are the most valuable sources of insight into the significance of a statement. Thus, both the content and tone of the interviews were important at the stage of analysis. These might have been lost had conventional questionnaires been relied upon. In addition, other sources of insights seemed to be facilitated by the more free-flowing style offered by the non-schedule standardized interview. It made more likely the possibility that discussion occurred in the course of child-care activities that the interviewer could observe and bring into discussion. Also, as Oakley (1981a) has suggested, 'asides' and questions to the questioner are inherent in the relationship that builds up around social investigations. As a woman interviewing women, therefore, discussions of my plans and circumstances compared with theirs were important not just as part of the rapport but as further sources of insight.

In the event, I had little difficulty in encouraging the women to become involved in their accounts of their lives as mothers. The interviews afforded an opportunity for them to describe to a sympathetic listener what it was like to be a mother at home, looking after her children, and the majority of them warmed to the task. Even those who were less enthusiastic at the beginning welcomed me warmly on my second visit. This was the case equally among women who enjoyed looking after their children and among those who did not. A number of women commented that mother-hood had turned out to be quite different from what they had expected and they were anxious to present a more realistic picture of their daily life. As a childless woman several years younger than themselves, it made sense to the women to whom I was talking that I should want to know what it was like to be a mother. They, in turn, seemed pleased to tell me. Indeed, several women said that they wished someone had told them what they were telling me when they had been in my position. When the tape-recorder was switched off, such comments inevitably led to questions about my own plans to have children and my own views on motherhood.[2] The effect on the interviews of my status as a middle-class woman is more difficult to judge. It seemed that the fact that I was also a foreigner from Canada put me at a social distance from the working-class and middle-class women alike, both in their eyes and in my own. While this meant that I noticed, and questioned, many things which both middle-class and working-class women took for granted, my own middle-class background may have made it comparatively more difficult for me to interpret the working-class women's accounts as they intended.

The interpretations that I have made of the women's accounts and the conclusions that I have drawn from them apply, strictly speaking, to the research sample only. There are, however, a number of grounds for believing that they have a wider applicability. It is generally accepted that in our society the mother holds ultimate responsibility for her children and that, on a day-to-day basis, she looks after them on her own at home. It is also widely reported that the quality of the marital relationship is at a particularly low ebb during this stage of the family lifecycle. In addition, there is growing evidence that for a substantial proportion of women the period of full-time motherhood before children start school is characterized by psychological distress and marked dissatisfaction. To the extent that these features of the situation of the women in the sample are also features of the situation of other women with pre-school children, there is good reason to believe that the observations, interpretations, and explanations presented in this book pertain to other women in society as well. At the same time, it must also be remembered that the sample was chosen so as to exclude women with marked social problems, such as severe housing difficulties or single-parent status. Such difficulties, however, are a not uncommon feature of the situation of women with young children: more than a third of children under fifteen live in households which are in poverty or on the margins of poverty and single mothers living with their children constitute one of the most important groups of poor in our society (Townsend 1979). (These figures are themselves a telling comment on motherhood as an institution.) To the extent that social problems detract from the rewards and heighten the frustrations in women's experience as mothers, there is thus reason to expect that the experience of motherhood is much more distressing for a significant proportion of women than the results of this study would suggest.

Notes

1. In Chapter 11, however, I categorize the women according to their own prior occupations because, when looking at their satisfaction with their lives as mothers, there is a case for doing so.
2. For a fascinating discussion of the realities of interviewing, see Oakley (1981a); also Woodward and Chisholm (1981).

PART TWO
THE WOMEN'S EXPERIENCE

· 3 ·
THE EXPERIENCE
OF MOTHERHOOD

As the review in Chapter 1 has suggested, the way in which women experience motherhood has rarely been the subject of research interest. Biologically based theories have assumed that motherhood is natural and naturally rewarding and have directed research towards describing the physical and psychological processes that bring this about. Social research has challenged these assumptions, but in describing women's experience has used inappropriate concepts, which have presented a fragmented and disjointed picture of it. The research presented in this book therefore set out to provide a more coherent description of women's experience as mothers, which reflected their own perspective. This inevitably entailed, as a first step, the development of new concepts for describing women's experience which were grounded in their accounts of their lives and reflected their main concerns. These concepts, and the measures for assessing them, are the subject of this chapter.

The concepts

In their accounts of their daily lives, the fifty women in the study conveyed that they experienced a wide range and variety of feelings about looking after their children. Within this multiplicity of feelings, however, two main themes could be distinguished. First, the women described how they felt about looking after their children while they were looking after them. The feelings they conveyed in this context ranged from frustration, irritation, and boredom to delight, pleasure, and enjoyment. Second, many women also described feelings of meaningfulness, personal worth, and significance as mothers. In contrast to the first set of responses, these essentially reflective responses emerged when they talked more generally about the aims and purposes their children gave them. It was from these two main themes in the women's accounts that the concepts for describing their experience were developed.

IMMEDIATE RESPONSE

The most common theme in the women's accounts concerned the pleasure and enjoyment, or conversely the frustration and irritation, they felt in the course of their day-to-day activities. This was conceptualized as their *immediate response* to looking after their children and defined as their response to their activities as they were carrying them out. The nature of a woman's immediate response was assessed on the basis of the feelings she reported and expressed in describing her activities of the previous day.[1] With the help of extensive interview material, each woman was assessed as predominantly enjoying or as predominantly frustrated and irritated with child care. The women who enjoyed looking after their children emphasized the positive aspects of their daily lives and expressed a good deal of pleasure in their interaction with their children. By contrast, the women who were assessed as frustrated and irritated emphasized the negative aspects of their day and expressed a good deal of irritation towards their children. The differences in the experience of the women in these two groups can be seen in the contrasting accounts of a woman from each group. First, Janet Hobson, a working-class woman with a daughter 5½ and a son 2, who is typical of the women who enjoyed looking after their children:

(Q: 'Do you enjoy looking after your children?')
'Oh, yes! . . . With Nicola because she's a very bright child so she stands out by herself. Wherever she goes, she's the centre of attraction herself. He's very good too. Sometimes I think he's too perfect. I'll say to him, "Put the toys away" and he'll take them into the other room. They get undressed down here in the morning and I'll say to him "Take the clothes upstairs". He does all things like that. And if I'm washing up, he'll get a chair and stick his hands in the soap. He's very easy . . . I wanted my children and I enjoy them. About 3.30 there's usually about

seven or eight children running around here. They always come in here of a night. I'd rather Nicola's friends come in here than her go to play with them. I like children around me. I don't like it quiet. If she goes to play with her friends, he goes with her and I'd rather have all of them around me here.

Nicola goes dancing, so when they came home from school – they're learning a song and a dance routine at the moment. The teacher tells me, because I used to go dancing, and I teach *her* now. Some nights they come in here and I teach them the words and the steps. I do that with them. Or "old woman says" or writing or singing. We do that with them when they're fed up. I'll give them some songs or drawing or something. I've got patience to teach them anything really. Before she went to school she knew most of her ABCs and her counting and her name. . . . She's a real little chatterbox herself. In the mornings it's "Mum . . ." all the time. All the time she's home it's questions.' (Q: 'Do you find this annoying?')
'Oh no! It's really interesting. She came home yesterday and she's learned about wool. She said it comes from the lamb and she wanted to know how they get the wool from the sheep and how it becomes a jumper (*said with warmth*). . . .

She went to bed about 7.30 last night. If anyone else is in, like my brother, they always want a story from them, but if I put them to bed, they settle down quite well. They're very good, both of them. We don't get any of this "I don't want to go to bed" or anything. . . . They always have a kiss and a cuddle and Nicola is always on about Nanny who's in heaven. She's so sweet. If any of us have a cold, it's always "Hope you feel better in the morning". She'll always go through the things she wants to happen the next day then. She's very thoughtful like that. . . .

I feel quite content really. We're young and we've got a house and we can run a car and we can afford holidays, which a lot of people can't. I've got my own family and they're both perfect. I like taking them out, especially holiday times. You see couples sitting on the beach without children. Surely there can't be the same pleasure as playing with kids on the beach. I wanted my children and I enjoy looking after them.'

Overall, the tone of Janet Hobson's account is highly positive: she describes herself as enjoying looking after her children and she expresses a great deal of warmth and pleasure in doing so.

By contrast, Dawn Straker's account is highly negative. In discussing the same aspects of her day, she both reports and expresses substantial irritation. Dawn Straker is a working-class woman, with a son 4 and a daughter 1:

(Q: 'Do you enjoy looking after your children?')
'I suppose you enjoy it to a certain extent. I suppose you do. It's just that he's such a little terror. He's jealous. I can't treat her the same as I treated him. Anything I try to do with her, he's down there interfering. I can't enjoy her as much as I enjoyed him. I don't do as much with her as I did with him. Maybe with two you don't have as much time. And at one she seems much more of a baby than he was, and I wonder if it's because I don't have time to treat her the same way. And the jealousy. . . . If I go up for a wash in the morning and leave these two down here, I hear her crying and I think "What's he done!" I have to come down and get her. Then I'm telling him off. It's a *strain*. What has he done to her? Or has he just taken a toy off her? If you're upstairs and hear her cry you don't know why she's crying so you've got to come down and get her. . . . I keep on at him. Then sometimes I give him a good smack. But unless I smack him really hard, it makes no difference to him. He's so stubborn and so hard – he's really got a mind of his own (*said with intense irritation*). Sometimes he gets a smack but you go on at him so much that sometimes he gets away with things (*said with great bitterness and resentment*). . . .

(*Last night at tea*) she was crying because she was tired and I hadn't had time to get her ready for bed. He was picking at his food and I was yelling at him to get on with eating it (*all said with extreme irritation*). You get to the stage where you're on and on at him all the time and you wonder if it's worth it. He was chatting on and on because his father just come in and you can't stop him!! (*said with growing exasperation*). . . .

He could talk the hind leg off a donkey (*said caustically*). Sometimes it gets too much – he does go on and on, really, and I just wish he'd shut up. . . . I wouldn't say it's interesting. It's interesting when he comes home from school and says "The teacher told me off". And I say, "What did you do and why did she tell you off?". But sometimes he goes on and on about things that happened years ago. He might talk about it, and a week later he's talking about it again. And you can't say *that's* interesting. . . .

One thing that gets me down is bedtime. Bathtime. Especially in the summer. He's been in the mud and it's light till quite late and he has to have a bath every night. And by the time I have him in bed and bathed and sit down – that annoys me. Because you've had them all day long and then you have dinner and wash up and then you've got to start getting them ready for bed. And it's a long day. By the time you sit down, you just want to sit. . . . Sometimes I read to him, but it's so late now. I know I should, really, and sometimes I do, only a quick one. I think "You've had all day!". But it was so late last night because he did watch the television. So it was gone 7.00 when he got up from here (*said with resentment*). . . .

I'll feel relieved when he goes to school. I am looking forward to them growing up. Not sort of really getting off my hands, you know, I'm not being nasty or anything but obviously after going through all the baby stages and all the stages they're going through, it is nice, really, to look forward to them growing up and becoming more independent.'

The frustration and irritation that Dawn Straker felt in looking after her children are evident throughout her account. Also evident is the fact that her negative feelings were felt and expressed in relation to both her *children* and her *child care* activities. She did not respond to the two independently and it would misrepresent her experience to consider her feelings about the two separately. This is clear in Janet Hobson's account as well: her enjoyment was of her children in the context of child care and of child care in the context of her relationship with her children.

Table 3(1) *Immediate response to child care and social class*

| Social class | Immediate response to child care | | |
	enjoyed no. (%)	irritated no. (%)	total no. (%)
working class	14 (56)	11 (44)	25 (100)
middle class	10 (40)	15 (60)	25 (100)
total	24 (48)	26 (52)	50 (100)

$x^2 = 1.28$ $p > 0.05$

The distribution of the women according to their immediate response to looking after their children and their social class is given in *Table 3(1)*. A surprisingly high proportion of women did *not* enjoy looking after their children and the difference between working-class and middle-class women is very slight. Middle-class women more often did not enjoy looking after their children: for every two women who enjoyed child care, there are three who did not. Among working-class women, the proportion is reversed with slightly more enjoying child care than not. The important result, however, is the first: that overall, more than half the women found looking after children a predominantly *irritating* experience. This finding is particularly interesting because it casts doubt on the view that looking after their children is 'naturally rewarding' for mothers. With over half of the women rated as predominantly irritated, it is difficult to claim that looking after children is inherently rewarding for a mother or to try and explain negative experience in terms of the 'personality problems' of individual women.

SENSE OF MEANING AND PURPOSE

The second theme in the women's accounts concerned the sense of meaning, value, and significance they felt in reflecting on their lives as mothers. The women who described these feelings said that they felt needed and wanted by their children, a feeling which both conveyed and fostered their commitment to their children as a valued purpose or aim in life. This commitment to their children in turn gave rise to a sense of meaning and significance when, in reflecting on their lives as mothers, they saw themselves as fulfilling their purpose. This theme was therefore conceptualized as their sense of *meaning and purpose* in motherhood and defined as the response felt when reflecting on their lives in relation to their goals or purposes for the children. In contrast to her immediate response to child care, a woman's sense of meaning and purpose was not an automatic response but required both a positive commitment to her children as a purpose in life and a reflection on her life in terms of that purpose. A sense of meaning and purpose in motherhood, therefore, could at times be submerged by more immediate responses to child care. The need to look after her children concentrated a woman's attention on the situation she faced and hence on her response to her activities as she was carrying them out. The enjoyment or irritation she felt in this was direct and unavoidable. A sense of meaning and purpose, however, emerged more in the context of reflection and so required a shift in attention away from the immediate situation.[2] The way in which a woman reflected on her life, I shall argue in later chapters, could be viewed as a social process, in the sense that it was influenced by the perceived values and attitudes of significant others. The strength of her sense of meaningfulness therefore reflected more complex and subtle dynamics than her enjoyment or irritation in child care.

The strength of a woman's sense of meaning and purpose was assessed on the basis of the feelings she reported and expressed in reflecting on her life as a mother.[3] This included both the feelings that she conveyed when she described such reflections and the feelings she conveyed when she reflected on her life in the context of the research interview itself. Through the use of this varied interview material, the women in the study were divided into two groups: those who conveyed a strong sense of meaning, value, and significance in relation to their children and those who did not. The women who did not convey any strong sense of meaning and purpose talked only about the enjoyment or irritation they felt in looking after their children. They said nothing about the children giving them an aim or purpose in life, nor did they try to view their daily activities in any broader context. By contrast, the women for whom a sense of meaning and purpose was a central theme both described their children as giving them a purpose and tried to relate their daily lives to this purpose. It is not feasible to present examples of the accounts of women who did not find a sense of meaning and purpose in motherhood since it is difficult to document the *absence* of a theme. The best that can be said is that the clear comments in some women's accounts about their sense of meaning, value, and significance were conspicuously missing from the accounts of these women. Typical of such comments are those made by Debra Lennon and Jane Crawford. Debra Lennon is a working-class woman with two sons, 5 and 3:

'I think I'd sooner be a mother than anything else, although I'm not very good at it and I don't 100 per cent enjoy it. It's very *responsible*, very important. . . . My children are an anchor for me. It was too easy before just to grab a handful of pills and shove them down my throat and that was that. (*Note: She was hospitalized twice after suicide attempts.*) I wasn't *responsible* for anyone then, but now I am. Now I've got to get hold of myself and talk to someone – anyone – just to get it out of me. Now I feel I've got a *purpose* in life. Now I feel my children and my husband, it's not fair on them. They need me and I must carry on for their sake. . . .

It's little things make you realize what it's all about. My Stewart, when he comes to the school door, he has a look round and a great beam comes across his face when he sees me. And he comes tearing across the playground – he's happy because Mum is there. By 5.00 things have gone to pot – I'm yelling at them to stop fighting and trying to get on with tea. But Stewart comes up and says "I love you, Mum". That makes it all worthwhile. Or "You're the best Mum in the world". That makes you feel ten feet tall. It's worth all the heartache and annoyance and trouble being a Mum.'

Jane Crawford is a middle-class woman with twin daughters 2½:

'At the moment they need somebody all the time. They do *need* you. Somebody's got to take care of them. You really are *needed*. You realize you've created somebody who really needs to be looked after and that's *your* responsibility, as best you can, to look after them. It's a tremendous responsibility but it's a *great* responsibility. . . .

In many ways the children have brought us together. They have given us a joint *aim* in life, something to do and something to get on *for*. It's worth going on and getting things better and working hard because of the pleasure we can get from the children and what we can do for them. It gives you a reason for doing it all, for going on. . . .

There's nothing I would say that makes me feel the fully satisfied mother figure, but when you go in at night and look at them when they're asleep, and you might have been swearing at them all day and there they are. They're just little creatures and you realize how *vulnerable* they are. I think that sometimes hits me as a big responsibility. . . . It's all sorts of little things, really. When they come up to you and do little things. When you are just sitting there and they come up and give you a cuddle. Sentimental things like that. You think, "It's worth it, really".'

In these comments, the women convey the sense of meaning, value, and significance they felt as mothers. They describe how their children gave them an aim or purpose in life which they valued and to which they were strongly committed, and how this, in turn, enabled them to see meaning and value in their daily lives. In seeing themselves as fulfilling their purpose – and in describing their lives in these terms in the research interview – they felt and conveyed a strong sense of meaning and purpose as mothers.

Table 3(2) *Sense of meaning and purpose as mothers and social class*

| Social class | Sense of meaning and purpose | | |
	strong no. (%)	weak no. (%)	total no. (%)
working class	12 (48)	13 (52)	25 (100)
middle class	17 (68)	8 (32)	25 (100)
total	29 (58)	21 (42)	50 (100)

$x^2 = 2.05$ p$>$0.05

The distribution of the women according to the strength of their sense of meaning and purpose and their social class is given in *Table 3(2)* which shows an interesting, though small, class difference: while two-thirds of the middle-class women conveyed a strong sense of meaning and purpose, only half of the working-class women did. This finding, that middle-class women more often experienced meaning and purpose in relation to their children, is particularly interesting in light of the previous finding that working-class women more often enjoyed child care. It suggests that the majority of middle-class women found motherhood rewarding despite the fact that they did not always enjoy looking after their children. It may also go some way towards explaining why fewer middle-class women than working-class women have depressive breakdowns despite the fact that they experience greater frustration and irritation in child care (Brown, Ni Bhrolchain, and Harris 1975): the experience of meaning and purpose in motherhood may be more important to a sense of psychological well-being than the feeling of pleasure or irritation in child care.

Summary

The first task of this research was to develop concepts for describing women's experience as mothers which would allow the women's own perspectives on their lives to emerge. The two concepts developed for this purpose distinguish between a woman's *immediate response*, in terms of the enjoyment or frustration she feels as she looks after her children, and her *sense of meaning and purpose*, in terms of the strength of the meaning, value, and significance she feels when she perceives her life as fulfilling the purpose to which she is committed. As I describe in a later chapter, this latter dimension takes account of the bond that develops between a mother and her child and the hopes and fantasies she invests in him. These are important sources of any strong commitment to her children as a valued purpose in life which is, in turn, the basis for any experience of meaning, value, and significance in motherhood. While psychologists argue that the bond between a mother and child makes child care *enjoyable*, I have argued that her commitment to her children makes child care *meaningful* but does not necessarily make it enjoyable. Psychologists and psychoanalysts see this bond or attachment as part of the psychic structure of a woman and so tend to see her experience as a consequence of her own psychology. By contrast, I will argue that a woman's continuing commitment to her children, and any resulting feelings of meaningfulness, are influenced by a woman's interaction with others, which is largely the product of social structure.

When these concepts are used to make sense of the women's accounts of their experience as mothers we find a more complex and interesting picture than previous reports of their 'satisfaction' have presented. On the one hand, about half the women in the study felt frustrated and irritated with looking after their children while they were involved in doing so. On the other hand, well over half the women felt a sense of meaning, value, and significance as mothers when they reflected on their lives in relation to their aims and purposes in their children. Motherhood is neither 'naturally rewarding' nor 'inherently frustrating' but, rather, a woman's experience as a mother is the product of a complex set of social and psychological factors. Describing the women's experience in terms of the two concepts defined in this chapter tells us a great deal about the nature of their experience as they themselves perceive it. To understand it fully, however, we need to look not only at each dimension separately but also at both dimensions together and at the relationship of each to the other.

Notes

1. The women's immediate response to looking after their children was assessed largely on the basis of information obtained during a 'time budget' and a discussion of six chosen child care routines. The women were asked to describe at length everything they had done during the previous day and then were asked about how typical this had been and how much variation there was in their activities. They were also asked in detail about six designated child-care tasks: getting the children up in the morning, mealtimes, general supervision of the children playing, tidying up after children, keeping children clean and tidy, and putting children to bed at night. Throughout the interviews the women were encouraged to say how they had felt about what they were doing and about their children while they were looking after them. Whenever possible, the women were encouraged to relive their experiences and to express spontaneously their feelings towards the children and child care. For the full interview schedule, see Boulton (1982).

   Both the feelings they reported and the feelings they expressed in the non-verbal aspects of their speech (tone, pitch, and rhythm) were used in assessing the women's immediate response. The expressed emotion was particularly important since women could acknowledge the difficulties they faced without expressing negative feelings about them; similarly, they could talk about the advantages without expressing any positive feelings about them. In general, however, the women conveyed their feelings about looking after their children in which of these – the difficulties or the advantages – they chose to talk about as well as in the feelings they reported and expressed in doing so.

2. Any number of things could trigger a change in perspective. For many women, it was the children's comments at a particular moment which reminded them of their wider purpose; for others it was 'quiet times' which routinely prompted reflection and a summing up of the day's events. At times like these, women viewed their lives through the framework derived from their commitment to their children and they did so on their own. This sort of autistic enjoyment, however, put the burden of initially changing perspective entirely on the women. Conversations with others about the children, on the other hand, provided a more external prompt to a woman to change perspective and a more structured opportunity to create and enjoy her view of her efforts as worthwhile and her life as meaningful.

3. The strength of the women's sense of meaning and purpose as mothers was assessed in part on the basis of their account of their daily experience obtained during the time budget section of the interviews, and in part on the basis of their answers to questions on how important it was for them to see themselves as mothers; what they found most rewarding as mothers; and what they enjoyed most about each of their

children. Because the concept had not been worked out *before* the interviews were carried out, but emerged from the interviews themselves, no questions were asked *directly* about the sense of meaning and purpose they felt in relation to their children. Spontaneous comments, therefore, were critical in making the assessment.

In these circumstances, it is possible that more women felt a strong sense of meaning, value, and significance than was apparent in the interviews. It seems unlikely, however, that a strong sense of meaning, value, and significance could have been an important part of a woman's experience without this emerging from the lengthy intensive interviews.

· 4 ·
DEALING WITH PRE-SCHOOL CHILDREN

The concepts defined in the last chapter allowed a description of the women's experience in terms of their immediate enjoyment or frustration in looking after their children and in terms of the strength of their sense of meaning, value, and significance in reflecting on doing so. To provide greater insights into both the nature of their experience and its social basis, in the next four chapters I shall fill out some of the details in these summary measures. The chapters are organized in terms of seven features of their situation, which emerged as the main themes in the women's accounts. The first four relate to their immediate response to looking after their children and include the nature of pre-school children, the organization of child care, the setting of child care, and the impact of maternity on their lives as a whole. The last three relate to their sense of meaning and purpose as mothers and include their feelings of being needed and wanted by their children, the way in which they invest their hopes and dreams in the children, and their pride in their children. The present chapter deals with the first feature and the following three chapters with the others. The women's accounts of their reaction to these features of their situation provide an insight into the social experience of women as mothers. They should not be taken at face value, however, as the explanation of their frustration.[1] A partial explanation in terms of other features is outlined in Chapters 9 and 10.

The characteristics of pre-school children

Perhaps the most fundamental feature of their situation towards which the women in the study expressed irritation was the particular nature of their pre-school children. Although the pre-school years are a period of rapid change, children do not attain their full intellectual and social development during this time and pre-school children are essentially immature, both intellectually and socially. Their capacity to understand abstract ideas is limited and they do not follow the rules of social living. For their mothers, who have to look after them in the context of an adult, social world, these characteristics make doing so a frequently stressful and frustrating experience.

Four characteristics came through in the women's accounts as particular sources of irritation. The first was their children's limited ability to grasp ideas and their short attention span which made looking after them a dull and boring chore:

> 'I find I run out of ideas. There's a limit to what Mark can do. With her, I've been through it all before, so I know what I can do with her: building bricks, clap hand games – yuck. With Mark, it's all pastures new and I tend to run out of ideas. What can they do, really? They're so limited. I rack my brains for ideas!'
> (Angela Bourne, middle class, son 3½, daughter 1½)

> 'I started trying to help her do the alphabet after lunch, but I found it wasn't working because he was distracting us. Then when I was giving him piggybacks, she wanted piggybacks, too. So I'm *occupying* them all day, rather than playing with them. I'm *distracting* them, that's all.'
> (Victoria Milton, middle class, daughter 3½, son 1½)

The tedious task of occupying their children was particularly frustrating because the children's short attention span and the ease with which they were distracted meant that the women had to provide a succession of new activities. They not only felt under a strain because of this but felt denied any sense of achievement or appreciation of their efforts. Victoria Milton continues:

> 'I try to settle one with doing something and then the other one, but it's a fulltime job. And each escapade of what they're doing lasts only five or ten minutes. You think, "Yes, she wants to paint". So you get the newspaper out and the painting book and the water and the paints. And she paints for three minutes and then she sees him trying to climb up and feed the fish. And she'll get down to do what he's doing. So you've gone to all that

trouble to get it out and she's not interested! To hold a three-year-old's attention is very, very difficult.'

A second characteristic of pre-school children was their limited ability to anticipate danger in their environment. A child's natural clues to danger (loud noises, looming objects, and so on) do not cover all contingencies in modern homes so his mother must be constantly vigilant and ready to intervene to save him when necessary. This situation tended to engender a crisis orientation in mothers and the tensions and nervous exhaustion associated with it. Victoria Milton goes on to describe some of the situations she had had to deal with in the previous twenty-four hours and the strains she had felt:

'He's terribly adventurous for eighteen months. He opened the back door yesterday, unbolted it, and turned the key and then fell out backwards when he leaned on it. Ideally I would like to have someone come in to look after Peter and I would go out to work. Only, of course, if I could trust the person because he's at a dangerous age. I know what he will get up to, but other people wouldn't. He pulled the wardrobe down on top of himself this morning. I knew this could happen because he's like that so I don't have heavy things on it. Or he puts things in the toilet and pulls the chain. I'm prepared for this but someone else might not be.'

It was not only in dealing with crises that she felt strained, but also in having to be constantly alert to prevent such crises from ever arising:

'With a three-year-old you think, "Don't give her a glass, she'll fall with it". But I went to one girl's house (*who was looking after her daughter*) and Sharon was running around the garden with a glass in her hand which she could have smashed and cut herself. When I saw her with this glass, I went out the next day thinking, I bet she's in the garden with that glass again. It's nerve-racking. With the other one you wouldn't worry because you wouldn't give him a glass anyway. You worry about other things with him.'

The third characteristic which made looking after children frustrating was their limited ability to express themselves rationally and to understand rational explanations from others. With babies, the problem was straightforward: they had no language with which to express themselves. This created a barrier between mother and child which was at times a major source of frustration, as one woman describes:

'I seemed to get in a state when they started crying too much. I felt *why*. I felt I could quite easily strangle them. The irritation, the noise. If they would only stop crying – this is what I felt when they're little. If only they could tell me what is wrong. At least now Martin is nearly four you can talk to him. You can say "Stop crying, tell me what's the matter". But when they go on and on – I can quite understand people who hit them, because I've felt like doing it myself. I can remember throwing them down in the corner of the cot and saying "Shut up!". In the middle of the night you feel so useless. You feel like screaming at the wall. And the baby just goes on crying.'
(Margaret Samuel, middle class, sons 4 and 2)

As they grow up, children gradually learn to understand and to use language, but pre-school children do not necessarily grasp the full implications of what is being said to them nor feel they have to accept it. By ignoring their reasons and explanations, children challenge the women's taken-for-granted methods of operating in a social world:[2]

'Before I was used to living with reasonable beings. That's what is so hard to get used to: you can't *reason* with children. If anything makes you cross – if they want to play with the gas cooker and they *can't* – you've got to try and reason with them, to explain why they can't play with it because they'll burn themselves. But you can't. They don't understand. They can't follow it, they aren't interested. Mummy is just being mean.'
(Jane Crawford, middle class, twin daughters 2½)

'Mine are too young to explain things to. You can't say, "Be good while I do this and then we'll go out", because once you've said you're going out, they just go and get their coats. They want to go out *now*. As far as they're concerned you've said the word, so you're off. I only hope when they get older, surely they'll understand more.'
(Mandy Turner, working class, son 3, daughter 2)

As Mandy Turner implies, the children's incomprehension of rational arguments also made it difficult for the women to enlist their co-operation when it was necessary:

> 'They just can't co-operate yet. Like in the morning everyone is in a rush. We've got to get on with things. And you can say *ten times* "Take off your pyjamas, I want to dress you". And they just carry on with what they're doing and take no notice! They just don't understand, I don't think, at this age.'
>
> (Jackie Schneider, middle class, sons 4 and 1)

> 'They always take their socks and shoes off just at the point when you're going out the door. You look round and there are socks and shoes missing! Always! And they're very difficult to get on, socks and shoes, on children this age. And they *always* do it!'
>
> (Victoria Milton, middle class, daughter 3½, son 1½)

Though the women generally believed that their children were not consciously awkward, at times they found their actions not only unco-operative but purposely contrary. This apparently pointed opposition could be particularly irritating to deal with.

Related to this contrariness was the fourth characteristic the women singled out: the self-centredness of children. Children are at the centre of their own world, and throughout the pre-school years they tend to see others only in relation to themselves. They consider themselves and their own needs only, and therefore make demands without regard to their effect on others. When they are very young, the demands they make are to meet very basic and urgent needs. While the women accepted these demands as legitimate, they often resented them as well:

> 'There are times when I feel like saying "I will feed you twice as much today so tomorrow I can just have a break". Before, I could say, "The fridge really needs to be cleaned, but I can leave it". With children, they need feeding when *they* need feeding. Their nappies have to be washed every day. It's as simple as that. When they cry, you can't say, "Well, I'll see you in an hour". That is what hits you: the fact that it's seven days a week, twenty-four hours a day, and *they* make the rules.'
>
> (Jane Crawford, middle class, twin daughters 2½)

As children got older, their demands were less to meet physical needs and more to meet psychological and emotional needs. They were made just as peremptorily and just as frequently, however, and were more difficult to deal with because the children's will had to be taken into account as well:

> 'When they're babies and you *have* to do everything for them, it's a matter of getting on with it and doing it. You've got better control over them. Now they're older, they've got more independent and it's always my will fighting against theirs.'
> (Debra Lennon, working class, sons 5 and 3)

> 'With a baby you give them their dinner and you put them to bed and that's finished. With an older one you have to say, "I think it's a time for you to have your bath now", and they may well say "No, I don't want to". And then you have problems.'
> (Susan Griffiths, middle class, sons 6½ and 1½, daughter 4½)

At the same time as they made demands on others, their self-centredness meant that children often ignored the demands that others made on them:

> 'I get very irritable at times, I get very impatient. If things don't go the way I want, I get very irritable. But you can't expect children to do what *you* want. If they don't feel like it, they don't. I think they really do what *they* want to do, so there's a battle of wills at times. And then I get very impatient.... They're very self-centred. They can be terribly co-operative but you can't say they will be co-operative at a specific time. Because they are never co-operative when *you* want them to be. Only when *they* want to be. They're terribly unpredictable on the whole. It's difficult to organize. When they're small and you've got to do everything for them, you want them to conform at specific times. When they get older it won't matter so much. They'll be more independent then.'
> (Anne Wootton, middle class, daughters 5 and 2, son 3)

The children's self-centredness was not limited to their dealings with their mothers but pervaded their relationships with other children as well:

> 'Martin's got this wretched railway which does keep him amused for hours on end, but he does get het up if he can't get it going

like he wants it to and then he gets into a temper tantrum. And you've got to stop Andrew from stepping on it and breaking it up and generally interfering with it. But Martin spreads it across the threshold of his room so you can't close the door and then you can't stop Andrew from breaking it, though you constantly *try*.'

(Margaret Samuel, middle class, sons 4 and 2)

'I always thought two children were as easy as one. It was a great disillusionment. It's not the *work* as such, it's the strain, the mental strain involved in separating the two. Just keeping peace between them.'

(Victoria Milton, middle class, daughter 3½, son 1½)

Having two pre-school children, then, brought with it a whole new set of problems not encountered with one alone.

Ways in which children were enjoyed

Although the emphasis in this and the next two chapters is on describing the frustrations which the women experienced in looking after their children, two themes concerning their enjoyment of their children are sufficiently interesting to warrant discussion here as well. These themes bring out social-class differences in the way women looked to enjoy their children and set in context the way they managed their interaction when they no longer found it enjoyable.

The first theme concerns the way in which the women viewed their children as companions for themselves. Among working-class women, children were usually looked on as interesting and enjoyable companions (*see Table 4(1)*). Indeed, their children's companionship provided them with rewards which to some extent overcame the negative experience of those who were predominantly irritated with child care: eight of the eleven working-class women who were irritated with looking after their children nonetheless found their children rewarding and enjoyable companions (*see Table 4(2)*). Among middle-class women, however, their children's company was only infrequently a source of pleasure and enjoyment (*see Table 4(1)*): even among those who enjoyed looking after their children, well over half did not find their children rewarding as companions (*see Table 4(2)*).

Table 4(1) *Enjoyment of children as good company and social class*

	Enjoyment of children as good company		
Social class	enjoyed no. (%)	not enjoyed no. (%)	total no. (%)
working class	22 (88)	3 (12)	25 (100)
middle class	6 (24)	19 (76)	25 (100)
total	28 (56)	22 (44)	50 (100)

$x^2 = 20.78$ $p<0.001$

Table 4(2) *Enjoyment of children as good company, social class, and immediate response to child care*

Enjoyment of children as good company	Immediate response to child care				
	enjoyed		irritated		
	working class no. (%)	middle class no. (%)	working class no. (%)	middle class no. (%)	total no. (%)
enjoyed as company	14 (100)	4 (40)	8 (73)	2 (13)	28 (56)
not enjoyed as company	0	6 (60)	3 (27)	13 (87)	22 (44)
total	14 (100)	10 (100)	11 (100)	15 (100)	50 (100)

$x^2 = 11.2$ $p<0.001$ $x^2 = 9.46$ $p<0.01$

In their accounts of their daily lives, working-class women built up very clear pictures of their children as important and valued companions. They chatted to their children on their own level, shared their interests with them, and spent much of their time with them:

'Yes, they're good company. Especially the eldest one, because he chats more. They always tell me if anything happened. Apparently the boy next door broke his arm and went into hospital. The boy downstairs is moving and I was telling them he's moving into a new flat. I tell them everything and they tell me what they know. Just general news.'

(Vera Watson, working class, son 6½, daughter 3½)

'Well, they're company. When they're not here I miss them. When they're here I tell them off because these two fight. But when they're not here it's *too* quiet. . . .

I've always got someone to talk to, no matter what age they are. I don't like being alone. If I had my preferences I'd like the children. But it doesn't worry me. If I have a visitor we chat. But we don't socialize. We haven't got time.'
(Helen Mowbray, working class, son 6, daughter 2½)

This attitude towards their children was particularly apparent when the women, left alone by their husbands in the evenings, kept their children up as company:

'I usually do let her stay up on Friday nights. I usually do let her stay up and watch TV because I'm usually on me own, so I keep her up for a bit of company for me'.
(Tracey Allen, working class, daughters 4 and 11 months)

'I think they can be good company. My husband usually goes out on a Friday night. Sometimes I look forward to him going. Usually we play a game or something for a little while and watch TV and I'll say, "Oh, I have some cakes!" and we'll have a cup of coffee and some cakes. They don't usually have coffee, just on Friday nights. They go to bed later and I say "Why don't you come in my bed and we'll have some stories". They're amusing if you've got the time. But perhaps if you did it every night, it would get on your nerves.'
(Sheila Wallace, working class, daughter 6, son 3)

(Q: 'Do you find your children good company?')
'It's a case of having to, really. With my husband away so much, they are all the company I have. I'd be lost if I didn't have my children.'
(Debra Lennon, working class, sons 5 and 3)

As Debra Lennon suggests, it may have been because their husbands were away a great deal that the women turned to their children for company.

Whatever the reasons, the working-class women on the whole looked on their children as interesting and enjoyable companions. By contrast, the middle-class women on the whole did not look on their children as companions and did not particularly enjoy their company as such.

'I don't fancy staying home all day. I want to get closer with other *people*. I want to be with *people*, instead of being with children all the time. Because you get rather washed out, if you only live in that circle and never get out. You get stupid in the end.'
(Gillian Nichols, middle class, son 4, daughter 2)

Gillian Nichols's stated reason for turning away from her children was not the irritation she undoubtedly felt in dealing with them but the fact that they were inappropriate and insufficient company for an adult. This attitude was apparent even among middle-class women who enjoyed looking after their children. Naomi Hilde-brand, for example, explains:

'I get bored with them sometimes. I do. Because there's no mental stimulation in it at all. Although you're playing with the children and you *love* the children – I've had a good education and I can't use it at all. My mind is just blank. You enjoy it because *they're* enjoying it. They're happy, and that's lovely, but you're bored too.'
(Naomi Hildebrand, middle class, daughters 4 and 1)

Her boredom with her children as companions did not spoil her enjoyment in looking after them: it simply led her to look elsewhere for interesting company.

These social-class differences in attitudes towards children can also be seen in the women's respective attitudes towards playing with children.[3] On the one hand, working-class women generally looked on their children as people to be enjoyed and playing with them as one way of doing so. 'Play' was defined as something enjoyed and most working-class women were therefore willing to bring it to an end when they themselves were not enjoying it. Middle-class women, on the other hand, more often looked on their children as people to be *brought up* and playing with them as one aspect of bringing them up. 'Play' was defined as something that children needed, and most middle-class women therefore continued it out of a sense of duty, even when they were not enjoying it themselves. These different approaches can be seen in the contrast-ing accounts of two working-class and three middle-class women.

One working-class woman, for example, described this incident from the previous day:

'Some days he's a nuisance, because Susan's got a record player and he wants me to play the records for him. You put on about

six records and then he says "I don't want that record", and you say, "It will go off by itself in a minute, if you let it". But no, that's not good enough for him. He "tuts". He goes "tsts, tsts", like that. Then I got annoyed and I packed it all in yesterday.'
(Sheila Wallace, working class, daughter 6, son 3)

Another describes similar behaviour:

(Q: 'Do you have a set time to play with them?')
'No. I'm in here with them after school. But I don't always play with them. Sometimes we have a rough and tumble on the floor. But I get fed up with that pretty quick. Then they have to play their own games where they don't want me to join in.'
(Jean Elliott, working class, sons 6, 4, and 2)

These women played with their children so long as they enjoyed doing so; when they lost interest they stopped playing. By contrast, the middle-class women felt it was their duty to play with their children and devoted a significant amount of time every day to doing so regardless of their own enjoyment.

'I try to not do any typing *(for her job which she loves)* when Daniel is around. I think it is a bit unfair to him, because the afternoon *should* be his time, really.'
(Jackie Schneider, middle class, sons 4 and 1)

'For a couple of hours or an hour and a half after lunch I always try to devote to *them*. But it's terribly difficult because the games that Mark can play are many and the games Emma can join in are few and she always wants to try to join in. She's too young. She can't play dominoes, picture dominoes, which I've started to play with Mark *(said with growing irritation)*.'
(Angela Bourne, middle class, son 3½, daughter 1½)

'I feel as though I *ought* to take them for a walk after lunch, though I don't always feel like it. I feel I *ought* to. I know they like it. I know they love going to the park and they love a walk and I feel they need the fresh air. I enjoy a really nice walk, but pushing the pram and going to the park and they go on the swings – I can't say it's the most enjoyable occasion.'
(Susan Griffiths, middle class, sons 6½ and 1½, daughter 4½)

In contrast to many working-class women who were simply 'with' their children all day and available to them if they called, most

middle-class women set aside time from their household responsibilities specifically for playing with their children. And because
play was defined as a duty, they set this time aside even when they
did not enjoy it.

On the whole, then, the working-class women's relationships
with their children tended to be relatively straightforward: they
looked to their children for companionship, they generally enjoyed
playing with them for a time, and when they got bored with playing
they turned to other activities. In contrast, the middle-class
women's relationships with their children tended to be more
complex. On the one hand, they did not look on their children as
appropriate companions for themselves, but on the other, they felt
they ought to play with their children for their children's sake.
While some women enjoyed this, others did not. Those who did not
nevertheless determinedly went through the motions of playing
with their children, possibly conveying to them the contradictory
feelings they felt.

Notes

1. The women's accounts of their frustration with these features of their
   situations are their proximal explanations for their frustration: that is,
   the women themselves saw these features as the cause of their feelings.
   While they may have been basically correct in seeing things this way,
   their explanations cannot be taken at face value because their reaction
   to each of the features of motherhood was not *independent* of their
   reaction to each of the others. First, the irritation they felt in response to
   one aspect of child care would probably have affected their feelings
   towards other aspects. Frustration with the setting of child care, for
   example, might well have lowered a woman's *threshold* for finding
   many things about her pre-school children irritating. Second, frustration arising in one area would probably have been expressed in other
   areas as well. For example, irritation arising from 'work overload'
   could also have been expressed in terms of irritation with the setting of
   child care. Finally, the women's particular situation in one aspect would
   probably have affected the way she experienced the others. The
   characteristics of pre-school children, for example, could have been
   more or less irritating to deal with depending on the way child care was
   organized in the family.
2. As the Newsons point out, the professional-class mother has 'committed herself heavily to the theory that friendly verbal explanations will
   produce rational co-operation in the toddler' but finds 'that he is
   rationally unco-operative and that in practice her careful explanation

tends to degenerate into an exasperated scream of "get on and DO it!" '
(Newson and Newson 1974: 77).

3. The patterns described here are remarkably similar to those described
   by Rainwater, Coleman, and Handel (1959) and J. Klein (1965).

· 5 ·
THE ORGANIZATION
AND SETTING
OF CHILD CARE

In this chapter I shall continue to document the experience of those women who did not enjoy looking after their children, focusing on their frustration with the organization and the setting of child care.

The organization of child care

In our society, the sole and final responsibility for children is given to the mother. She alone is responsible for them and she is responsible for them all the time. Her duties as a mother therefore necessarily entail diffuse and comprehensive obligations for their care. In terms of her day-to-day life, this gives her work an unbounded quality which many women find overwhelming and exhausting. Further stress is also created when children and child care interfere with other activities or conflict with other responsibilities.

RESPONSIBILITY WITHOUT BOUNDS

Because their responsibility for their children was constant and complete, many women I interviewed felt overburdened by their workload and out of control of their situation:

'I feel exhausted. I used to be cool, calm, and collected before I had children. Nothing really bothered me; I wasn't a worrier. But I do find they get me down. They do seem to get on top of me. You find that with two children both in nappies and every day or

every other day it's nappies, things become a bit of a drudge. People who say have children close together! When they're grown up it's probably lovely, but they tend to gloss over the fact that when they're young, it's a lot of hard work. I find I'm getting up at about 6.00 in the morning and still working at 9.00 at night; I'm still doing things. And it's too much. It's definitely tiring because you're on the go all day long. Every minute of your day is filled. It's not even like going to work where you've got a lunch hour. In that hour you're completely away. You sit down for lunch with the children but you're still at the job aren't you.'
(Mandy Turner, working class, son 3, daughter 2)

'Just the fact that everything's a constant rush. You haven't got time to do anything in between. In the morning you have to get them dressed, then do the washing. By that time you have to change the baby's nappy again. Then it's time to start getting lunch ready and it just goes on and on. You don't stop at all. There's so much to do, all the time. You're constantly *rushing*.'
(Margaret Samuel, middle class, sons 4 and 2)

'I taught in the East End. I taught little horrors in Hackney and I thought that was hard work, but it's nothing compared to this. Because when you went home, that was it. And Friday evening you didn't see them again till Monday. And if you didn't feel up to it, you didn't go in. I think a lot of women probably regret their children in that sense. With your own children, there's no end to it.'
(Jane Crawford, middle class, twin daughters 2½)

As Jane Crawford points out, child care was felt to be particularly burdensome because it had no natural limits to it. This tended to give rise to a sense of being overwhelmed by the work and out of control of the situation (*see Figure 5(1)* overleaf).

In order to restore a sense of control in their lives and cope with their workload, most of the women tried to create a structure in their work. One way of doing this was by imposing boundaries, in both time and territory, which children and child care were not allowed to cross. Ruth Venables and Claire Hughes, for example, created space for themselves in *time*:

'I would like to give them more of my time. Instead of putting them down for the afternoon, I'd like to be able to do something

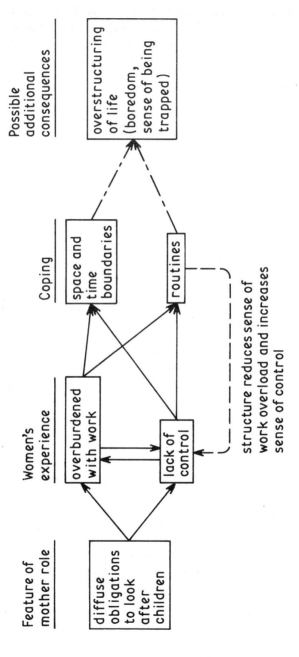

Figure 5(1) *Simplified causal model of frustration and irritation related to diffuse responsibilities*

with them. But I do think if I don't have a break, then before long I shall blow my temper. Their afternoon sleep is very important to *me*. Once I get them up from their rest, we go off to the lake and feed the ducks or we go to friends. But that break is important to *me*.'
(Ruth Venables, middle class, daughter 5, sons 3 and 2)

'One thing, too, is to organize little treats for yourself. I know it sounds awfully childish. Even if it's just an hour with a glossy magazine and a cup of coffee by yourself. But some time during the day, just to keep sane. Because I could dash around, morning till evening, doing all the necessary things. But I just make myself stop. James is changing over from a morning to an afternoon nap but he'll play well by himself if he isn't asleep. An hour and if I'm lucky, an hour and a half. And that's *my time*. You'd be amazed – there are all sorts of things you can't do with very young children around. And that's when I do those things.'
(Claire Hughes, middle class, daughter 5½, son 2½)

For similar reasons, Nina Lockwood and Rosemary Penrose created *physical spaces* for themselves:

'The living room is the room where they mustn't take their toys. Normally during the day I keep it shut because that's the place we like to keep clean, in case someone happens to come over and doesn't want to be knee-deep in children.'
(Nina Lockwood, working class, son 3, daughter 11 months)

'In the kitchen they can do what they like, and in the morning room there's a big table and they can play in their bedrooms, too. But I don't want the living room and the dining room and my husband's study to be an extension of the playrooms. I couldn't stand to have the children *everywhere*.'
(Rosemary Penrose, middle class, son 4½, daughter 2)

The creation of time and space boundaries for children allowed women to feel that child care was limited and contained, and therefore manageable and under control. Women also created important opportunities for the many specific tasks of child care to be handled through *routines* (Oakley 1974a). The development of routines allowed a woman to organize her work so she could deal with the children's demands and get through her work in the time she had available. One woman describes the difference that such routines had made to her:

> 'I feel life is much easier now than it was a year ago. It was much more of a struggle then. I always felt I was fighting against time. Things now seem to run themselves much more smoothly without too much stress or strain but it wasn't always like that. It's because I have a *routine* now, and things seems to fit into it quite well. Everyone fits into it quite easily.'
> (Pauline Lewis, middle class, daughters 9, 5, and 2, son 7)

The creation of an internal structure in their work was undoubtedly valuable to the women in containing the endless burden of their responsibilities and in establishing a sense of order and control in their lives. At the same time, however, the structure they created could give rise to a different kind of frustration when too many boundaries or too rigid routines destroyed the freedom and flexibility that they valued in their domestic roles (*see Figure 5(1)*). Jane Crawford describes this paradox:

> 'Before I was fairly slap happy. I didn't have any set routines. If I thought it was about time I did such and such, I'd do it. And I'd do what I wanted the next week. With children you've got to have a routine. *They* need the routine and *you* need a routine to cope with it all. Even if you feed them on demand, there are certain things which have to be done every day that *have* to be done every day and that I never had before. So you're *stuck* to a routine, but you *have* to have it.'
> (Jane Crawford, middle class, twin daughters 2½)

She needed a routine to cope with the work and she appreciated her routine for that value; at the same time, she resented the way it restricted her day and destroyed her flexibility.

CHILDREN'S INTERFERENCE WITH OTHER ACTIVITIES

Because of the diffuse nature of a woman's responsibilities for her children, children must be looked after at the same time as other activities are performed and other activities carried out at the same time as children are cared for. As a consequence of this temporal merging, children may disrupt their mothers' other activities, which spoils the women's enjoyment of these activities and generates resentment towards the children themselves.

In this study, housework was the most obvious activity that children disrupted, while shopping was most frequently mentioned as an inherently enjoyable activity which children made a stressful chore:

'I like shopping, going down to Croydon. But I don't like it for shoes because I have to take him with me as well as the baby. He has to stop at all the toy shops and he wants things, and I have to tell him he can't have them. And it slows me down. I like to have a quick look around before I buy anything but I can't because he gets tired walking around. And he whines. And he does play up a bit while you're waiting to be served. He runs about and disappears. I can't think straight when I'm trying to keep track of him and to do my shopping as well. It spoils it. I don't enjoy it with him there.'
(Dawn Straker, working class, son 4, daughter 1)

Car journeys were also mentioned:

'I do a lot of driving – chauffeuring – and I thought how marvellous if I could just go off. Because I quite enjoy driving, but I loathe driving with the children. They're not awfully good in the car. And I thought how lovely to go off for a long drive. Go off and see somebody by myself without the children squeaking.'
(Anne Wootton, middle class, daughters 5 and 2, son 3)

And so were telephone calls:

'The thing I find the most difficult with children is being on the 'phone. That is impossible. I dread it when the 'phone rings because I can't talk to anyone. If I take the telephone upstairs, Isabelle is going to start going in all the other rooms so I've got to put the 'phone down every two seconds so I can see where she is because I'm afraid she's going to eat my make-up or something. Or go into my husband's study. So you've got to be watching all the time. When I'm on the 'phone they love to go there and open the drawers and take everything out. That drives me round the bend.'
(Rosemary Penrose, middle class, son 4½, daughter 2)

In each case, the women found it impossible to concentrate on their immediate task with their children also demanding their attention. This tension between the two sets of demands spoiled their enjoyment of the occasion and created a great deal of stress for them.

This twofold complaint was expressed particularly clearly when the women talked about visiting friends. On these occasions the obligation to 'manage' the children was often especially salient and its disruptive effect therefore particularly obvious:

> 'She objects to me talking to someone else. They seem to think their mothers are something that are theirs and no one else can talk to or . . . she will do her utmost to get my attention, when I'm with someone else – shout, scream, throw things. She *always* spills a drink, sometimes on purpose for attention, which is mortifying. You can't think along the lines of what you're saying. It's distracting. It's very, very hard on your nerves. And I'm sure I tell people the same thing over and over again.'
> (Victoria Milton, middle class, daughter 3½, son 1½)

Like most of the other women in this group, she concludes that she would rather not go visiting:

> 'I'd rather not go visiting people. It's too embarrassing. And I'm terrified something's going to get broken with him. Rather than risk going and having him break something, I'd rather them come here. Which means, of course, that I never go out and have someone else make the coffee.'

The implications of this are obvious: she stayed home rather than go out to different places; she saw a limited number of people and only those who, like herself, had young children; and she never escaped from a child-centred world.

THE CONFLICT BETWEEN DOMESTIC RESPONSIBILITIES

While the temporal merging of child care and domestic duties may give rise to irritation when children disrupt a woman's activities, the more basic merging of responsibilities for husband, house, and children may also give rise to irritation when child care obligations conflict with the obligations of housework and husband-care. The most common type of conflict encountered by the women I interviewed was that between the responsibilities of a mother and those of a housewife. On the one hand, current psychologically oriented theories of child rearing prescribe a free atmosphere for children to explore, learn, and grow in: stimulation and individual discovery are desirable and restriction and repression are to be avoided. On the other hand, the standards of housework require a clean, tidy, well-ordered house, with a place for everything and everything in its place. The two clearly conflict and must be coped with in some way.

Virtually all the women in the study coped with this potential conflict by giving priority to children and child care:

'I like my house to look reasonable: clean and tidy. But during the day I don't bother too much with the children around. I don't think it's fair on the children if you're forever clearing up. If they're both home and have their toys around, if you keep tidying up after them, I'm sure they'd tend to not play with their toys and not want to play with them. And then how would they learn? They'd just sit there and be pretty little vegetables.'
(Colleen Johnston, middle class, daughters 6 and 3)

'At one stage I was houseproud, and I was forever dusting and polishing and cleaning. But now, once they are enjoying themselves, I just let it go. As long as *they* are clean: that's my first priority.'
(Ruth Venables, middle class, daughter 5, sons 3 and 2)

'I look forward to the time when I can be more houseproud. But I'm not prepared at the moment to say "You mustn't touch this, or have that", for the sake of neatness. It isn't fair to them, to be always restricting them. But I hope as they get older they can learn to do things, like, if we have a record-player out, you don't fiddle with it.'
(Jane Crawford, middle class, twin daughters 2½)

As Jane Crawford implies, the strategy of subordinating housework to child care did not do away with the conflict between them: it simply reduced the tensions to a more manageable level. By concentrating on their children and by reminding themselves it was only for a short time, the women were able to accept the drop in their housework standards. The tensions themselves, however, continued to percolate beneath the surface and it required constant efforts to keep them submerged.

Another way of resolving conflict was to try and maintain high standards in both roles. Naomi Hildebrand describes how:

'At 9 o'clock, I let them get all their toys out; I put the gate up on the stairs and I just leave them to it. It's been very good because it's let Ann get to know the baby. I find they play so much better on their own than when I'm around. That takes an hour or so while I'm going around the house, putting the washing in the machine, clearing up, dusting, and then I get myself dressed. I like the house to look tidy. Very tidy. Except for toys. I don't mind any toys. You can see there are a lot of toys out now, but things that I control myself have got to be tidy. Toys are a different matter. I think children have got to have toys out. And I don't like a house that hasn't got toys out. I don't think it looks like children are in it. At night they all go back in the cupboard and we start fresh in the morning.'

(Naomi Hildebrand, middle class, daughters 4 and 1)

Her morning organization was such that she felt she was both caring for her children well and getting all her housework done efficiently. Similarly, her distinction between the basic cleanliness and tidiness of the house on the one hand and the clutter of toys on the other separated the two sets of responsibilities and drew them out of conflict. By keeping the house basically clean and tidy she saw herself as fulfilling her housewife obligations and maintaining a high standard of housekeeping; by having toys about she could fulfil her obligations to her children and maintain a high standard of child care.

This emphasis on liking toys around was a common theme. Mandy Turner repeats it:

'They get out their toys and they have their toys all over the place and all day long this goes on, and it doesn't bother me one bit. I think, "This is their life". But just as soon as my husband comes in, he doesn't like to see it and he says, "Come on, let's pick all these toys up".'

(Mandy Turner, working class, son 3, daughter 2)

The emphasis on toys was perhaps because the women needed to reassure themselves that they had resolved the conflict in the way they believed was best and were not letting housework impinge on the children. It appeared to be for some a symbol of allegiance to the current trends in child rearing, or at least visible evidence that they gave priority to their children. It was not always successful, however, as a strategy to resolve the conflict between housework and child care or to reduce the tension which the conflict engendered. Mandy Turner continues:

'I worry if the place is untidy if anyone comes. I must dust and I must hoover and I must get this done. Probably that must worry me. I have to make sure everything is done. There are days even now where I think I must do this and this and they think *they* should have your attention. Sometimes I push them away or ignore them crying even and do what I was doing.'

Another woman echoes her feelings:

'I always have a scurry round when people are coming for dinner. It takes me all day to clean. Otherwise, if people drop in, I just apologise.'
(Q: 'Does it worry you when people drop in?')
'Well, deep down it does, I suppose. I wish I had an immaculate house. Some people's houses I go to, I don't know how they do it. It looks like they've got no children living in it at all. I wish mine could be like that, but it doesn't matter what I do. I do try, but it doesn't matter what I do, as soon as I get it looking spotless, the children bring all their toys in again. Which I suppose they have a right to do, but. . . .'
(June Robertson, middle class, daughters 3½ and 2)

For some of the women, then, there was a pressure to maintain their housekeeping standards that was in direct conflict with their desire to follow the child-rearing principles they also subscribed to. This may have been because the housewife role was an older and more established role with which they had already identified before having children. It may also have been because housework standards were more clearly visible: the effort put into housework gave immediate concrete results and therefore an immediate feeling of accomplishment and of using time profitably. A clean well-ordered house also reflected well on the woman as housewife: others could see the results of her effort and judge her accordingly. Whatever the reasons for it, this felt pressure to maintain their housework standards meant that maintaining their standards in child care had become difficult and stressful for a number of women. This was particularly noticeable among the working-class group, who described feelings of role conflict more often than the comparable middle-class group. This class difference may have been due to a stronger identification with the traditional housewife role on the part of working-class women which made it more difficult for them to distance themselves from it in the way the middle-class women tended to (Komarovsky 1962; Oakley 1974a). It may also have arisen from the fact that middle-class women on the whole had more space and labour-saving devices which enabled them to avoid the conflict to some extent and, as Naomi Hildebrand did, to maintain high standards on both fronts.

The setting of child care

Child care is set within the domestic sector of society and within this sector, in individual household units. Women who look after children are therefore largely excluded from the productive sector of society and to a great extent tied to their individual homes. This tie is reinforced by the particular needs and demands of young children which make it difficult for women to leave their homes and which further prevent them from integrating into the larger world of paid employment.

ISOLATION FROM REWARDING COMPANY

Only three of the 50 women I interviewed felt that they spent too much time on their own during the day. Most of them saw, or spoke to, several friends every day. Nonetheless, many of these women described themselves as dissatisfied with the company they had and, if not isolated, then at least cut off from the sort of varied company they felt they needed:

'Yesterday, for example, I had two girls in and looked after one girl's baby while she went to the doctor. Then I had another girl this morning for coffee. And I had another at lunch time with two children. I see several different people every day. But the conversation always ends up with babies and things, because they all have one child only. And I've got to the stage where I've had enough of babies and children. I'd rather go somewhere where I can talk to people without any interest in babies. I've joined a badminton club again, and on the rare occasions when I can go, it's lovely to be there because they're not talking about babies. With the first child you'll find you accept "Let's all compare notes and sit down and talk about babies". But with the second one, you're fed up.'
(Victoria Milton, middle class, daughter 3½, son 1½)

'Most of the people I mix about with are like myself. The people here, we all know each other fairly well and we know each

others' children. So of course she'll have a moan at me about the kids and I'll have a moan to her. And really, what else is there to talk about? When I went to Keep Fit we never spoke about the kids. Yes, I think I would like a bit more of that sort of company. I get a bit weighed down with the children, conversation-wise.'
(Sandra Keating, working class, daughters 7 and 4)

It is unlikely that they will find the sort of companionship they are looking for among their friends since they, like themselves, are largely confined to the domestic sector of society and have no new perspective to spark the imagination. One woman makes this point:

(Q: 'Do you feel you are on your own too much during the day?')
'No, not really. I've got the telephone. And we go out quite a lot. But I'd like to have more *varied* company sometimes. People with interests other than my own. Your friends tend to be leading the same sort of life you lead, so the same daily happenings are happening to them as well. So like on holidays and Christmas, you mostly discuss *children*. You never discuss anything unusual.'
(Sarah Hepburn, middle class, daughter 6, son 2)

Several of the women added that even among those who wanted to broaden their conversation, their children prevented a stimulating, thoughtful, or coherent discussion. Jackie Schneider, for example, says:

'One does become a bit of a cabbage in many ways. Because when we do meet in the afternoons, we don't discuss politics. You can't because with one eye you've always got to watch the kids. So you can't have a proper conversation anyway. And I suppose one does compare notes. Perhaps your child doesn't want to know about the potty so you ask your friends how they managed to train theirs.'
(Jackie Schneider, middle class, sons 4 and 1)

Although the company of other mothers was frequently mentioned as a source of frustration, the very same feature was mentioned as a source of positive pleasure and reward by thirteen women (*see Table 5(1)*). These women emphasized the sense of community support and companionship among their friends:

(Q: 'Do you feel you are on your own too much during the day?')
'No, we have a close community. I need people around me. And it helps life all the time.'
(Q: 'Are these the other mothers in the neighbourhood?')
'Yes, mostly very much the same as me. We have a lot in common. In the *evenings* I don't like to talk about children too much. I like to talk about other things, but I don't mind talking about children. I don't appreciate an evening where it's baby talk the whole time. But when we're on our own during the day. . . .'
(Naomi Hildebrand, middle class, daughters 4 and 1)

Table 5(1) *Enjoyment of 'community of mothers' and social class*

| Social class | Enjoyment of 'community of mothers' | | |
	positive no. (%)	negative or neutral no. (%)	total no. (%)
working class	10 (40)	15 (60)	25 (100)
middle class	3 (12)	22 (88)	25 (100)
total	13 (26)	37 (74)	50 (100)

$x^2 = 5.09 < 0.05$

'We know a lot of people around here. It's like a little community. All the Mums know each other because nobody goes to work. There's about eight Mums and we all met at the clinic. We used to go to playschool together and now we take the kids to school together. We've got a lot of friends because we do know the same people really. We pop in on each other all the time. There's two big blocks of flats over there and in the summer we see everyone. We all go to the park with the kids or go and sit in someone's garden.'
(Tracey Allen, working class, daughters 4 and 11 months)

(Q: 'Do you feel you are on your own too much during the day?')
'No, not really, because we do coffee mornings. We take turns, ten or twelve of us. All the neighbours come in. We did our coffee morning today. It's all friends we've had since nursery school. I go to Keep Fit Tuesday nights and they all go as well. We talk about everything. If someone is going on the Pill and is worried,

we tell them what we think, and things. We compare things with the children – silly little things.'
(Vera Watson, working class, son 6½, daughter 3½)

They enjoyed such companionship because they felt their friends were friends in the true sense of the word: they were people with whom they shared personal activities, and people with whom they could discuss things on a personal level. It is interesting to note that five of the women who spoke warmly about the companionship and support they found in the community of mothers did not enjoy looking after their children. While their friendship with the other women was based on their role as mothers they saw it as largely independent of their child care responsibilities. It was one of the 'perks' of their domestic roles which, though enjoyed in itself, did not make motherhood a rewarding experience.

Their range of social contacts was seen as a source of frustration by a larger proportion of middle-class than working-class women. This may have been because the sort of companionship the working-class women had as mothers was similar to that which they had had before they had children. The contrast with their previous experience was not so sharp, nor the gap between expectations and experience so wide: their contact with others was therefore not so often *perceived* as a source of frustration. In addition, working-class women may have found some companionship in their children, and so may not have felt the lack of rewarding company so keenly. (Chapter 4 described how working-class women looked to their children for companionship.) Though probably unsatisfying in the long term, so long as the children provided them with some sense of companionship, this might have militated against working-class women perceiving their range of social contacts as a source of frustration.

CHILDREN AS A TIE TO THE HOME

The way that children tie their mothers to the home is frequently cited as one of the main frustrations of child care (Gavron 1966; Lopata 1971; Comer 1974; Oakley 1974a, 1980). Indeed, 'loss of personal freedom' is almost universally accepted as inherent in maternity and it is the reason for avoiding childbirth most frequently given by 'intentionally childless' women (Veevers 1973a; Baum and Cope 1980). It is not surprising, then, that the majority of women in this study who did not enjoy looking after their children referred to this aspect of their lives in particular.

Children tied their mothers to the home in three main ways. First, the time-consuming task of getting young children ready to go out discouraged many women from even trying to get away from the home:

'I'm stuck here with the two kids and he can just go off when he wants to. I wish sometimes that I could just get ready and go out and not worry about the kids. But it's such a hassle getting them ready too, I can't be bothered. That's why I think that if anybody doesn't want kids, I don't blame them. Because they do tie you down. It's just that you have to put up with it. But it would be lovely to be free, to get out more.'
(Tracey Allen, working class, daughters 4 and 11 months)

'I sit here and say, "It's not worth it, to go to Peckham (*where her mother lives*). By the time you get ready and get them ready and get on that bus, no, it's not worth it". And I *pounce* on my husband when he comes in, as a grown-up to talk to. But I don't *say* anything, because I haven't been anywhere.'
(Sheila Wallace, working class, daughter 6, son 3)

Second, the difficulty in getting around with children and the supplies they require severely restricted the distances most women could go.

'You have to be strong to be a mother. Because, try lifting a pram plus a child plus another child up a hill. Buses should be *banned*. It's absolutely impossible: they never wait till you're on and sitting down before they start. It's a continual battle.'
(Victoria Milton, middle class, daughter 3½, son 1½)

'When we first moved here, we had a car. Then we sold it. And I noticed the difference being bound indoors, because it's impossible to take two small children out without a car. I find that very constricting. We're stuck here and the furthest I can go is the high street except when someone gives me a lift which is rare.'
(Colleen Johnston, middle class, daughters 6 and 3)

While Colleen Johnston implies that a car would lessen the tie children impose, six of the seventeen women who had the use of a car during the day felt it provided less of a release than might have been expected. They pointed out that the difficulties involved in taking children out in a car meant that they did not use it often and that, when they did, the stresses entailed in visiting further discouraged them from doing so frequently. This is the third way in which children tied women to the home: they made the whole experience of visiting friends so difficult that many women 'preferred' to stay at home. This is not to say they necessarily enjoyed staying home but simply that it was preferable to an even more stressful alternative. Jackie Schneider, for example, was bored at home, but explains why she chose not to visit people, despite having her own car:

> 'My sister-in-law, for example, her children are older. She's got the sort of house where it's forever "Don't touch this", "Don't touch that". I just can't bear it. So I don't go there any more. I feel uneasy because I know he's going to be told off.'
> (Jackie Schneider, middle class, sons 4 and 1)

Mandy Turner, too, regretted the fact that she had had to give up visiting friends because 'it wasn't worth the effort, I didn't enjoy it':

> 'I prefer people to come to visit me, than for me to visit them, because I know what they're like. They're always into things. I always find when we go out somewhere, other people aren't prepared and they usually end up breaking something which is embarrassing. And all the time I'm not relaxed when I'm out because I'm watching what they're doing and making sure they aren't into things.'
> (Mandy Turner, working class, son 3, daughter 1)

When the home is the only place that is suitable for children in the sense of allowing a mother to cope with them relatively smoothly, it is not surprising that there is a tendency to remain there despite the frustration it entails.

· 6 ·
MONOPOLIZATION AND
LOSS OF INDIVIDUALITY

The description of the women's experience as mothers has so far caused three social-class differences to emerge. First, while working-class women generally looked to their children for companionship and played with them so long as they enjoyed it themselves, middle-class women on the whole neither expected their children to be good company nor regulated their play according to their own pleasure in it. Second, a significant proportion of working-class women, perhaps strongly identified with the housewife role, found it difficult and stressful to resolve the conflict between housework and child-care responsibilities; more middle-class women, in contrast, experienced relatively little tension and guilt in this area. Finally, getting on for half of the working-class women enjoyed the companionship of the local community of mothers whom they knew through their children, while only three of the middle-class women did so.

A broader look at the women's accounts of their experience of motherhood shows a further and perhaps more important class difference in the way the working-class and middle-class women described and explained their frustration in looking after their children. In describing their daily experience, the working-class women on the whole emphasized the practical difficulties they faced in carrying out their responsibilities as mothers: they concentrated largely on the difficulties in getting through their work and the problems in getting away from the house with young children. Implied in their accounts was the view that the solution to their difficulties lay in greater material wealth and the household aids which would make child care easier. The middle-class women, on the other hand, tended to emphasize more basic difficulties rooted in the way the care of children is organized in our society: they stressed the difficulties that arose from looking after children while at the same time engaged in other activities, and the problems they faced in mixing more generally in society while still responsible for children. In addition, they conveyed a frustration with the overall impact of motherhood on their lives in describing a sense of 'monopolization' and 'loss of individuality' in motherhood. The implication of their accounts – though never stated explicitly – was that the solution to their problem lay in a more fundamental change in the way the care of children is organized at societal level.

This class difference in the way the women described their frustration and the level at which they attempted to account for it (implicitly or explicitly) is very striking. The working-class women almost always described their frustration only in terms of specific features of child care. The middle-class women, although they described such specific features as frustrating, always mentioned the more fundamental sense of monopolization and loss of individuality as well. That is, all fifteen middle-class women who were irritated with looking after their children described the way they experienced the basic features of the mother role – exclusive responsibility for children and responsibility for them all the time – as inhibiting their personal freedom and autonomy and as replacing their identity as individuals with their identity as mothers; this held for only two of the eleven comparable working-class women.

Typical of the middle-class women who felt monopolized by their children is Anne Wootton. She says:

'I think that children take away your whole life – your *identity* really. You can never be yourself with your children around. They're so demanding they take everything from you. Then come the evening, you're too exhausted to revert back to yourself. Your whole day, your whole life – you're completely involved with your children. Physically it's very demanding. But mentally, too; you can't think. Life's become much more restricted, much harder work, and generally the children have taken over. One can't sit down without being monopolized by children. You can't have any time to yourself. While the children are home, you have to just muck in with whatever *they* want to do, rather than pursue what you want to do. There's no doubt about it, that your children just *monopolize* you, mentally, physically, and emotionally. One is all day thinking about them. Even if you try to put them to the back of your mind – I don't think children allow you to. Especially if you've got three active children who demand attention all the time.'

(Anne Wootton, middle class, daughters 5 and 2, son 3)

The volume of work, the demands of the children, their interference in her other interests, and the restriction which children imposed all contributed to this overall response: together, they were experienced as a sense that 'generally, the children have taken over'.

Related to this sense of being taken over by the children was the sense that 'you can never be yourself with your children around'. Children took away a woman's identity:

'You give up a lot. I think you give up individuality. In that you are a mother with young children, you tend to remain as a *mother* rather than yourself. But it's very difficult to have an identity of your own, when you have so many people, not relying on you but *needing* you. So you tend to have to consider everyone else before you consider yourself and what *you* want to do. And it's very hard.'

(Colleen Johnston, middle class, daughters 6 and 3)

She traced her loss of identity to the need to 'consider everyone else before you consider yourself'. This was, for these women, the underlying rule of motherhood and the meaning of their sole and constant responsibility for the children. Their sense of monopolization and loss of individuality may be seen, on the one hand, as a response to this rule directly; on the other hand, the principle of 'putting the children first' gives rise to the various elements of child care described in the two previous chapters and a sense of monopolization and loss of individuality may also be seen as a global response to these specific elements. In either view, they are essentially responses to the experience of motherhood as a whole.

The majority of women who spoke of their sense of loss of individuality related it to the principle that the children should be put first:

'You have to be prepared to sacrifice. You have to sacrifice a great deal when you have children.'

(Q: 'What have you sacrificed?)
'Freedom. The freedom to do what you want without considering others. You can't – you have to think of them *first*. Whatever you plan, you can't plan unless you have taken care of your children. That's the first thing. If you want to go out, you can't. If you haven't got anyone to look after your children, you can't.'
(Gillian Nichols, middle class, son 4, daughter 2)

'You can't do *anything* without thinking of their welfare first. You can't even go to the loo. You've got to see that they're all right when they're around – *first*. Your life is not your own. You can pretend children aren't there, but they are and that's it. That's why I wouldn't advise anyone to go and do it light-heartedly.'
(Claire Hughes, middle class, daughter 5½, son 2½)

'Your life isn't your own once you've got children. You can never think, "I'll go to Croydon this afternoon", or "I'll go to the cinema this evening". You're no longer free. You're no longer able to do what *you* want to do.'
(Sarah Hepburn, middle class, daughter 6, son 2)

Many women found that thinking of their children *first* meant thinking of their children *only*:

'What surprised me most is how demanding they are and how little time one has left for oneself. One never realizes quite how much one's freedom is gone with children. We used to go out quite a lot during the week. Have our meal and just get in the car and go. But we can't do that now. Everything has to be planned. You can't *spontaneously* do anything.'
(June Robertson, middle class, daughters 3½ and 2)

Like Anne Wootton, June Robertson felt monopolized by her children and had no time or energy left for herself as an individual. Claire Hughes makes the same points in regard to more specific activities:

'It's a very difficult adjustment. I felt all the time I was battling with them. I wanted to do all the things *I* wanted to do, and James wouldn't let me. I have lots and lots of interests and hobbies, like sewing and painting and renovating furniture and collecting Victoriana. And I felt I just could not do any of these

things. I was all the time working towards it. I'd get up in the morning and I'd think, "When I've done such and such, then I'll do what *I* want". A bit of sewing or something. And I'd spend the whole day working towards this aim and never get there. . . . I started making toys and I got very involved in it. A toy shop ordered some and I thought I might pursue it. But I couldn't. I had all these toys arranged all over the house and I was going to do them Sunday after I washed the nappies. And this was really bugging me. Then suddenly I put all these things away out of sight and I felt much better. I thought, "I just *can't* do it and that's that".'
(Q: 'Is this different from what you expected?')
'It is different, I didn't expect it to be so involving. It demands all – or most – of you, most of the time. It takes you over, *completely*.'
  (Claire Hughes, middle class, daughter 5½, son 2½)

She had a number of projects in which she had a great personal investment but which the demands of her children prevented her from pursuing. Her own activities – and her own identity – were pushed out by those of maternity.
  The *timing* of children's demands had a similar effect:

'You can never forget yourself and just go off somewhere. Because the whole time you're clock-watching. Waiting to pick them up or something. So your whole day is run by your children, really. And I don't see how you can get away from it.'
  (Anne Wootton, middle class, daughters 5 and 2, son 3)

As she points out, the children's schedule broke up her day so much that she had no suitable time left for herself. She could not forget herself and so could not escape from the mother role even when the children were not around.
  Finally, the constant physical presence of the children also contributed to a sense of being monopolized. The women felt they had no suitable *space* in which to maintain an independent existence or a sense of separateness from the children:

'I think when you're a mother everywhere you go, the children got to go with you. You can't do anything on your own. They're always there, with you.'
  (Vera Watson, working class, son 6½, daughter 3½)

'You've got no privacy. And I can't stand that. It's all right when they're very young because you can put them to bed and they sleep. But as they get older, they're always there at your elbow.'
(Maureen Richards, middle class, daughter 3, son 11 months)

In both cases the women found that the constant physical presence of their children intruded into their personal space and disrupted their sense of independent existence. The implication was that they needed space as well as time in which to be themselves in order to maintain their sense of individuality.

Coping with a sense of monopolization was more difficult than coping with specific practical difficulties arising from child care and most of the seventeen women simply accepted that this stage of childhood was inherently frustrating. In order to sustain themselves through it, a number of women emphasized that it lasted only a limited period and would be followed by more enjoyable times. Looking forward to the future made it easier for them to accept their current frustration and to continue to perform their roles despite it:

'I wouldn't want to spend the rest of my life doing what I'm doing now, being constrained as I am now in these ways. But it's only for two more years, till this one is at school full-time.'
(Colleen Johnston, middle class, daughters 6 and 3)

'I'm not in a hurry to get rid of them because I know in a couple of years *I'll be all right*. It's only three years, four at the most.'
(June Robertson, middle class, daughters 3½ and 2)

'First of all I thought, "This isn't going to last for ever. My children are going to be grown up very soon and I shall be saying 'Weren't they lovely when they were tiny' ". And I thought "Well, I *must* enjoy it".'
(Claire Hughes, middle class, daughter 5½, son 2½)

This approach of tolerance and anticipation appeared to be quite effective in sustaining the women through difficult times. It was limited as a way of coping, however, as it did not appear to increase a woman's ability to enjoy looking after her children. The women regretted this, as Margaret Samuel suggests:

'It does get better as they get older, I'm sure. But I feel in a way that I am missing out because I'm not enjoying it, because I didn't enjoy Martin. So many people say to you, "Oh, you regret it when they're older. You'll look back and you'll say 'Oh, wasn't it lovely. I wish they were young again' ". I don't know. I think, "Once they are older. . .". But you are wishing their lives away which isn't right.'

(Margaret Samuel, middle class, sons 4 and 2)

One could almost say that she was frustrated and unhappy with the fact that she was frustrated and unhappy looking after her children.

A sense of being monopolized by children and losing individuality in motherhood was described much more frequently by middle-class women than by working-class women. This striking difference must raise the question of how far working-class women *experienced* something comparable to these feelings but found it more difficult to describe them in an interview setting. While it is difficult to be confident here, there are several differences in the situation of middle-class and working-class women which might well account for their different responses. First, it has been argued that working-class women are oriented more exclusively to domestic concerns and have fewer interests outside their families than middle-class women (Komarovsky 1962; Gavron 1966). It is possible, therefore, that the demands of their children were seen not as monopolizing them nor as taking over their identity as individuals but as giving them a focus of interest of a kind they had not experienced before. It is not that in any sense their children took up less of their time, energy, or attention; it is, rather, that because they had fewer interests to compete with the children they did not experience children as so monopolizing. Similarly, their main interests – and concomitantly their identity as individuals – may have been more thoroughly centred around their domestic roles and the need to put their children first may therefore have more readily tended to *express* their individuality than to undermine it.

A second reason for this class difference may be the fact that middle-class women had more material resources than working-class women which enabled them to cope more easily with the basic routines in their domestic roles. This in turn *appeared* to allow them the time and freedom to pursue more personal interests outside their domestic roles. It was when they tried – and largely failed – to follow these other interests, that they discovered the restrictions inherent in the way the mother role is institutionalized in our society. That is, when they were released from the constant burden of domestic chores the full implications of their sole and final responsibility for their children became clear: however light their immediate workload, they still had to subordinate their freedom and autonomy to their children and put the children first. Their sense of monopolization and loss of individuality reflected the frustration they felt as a consequence of these broad and fundamental restrictions.

By contrast, working-class women, with fewer resources, faced the more elementary problem of getting through their daily routines. They were usually not in a position to consider activities outside their domestic duties and so were perhaps less likely to confront the fundamental limits inherent in their role. Instead, practical difficulties tended to focus their irritation on much more specific issues within the bounds of their domestic roles. They were more likely to hint that their difficulties arose from their material circumstances – no garden, no washing machine, no car, for example – and to look to improved material conditions for their solution. They may have been quite realistic in expecting to enjoy child care more when they had more material advantages but they were not yet aware of the likelihood that new problems would arise when these practical problems were solved. Their accounts of their frustration and irritation as mothers reflected the limitations of their material circumstances and left untouched the more fundamental restrictions of their social position.

Summary

Although they have dealt with a variety of features in the women's situation, these last three chapters have considered only one dimension of the women's experience as mothers: their immediate response to motherhood. This is clearly an important dimension of their experience and it is the one about which the women had the most to say. It does not, however, present the whole picture: in addition to their immediate response, a number of women described their more reflective or interpretive response to looking after their children. This response was relatively independent of their immediate response to motherhood and was described in quite different terms. In the next chapter, then, I shall move on to consider in detail what is meant by a sense of meaning and purpose in motherhood and to present the kinds of experiences to which a measure of this refers. For this dimension, I shall document the experience of those who felt a strong sense of meaning and purpose as mothers.

· 7 ·
A SENSE OF
MEANING AND PURPOSE

In their discussions of the experience of meaningfulness, psychologists appear to agree that it derives from an individual's sense or view of herself as pursuing important aims or fulfilling a purpose to which she is committed. Klinger, for example, states that 'meaningfulness seems to arise out of people's relationship with their incentives' (Klinger 1977: 10): when they can pursue and enjoy important, valued incentives, their lives feel meaningful; when they are deprived of important, valued incentives, their lives feel less meaningful. Battista and Almond take a similar view, but spell it out in more detail. From their review of a wide range of philosophical and psychological works they conclude that:

> 'when an individual states that his life is meaningful, he implies (1) that he is positively committed to some concept of the meaning of life; (2) that this concept of the meaning of life provides him with some framework or goal from which to view his life; (3) that he perceives his life as related to or fulfilling this concept of the meaning of life; (4) that he experiences this fulfilment as a feeling of integration, relatedness, or significance.
> (Battista and Almond 1973: 410)

Fundamental to a sense of meaningfulness, then, is involvement in an important purpose or 'incentive' (in Klinger's terms) or commitment to a valued goal or 'concept of the meaning of life' (in Battista's and Almond's terms). For women especially, it is children who are expected to provide a major incentive or concept of the meaning of life and it is in caring for their children that they are expected to experience a sense of meaning, value, and significance.[1]

Although vague concepts such as satisfaction with motherhood have tended to obscure a sense of meaning and purpose as an independent theme in women's experience, a few authors have made some reference to it. Busfield (1974) and Busfield and Paddon (1977), for example, state that the meaning and significance children are believed to give people's lives is a central theme in their desire to have children. Blake too found that for high proportions of her respondents children were seen as having 'social investment value', that is, value 'for providing meaning in life, for giving women a status without which they would be unfulfilled and for cementing marriages' (Blake 1979: 251). Blood and Wolfe state that 'children give life purpose through providing something to work for, plan for, look forward to' (Blood and Wolfe 1960: 139). Rainwater felt that it was for working-class women, more than for middle-class women, that children provided an understanding of their 'reason for being' and a valued focus which defined their purpose in life (Rainwater, Coleman, and Handel 1959; Rainwater and Weinstein 1974). The Pahls (1971), however, obliquely suggest that many managers and their wives make meaningful their hard work and difficult career decisions in terms of their benefit to the children, and Goldthorpe et al. (1969) imply that a similar situation exists for the affluent workers, whose familistic orientation also suggests that they work for the sake of the family.

In this study, too, the majority of women (58 per cent) made it clear that their children were an important incentive in which they were emotionally involved and to which they were deeply committed. Their children therefore gave them a purpose and in pursuing this purpose, they experienced their lives as meaningful. In the rest of this chapter, I shall look at some of the ways in which the women found, and conveyed, this sense of meaningfulness in motherhood.

The nature of a sense of meaning, value, and significance

THE CHILDREN'S DEPENDENCE: BEING NEEDED AND WANTED

Each of the twenty-nine women who felt a strong sense of meaning, value, and significance in motherhood referred in some way to the children's dependence on them as a basis for it: they saw that their children needed them and they therefore felt that they had a purpose in their children.

When children were very young, their total dependence brought this home very forcefully:

'I love babies. They're dependent. They need you a lot.'
(Ivy Cullen, working class, sons 5, 4, and 11 months)

This sense of being essential to a baby was one of the greatest attractions of motherhood, and it was a common theme in the accounts of the twenty-nine women.

'This is my favourite stage so far (*eighteen-month-old son*). Susie's growing up now, but this is my favourite stage at the moment. I've never gone keen on everybody else's baby but mine. I like them because they are *dependent* on you. When they grow up, older, they get more independent. And though I want them to get more independent, in some ways I don't. It's nice to have someone who's *dependent* on you, someone who *needs* you.'
(Maureen Richards, middle class, daugher 4, son 1½)

The children's need for their mothers was felt as especially compelling because it was seen as a need for them as *unique individuals*: the children not only needed attention, they wanted it from their *mothers* in particular. The intensity of the feelings that this engendered is clear in the following comments:

'Just like a dog would be lost without its master, it will do anything for you no matter what you do to it. It's a lifelong thing. I think with a child it's the same sort of thing. When they're little, to them you're *everything*, the whole world. It changes, but when they're this age . . . being *wanted*. At the beginning even Father doesn't come into it really. They definitely know you if you're feeding them. I remember when they were babies and they were being held by grandmother and you leave the room. When you come back the head turns immediately in your direction. And people say, "He knows who his mother is". That's one of the things that makes it worthwhile. That's when they're very little. When they're older, they smile at you or say nice things to you. They're special to you and *you're special to them*.'
(Margaret Samuel, middle class, sons 4 and 1½)

Her description of her experience is remarkably similar to the psychologists' description of the process of bonding (Klaus and Kennell 1976; Schaffer 1977a). During the first weeks of looking after them, most women come to know their children intimately, to recognize their individuality of needs and expressions, and so to establish a sensitive relationship with them. The children in turn come to respond to their mothers' care and attention and soon to respond differentially to the mother. The result is that deep emotional bonds are formed between a woman and her children. This bond, or deep emotional attachment, is one reason for a woman's strong commitment to her children as a valued incentive or purpose in life which is in turn fundamental to her sense of meaningfulness and value.

The obvious *physical* dependence of babies gives most women a very clear-cut purpose which they can readily identify, strive for, and see themselves as fulfilling. But when children grow older and are able to do more for themselves they do not need their mothers in the same obvious ways and their mothers' sense of meaning and purpose may become more precarious. Ethological studies of animals suggest that, as the offspring become more independent, bonds may fade and a mother may eventually cease to recognize and care for her offspring. The women who felt a strong sense of meaning, value, and significance, however, said that, as they grew up, children became not so much less dependent as dependent in different ways. They stressed that their children still needed emotional support and attention and that this *emotional dependence* was as important as their physical dependence had been:

> 'They don't need you so much as they get older but at the same time I find he doesn't need me for the little things but he needs me to come home to. He needs a listener. If he gets stuck with something he needs me to help. They have great admiration for the teacher but the teacher is always someone who is a little aloof. They need someone who's familiar. If something goes wrong at school they need someone to come home to and if they've been unhappy they can tell you about it or they can just come to you for affection. *They need you in new ways.*'
> (Ivy Cullen, working class, sons 5, 4, and 11 months)

The children's selective dependence on the mother was seen just as clearly in their emotional dependence as in their physical dependence. The children singled out their mothers for confidences, support, and comfort and this special preference for their mothers again intensified the sense of meaning and purpose the women felt:

'My husband doesn't help with them because it's just *me* with Lisa and Lisa always wants *me*. She won't let her father do it. Susie was off her Dad for a while, too. She was always on me. It's their Mum they want, not their Dad.'

(Eleanor Gordon, middle class, daughters 5½ and 3)

'He's independent in his own way, but he'll always come to *me*. For advice and things. He'll always tell me about his own problems. If he had a fight at school, he'll always come to me and tell me about it. They're very close to me. All of them. They always come to me. They tell me everything. If they have something to say, they always come to *me*. They know I can be trusted.'

(Sally Friar, working class, daughters 12 and 3, son 10)

Many of the women in the strong meaning and purpose group could see their children's emotional need for them in almost any activity. Anne Fitzgerald, for example, saw it in her son's reaction when she went out:

'Last week I went out two nights in a row. The first night Tony *(her husband)* was here and the second night we had a baby-sitter. On the second night Graham said "Oh Mummy, you mustn't go out again. You mustn't go out every night". You could see he was terribly upset. I was very touched.'

(Anne Fitzgerald, middle class, sons 4 and 2)

Another woman saw it in the way her son played with them:

'Fraser is nervous on a swing. But he'll jump off the top of that ladder because his father will catch him. We were saying the other day, "Isn't it nice to be *trusted* to that extent". They do it instinctively. They *trust* you. It's a fantastic feeling, to think they trust you so much.'

(Judy Bennett, working class, daughter 6, son 3)

More commonly, however, the children's emotional dependence was seen in the way they shared with their mothers their thoughts, feelings, and activities. This was described as closeness between the women and their children: the children confided in their mothers, shared their lives with them, or looked to them for emotional support. Two examples illustrate this:

'She tells me about school and her little problems. Little things like she's beginning to be afraid of the dark at night. She's beginning to talk about bad dreams and a couple of times she's come in to us in the middle of the night and she's frightened. We're very close. Both children are extremely close to me. I'm very close to my children but I don't want to be over close because I was brought up being terribly, terribly close to my mother. Too close, so I was insecure without her.'

(Naomi Hildebrand, middle class, daughters 4 and 1)

'We're very close. She doesn't want to go away and spend any time with anyone else. She likes to play school and things that involve me. I have to be the child and she's the teacher. This sort of thing. We do a lot together. We used to go up to the West End quite a lot before I had him, on holidays, for the day. She loves looking through the stores and having meals out. She's quite an extrovert, I suppose because I always went out with her, every day. I think your children grow up with a similar interest to yours. Your own children, this is what I like, you *share* things with them, things you enjoy. She likes people, which again I like. I quite enjoy people. I think my daughter is very much like me. We're very close.'

(Lesley Dixon, middle class, daughter 7, son 11 months)

These women saw their children as emotionally dependent on them and so saw themselves as needed, wanted, and significant to their children.

Eleven women said that they felt close to their daughters in particular because it was with them that they could most fully share their lives:[2]

'She loves to help me with the housework. She follows me around with a toy hoover. And ironing, she gets her ironing board out, too. She is very much the little mother round the house. She tries to do the same things that I do, which I think is lovely. And also, having a new baby about has revived Ann's interest in dolls. Her dolls become her babies. I'm glad I've got girls. I do like the way girls copy your housework and things. I like the way you can share your interests with them.'

(Naomi Hildebrand, middle class, daughters 4 and 1)

'With a daughter you have a different instinct than with a son. There's a different bond between a mother and daughter than what there is with a son. With Mark, when Dad's around Mum

doesn't exist. Dad's his idol. But with Sarah, it's still Mum. She still wants to do things with *me*.'
(Vera Watson, working class, son 6½, daughter 3½)

'Boys are more boisterous. They like climbing trees and doing things outdoors. Little girls will always come and sit indoors and see what you're doing. When this one is older, about ten or eleven, I'll be able to take her out and buy clothes with me and that. It's not the same with little boys.'
(Janet Hobson, working class, daughter 5, son 2)

The emotional security and esteem they felt from their daughters was enhanced by the belief that 'your daughter's your daughter the rest of your life': they expected always to remain the adviser, the authority, and the friend to their daughters, as their daughters followed in their footsteps and became wives and mothers themselves.

The children's physical and emotional dependence on their mothers and the unique, close relationship that this engendered encouraged the women's commitment to their children and hence their strong sense of meaning and purpose in looking after them. Being needed and wanted was tremendously *rewarding* in these terms. But being needed and wanted was also experienced as a *burden*. As Chapters 4, 5, and 6 made clear, coping with the demands of a dependent child could be irritating and exhausting, and carrying the responsibility for them could monopolize women in the mother role and rob them of their individuality. In these terms, being needed and wanted was irritating and overwhelming. The children's dependence on their mothers and the women's sense of being needed and wanted could therefore be experienced in markedly different ways. Moreover, feeling overwhelmed and irritated by the demands of children did not necessarily preclude a sense of meaning and purpose in meeting the demands. The children's dependence on their mothers could be experienced in both ways by the same women. As I shall argue in Chapters 9 and 10, a husband's practical and emotional support for a woman was important in enabling her to feel a strong sense of meaning and purpose in looking after her children despite the irritation she may also have felt.

CHILDREN AS A FOCUS OF HOPES, DREAMS, AND AMBITIONS

A second reason for a woman's commitment to her children as a valued purpose or incentive in life is the opportunity they give her to realize vicariously the hopes and ambitions she has failed to achieve herself and to relive experiences from the past altered to be as she would have liked them to have been (Komarovsky 1962; Busfield 1974; Leonard 1980). These hopes, dreams, and ambitions are uniquely important goals for a woman and the avenues that her children present for fulfilling them make her children a uniquely important incentive. Her emotional investment in her hopes and ambitions becomes an emotional investment in her children; in pursuing them through her children she may feel a strong sense of meaning, value, and significance.

The variety of hopes, dreams, and ambitions that the women described fell into three main categories: the hope that their children have what they themselves missed as children; the hope that their children have a better life in the future than they have now; and the hope that their children achieve specific ambitions which they had failed to achieve themselves. The first of these reflected the women's desire to make up for what they themselves had missed as children and echoed a common theme in the psychoanalytic literature (Deutsch 1945; Coleman, Kris, and Provence 1953; Benedeck 1970a; Chodorow 1978). Judy Bennett, for example, was trying to be the mother to her children which she had wanted her mother to be to her. She says:

'I do cuddle my children an awful lot. I think this is why I tend to cuddle them, because I missed it. And I don't want them to miss it. I know what it's like to go without. Even when they're naughty you can be firm without being unkind. You've got to give them a cuddle. You can't just say, "Oh, no, you've been naughty", which is cruel. Which is what my mother done to me. It's cruel. I learned. And I always vowed I wouldn't do that to my children.'
(Judy Bennett, working class, daughter 6, son 3)

Lesley Dixon and Patricia Hawkins could also be seen as dealing with their own remembered tensions in the way they related to their children:

'I don't want to be distant from my family as I think my mother was from me. I don't want my daughter and my son to know I worry. I want to have as calm an atmosphere as possible for them. Because my home life wasn't particularly happy. There were so many arguments and tensions. I was very unhappy. I don't want that to happen here.'
(Lesley Dixon, middle class, daughter 7, son 11 months)

'I couldn't talk to my parents. Couldn't discuss things. They always shouted. My husband says he had rotten parents. He doesn't think his Dad did a very good job in bringing him up. He should have had more *understanding*. So we're trying to be more understanding with our children. His father didn't encourage him in the things he enjoyed doing, whereas we've always said we would encourage them in whatever they were interested in.'
(Patricia Hawkins, middle class, daughters 3 and 11 months)

Sometimes old problems were dealt with in a more materialistic way. One woman, for example, tried to compensate for her own deprived childhood through the toys and clothes she had missed:

'She has a lot more clothes than she'll ever wear. I didn't have that. We had a lot of clothes to wear indoors but there was just one best. And everywhere you went you wore the same thing. It was really embarrassing with my friends having new clothes. I don't want my children to feel that way. She'll always have more than she needs.'
(Sally Friar, working class, daughters 12 and 3, son 10)

In contrast, Maureen Richards was trying to give the more intangible experience of which she had been deprived as a child:

'I like to think, when they go to school, they'll be a *success*. Not top of the class, but well-liked. And have nice friends. And be able to bring home their friends quite freely, quite happily, like I never could.'
(Maureen Richards, middle class, daughter 3, son 11 months)

The other two themes in the women's accounts centred on their hopes for the future and for the achievement of ambitions through their children. The first of these was the general ambition that the children get on better and have a better life than their parents. This was a particularly important goal, for it could give a sense of meaning and purpose to *all* that the parents did. By relating their efforts and sacrifices to these goals, the women could feel that these efforts and sacrifices were worthwhile. Vera Watson, for example, says:

'If you're normal working class, you've just got to carry on. All the frustration, the money troubles, you've got to manage from week to week. It's all sort of working at things all the time. That's

why we've only got two children – so we can give them as much as we can. To make life as nice for them as it hasn't been for us.'
(Vera Watson, working class, son 6½, daughter 3½)

Finally, for some women their wish that their children get on better entailed them achieving specific ambitions:

'I'd like them, if possible, to have careers, proper careers, professions. Obviously you don't always get what you want. They might all three turn out to be dropouts. Of course, one shouldn't hope too much for one's children, I know that, or you'll be disappointed. I'm afraid I do hope for them, but I shall try not to. I would like very much that they all go to university and all have some sort of professional career that they would enjoy and feel important to them. I would like Daniel to be a doctor or solicitor. Jo-Ann too. Possibly because I messed up my chance (*at medical school*).
(Susan Griffiths, middle class, sons 6½ and 1½, daughter 4½)

For all these women, their children provided a second opportunity to relive their lives with the advantages of greater knowledge and control and the chance to realize their unfulfilled dreams and ambitions. By investing their personal hopes and fantasies in their children, they transferred to them some of the most emotionally compelling goals they had. These goals, invested in their children, both motivated the women to work hard for their children and provided a framework for giving meaning to their efforts. Thus, when they were seen as relating to these goals, their everyday activities were felt as meaningful and their sacrifices experienced as worthwhile.

A remarkable variety of events and activities were seen as worthwhile and meaningful in these terms. At one extreme, Maureen Richards and her husband had decided to leave London and the life they had established there and to start a new life in the country. This was done 'for the sake of the children' and the tremendous effort involved and the great sacrifice of family and friends were seen as worthwhile in these terms.

'We're moving for the sake of the kids. Because we think we should have free-range kids. They should have the sea and the green grass and everything the Island has. For the children it's fantastic. They've got good schools and greenery, open pastures, woods, sea. The house is marvellous. It has a huge garden where

we can grow our own vegetables and have the kids run. Stephen doesn't mind where he is. He'll have his best mate and he only needs two or three people. But I shall miss Ruth and Tim. I won't see them a lot. Acquaintances will never be the same as friends. People I meet there will never be the same as Ruth and Tim. But it's for the kids we're moving. It's worth it for the kids' sake.'
(Maureen Richards, middle class, daughter 3, son 11 months)

Vera Watson presented her forthcoming move to Milton Keynes in the same way:

'I think I will have regrets and then I think "Oh, no, I can't possibly". Going from a flat to a house. And it's all new ideas and young mothers. Good schools, baby-sitting syndicates on the estates. You can go to the sports centre and take your children with you. It's definitely for the kids' sake anyway. I think it will be a far better life for them. It's all countrified. Where we live now we couldn't let the children out to play. It's all main roads here. It will make such a different life for them. They'll have all the things that we never had growing up in London.'
(Vera Watson, working class, son 6½, daughter 3½)

These women saw their children as providing a reason for trying; the efforts and sacrifices they made on behalf of the children were perceived as *worthwhile*.

On a more mundane level, Ruth Venables' efforts at knitting were given meaning by their value to her daughter, and Victoria Milton's enterprise in attending the opening of Parliament was seen as worthwhile in the same manner:

'Lisa also likes to look nice. I stayed up all night last week knitting a little dress that was close at the waist and flares out at the bottom. We were going to my father's and she desperately wanted to wear it. And she stood in front of the mirror, spun herself around, and said "Do you like me Grandad? Do I look smart?" She likes to look nice. She's a bit vain for her age. I'm pleased I did it. I'm pleased I put in the extra effort because it really meant a lot to her.'
(Ruth Venables, middle class, daughter 5, sons 3 and 2)

'I went to see the State Opening of Parliament. I had my sister-in-law's daughter that day and she and Sharon immediately started to fight. It was a lovely day so I rang What's On. They said "It's

the State Opening of Parliament. The Coach will leave at so and so". I thought, "Super, this is just what they need". I got Sharon, Peter, and Jenny and went. A lot of people thought I was potty. But children need this sort of thing. And they found it all very exciting and it was a great success. I felt it was worth the effort.'
(Victoria Milton, middle class, daughter 3½, son 1½)

These gestures were not valued because of the intrinsic enjoyment they offered: both were, in fact, tiring and to some extent irritating at the time. Instead, they were seen as creating experiences which the women themselves valued and wanted to share with the children and both were seen as worthwhile and meaningful in those terms.

PRIDE IN THE CHILDREN

One other theme needs to be considered in this discussion of the women's sense of meaning and purpose as mothers: their pride in their children. It is of interest because, surprisingly, it does not distinguish those who felt a strong sense of meaning, value, and significance from those who did not. Instead, it runs through the accounts of virtually all the women in the study sample: virtually all of the women were pleased with how their children were turning out and held positive images of them. This was true for working-class and middle-class women equally, though there was an interesting difference in orientation between the two classes.

There are several reasons why all the women in this study were able to present their children in positive terms. First, because their children were still very young, most of the women did not expect specific successes or achievements. As a number of women pointed out, pride as such was something that was not generally expected in relation to pre-school children.

(Q: 'What things are you most proud of in your children?')
'I think this really comes as they get older.'
(Diana Hayes, working class, sons 10, 7½, and 3½, daughter 4½)

'I should think they're average. They're too young to say.'
(Nina Lockwood, working class, son 3, daughter 11 months)

'They're so young, I can't really say anything. If they were 7 or 8 I could be proud of *something*. Or maybe disappointed. But now I'm just pleased to have them, and pleased that, as far as I can see, they are healthy, happy children.'
(Jessica Lloyd, middle class, son 3, daughter 1)

Rather than feeling proud of their children, most women felt as Jessica Lloyd did: pleased with them and the way they were turning out. Their pride, then, was in their children 'in general':

'It's just everything in general. It's just them. I mean they're healthy, happy, well-made children. I suppose everyone is proud of their children. They're good, they're good-looking, they're bright, they're well. . . . You can't help it. I think everyone naturally thinks their children are fantastic. Yes, we're *very* proud. But it's difficult to say why.'
(Anne Wootton, middle class, daughters 5 and 2, son 3)

Because they took such a broad view of their children, most of the women in the study were able to concentrate on their pleasing features and to minimize or gloss over their shortcomings. June Robertson, for example, could 'balance out' differences and so feel that her daughter was progressing as she should:

'At Alex's age – 3½ – there's a terrific difference among children. Carol is much more advanced than Alex in talking but not so advanced in doing jigsaws. It all balances out. They've both developed to the same level on the whole. And I think too much worry about one's child's progress in comparison to other children is not good.'
(June Robertson, middle class, daughters 3½ and 2)

Despite what she says, comparisons among children were almost inevitable and in fact provided a second reason why the women found it easy to feel proud of their children. Patricia Hawkins, for example, used her neighbour's child to highlight just how good her own daughter was:

'She's a very good child. You never had to tell her every day, "Don't touch". It was only odd occasions she explored. She's obviously got an inquisitive mind, but she *asks questions* rather than just looks herself. But the boy next door – a week doesn't go by without him doing *something*. And he's old enough to realize you don't do that!'

(Patricia Hawkins, middle class, daughters 3 and 11 months)

Since they could choose with whom to compare their children and also which qualities to compare, most women were in a position to see their own children – at this young age at any rate – in a favourable light.

Although both working-class and middle-class women looked on their children with pride, they differed in the ways they went about evaluating their children. While middle-class women tended to judge their children themselves, working-class women looked to the judgements that other people made. This contrast is illustrated by the following two examples.

'I think they're pretty good. Comparing them with other people's children, I'm quite happy about mine. I've seen children who are spiteful, and I think, crumbs, I'm pretty lucky, my children are not. They're not spiteful children and on the whole they play very well.'

(Ruth Venables, middle class, daughter 5, sons 3 and 2)

'I have a friend who comes here with three children. They're so cheeky – they're such horrible children. I dread Thursdays when they're going to come. They run a riot. When I look at my children I think, "Oh God don't let my children be like that!" They're not, though. My friend down the road, if ever we go out, she usually has them, and she says they're very good. I've never had any bad reports. My Father, he's very strict and he seems to get on all right with them.'

(Sandra Keating, working class, daughters 7 and 4)

Sandra Keating has evaluated other people's children and let other people evaluate hers.

This concern for other people's views of their children may reflect a feeling among working-class women that their own prestige in the community is founded on the way their children are judged: their children are their 'products' and the way they turn out is a reflection on the women who have been responsible for them.[3] This feeling was expressed most clearly when they talked about their children's appearance, behaviour, and manners. Cathy Burgess, for example, says:

(Q: 'What about their appearance?')
'Indoors, I don't care if their clothes are old. My children indoors are very scruffy. I put all old clothes on them. When they go out I always change them. When we go out, I really like them to look really nice. So I can be *proud* of them, so people will see how good they look.'
(Q: 'Are they well-behaved children?')
'When they're *out* with me, they're very good. It's just when we are here they play me up. In the street they behave very well. They won't leave my sight or pick something off the shelf in a shop. I consider myself very lucky being able to take them out. Some people can't. I'm very lucky – I know exactly what they're going to do when they get on the bus. They're going to sit down and behave themselves. Everyone can see they are very good children. And people do notice. They are all right the way I brought them up.'

(Cathy Burgess, working class, son 6, daughter 3)

She was very concerned with what others thought of her children; what they were like with her alone was much less important to her. Alice Gray was similar:

(Q: 'What about their appearance?')
'I think when they go out it means a lot. But like indoors, he's only in his everyday clothes because all that he'd do playing is get mucked up which he has done anyway. But when we go out, I dress the two the same when they go out. Hundreds of people always ask me when I go out if they are twins.'
(Q: 'Are they well-behaved children?')
Most of the time. Only if they're tired or we go out late then they play me up a bit.'
(Q: 'How do you feel about this?')
'Shown up sometimes. If we go to people's houses and they start – I smack them and that still doesn't do any good. I feel terrible. It's embarrassing to me.'
(Q: 'Are they better behaved at home?')
'It's hard to say. When they're at home, there's no problem. They play up or they're good. It doesn't matter. It's only really when we go out that it counts.'

(Alice Gray, working class, sons 5 and 3)

Once again, she was concerned largely with the way others saw her children and with the way that reflected on her as their mother.

By contrast, middle-class women were not noticeably over-concerned with what other people thought of their children. They seemed instead to put more value on their own view of their children and then attribute their view to others as well. One woman, for example, talked about her children being bright and assumed that others thought so as well:

> 'I'm very proud of them. They're very bright. Sharon can read very well if she tries. They're obviously very bright lively children and I'm very proud of them.'
> (Victoria Milton, middle class, daughter 4½, son 1½)

Later, she expressed the same view of the children, in a different context:

> 'They seem to be very bright children. I can see, where other children tend to sit and not move about, mine are always on the go. I've never encouraged them to sit like lumps. I've always encouraged them to explore.'

The contrast with the statements by the working-class women is clear.

Despite the difference in their manner of evaluating their children, working-class and middle-class women alike were able to look on their children with pride. How this influenced their sense of meaning and purpose in motherhood, however, is difficult to say. With older children who are establishing their individual talents and achieving their successes, the women's pride in their children may prove an important incentive and a justification for their efforts. For pre-school children, however, success and failure lie in the future and it is perhaps the children's *potential*, and their mothers' hopes, dreams, and ambitions for them, that are more important. The women's views of their children as developing normally, as behaving well, or as healthy and happy children were probably the product of their wish to present their children as normal and themselves as good mothers. Such a wish arose out of their need to carry on looking after their children and to feel they were doing an adequate job. For the reasons discussed above, it was not difficult for the women to develop and present these positive views, which as a result may have had only little impact on the women's experience as mothers. They were important, perhaps, only in negative instances when the inability to see themselves and their children in positive terms could give rise to anxiety, tension, and a sense of helplessness among the mothers.

Summary

Getting on for two-thirds of the women in this study experienced a strong sense of meaning, value, and significance in looking after their children. They felt that their children needed and wanted them and they invested in them their hopes and dreams for the future. These aspects of their relationship underlay their active commitment to their children as a major purpose in life and the sense of meaning, value, and significance they felt in looking after them.

This dimension of their experience is in addition to their immediate response to looking after their children and therefore only part of the picture of their experience as mothers. It is a very important part, however, since feelings of meaning, value, and significance meet very basic human needs (Maslow 1954; Fromm 1975; Erikson 1959; Weiss 1969). For those who experienced these feelings, motherhood was a unique and rewarding role. This is an important point, for it suggests one reason why women may continue in their role as mothers despite the frustrations and stresses they also experience.

Not all of the women, however, felt a strong sense of meaning and significance in motherhood: over a third did not and among the working-class women the proportion rose to as high as a half. Children may bring a sense of meaning and purpose but they do not *necessarily* do so. Though they have the potential to give a sense of meaningfulness and intrinsic worth to a woman's life, children may bring no more than an 'appropriate' or socially desirable role. This, too, is an important point, for it belies the expectation and general assumption held about motherhood. A sense of meaning and purpose does not come automatically or inevitably in motherhood. It is not wholly instinctual and there is nothing as straightforward as the automatic fulfilment of a need. Rather, a positive commitment to her children and a sense of meaning and purpose in looking after them must be created and sustained in the values, meanings, and interpretations given to children and child care by those directly involved in it as well as by the society in which they live. Chapters 9 and 10 look at some of the issues within the family that influenced whether or not the women felt a sense of meaning and purpose in their lives as mothers.

Notes

1. Children may provide one important incentive or concept of the meaning of life *among several*: 'the more kinds of incentives people can respond to the greater their sense of meaning' (Klinger 1977: 8).
2. Five women also mentioned that they had wanted sons for their husbands so they, too, could share their interests and feel close to someone. Three of these women had sons already, but two had not. Both these women said that they were considering having another child in the hope of 'having a son for my husband'.
3. See also J. Klein's discussion of Ashton mothers and children. Women achieve their individual worth 'by doing the job of motherhood as well or better than their neighbours'. In this competition, emphasis is put on 'the outward signs – new clothes, new toys, well-fed children. It is by these standards that a mother is immediately judged' (J. Klein 1965: 114–15). Oakley, too, notes that among working-class women 'a greater importance is attached to the child's appearance and behaviour' (Oakley 1974a: 173).

· 8 ·
FOUR TYPES
OF EXPERIENCE
OF MOTHERHOOD

Overall experience of motherhood

Neither of the two dimensions so far discussed – the immediate response to looking after children and the sense of meaning and purpose – can, on its own, adequately describe women's experience as mothers. Both dimensions are important. The immediate response to child care is important since all women must experience motherhood on this level: children demand to be looked after and a woman must cope with the situations that arise. Her response to this, whether it be enjoyment or irritation, must be immediate and continuous. A strong sense of meaning, value, and significance, on the other hand, is far from inevitable and can be difficult to sustain. However, when it is experienced it is important since it can contribute a sense of positive identity and purpose which helps to make life seem comprehensible and worthwhile, and a sustaining sense of direction that can help to carry a woman through day-to-day difficulties. Without this sense of meaning and purpose, motherhood may be experienced as lacking something: as being enjoyable, perhaps, but not deeply rewarding.

Both modes of experience are important to a woman and both contribute to her experience of motherhood in complementary ways. They do not necessarily balance each other, nor draw each other into consistency, nor does one necessarily predominate over the other. To understand a woman's experience as a whole, therefore, we must consider both dimensions of her experience and the way they fit together. Given the two basic elements, we can distinguish four types of experience among the accounts of the fifty women: a strong sense of meaning, value, and significance may go with either enjoyment or irritation with looking after children and the lack of a sense of meaning, value, and significance may also go with either enjoyment or irritation in child care. These four types of experience can be labelled as 'fulfilled', 'in conflict', 'satisfied' and 'alienated' (see *Table 8(1)*).

Table 8(1) *Overall experience of motherhood*

Sense of meaning and purpose	Immediate response to child care	
	enjoyed	irritated
strong	fulfilled	in conflict
weak	satisfied	alienated

It must be emphasized that these categories represent types of experience, not types of women. As a woman's circumstances change, it is likely that her experience of motherhood will change and she may move from one category to another in this typology. Since the nature of these types of experience can be conveyed best by the women themselves, each will be defined and illustrated by excerpts from the interviews. While these comments by and large reflect the feelings and ideas expressed throughout the interview it must be remembered that they represent only a small proportion of the material used in rating the two dimensions.

FULFILLED (STRONG MEANING AND PURPOSE AND ENJOYMENT OF LOOKING AFTER CHILDREN)

The women in the *fulfilled* group found motherhood rewarding in all ways. Their commitment to their children made their daily activities seem intrinsically worthwhile and gave a sense of meaning and purpose to their lives. At the same time, they enjoyed domesticity and the lifestyle involved in looking after pre-school children as well as the content of their day-to-day activities.

Lesley Dixon's comments are typical of those women in the *fulfilled* group:

(*Q: 'Do you enjoy looking after your children?'*)
'Yes. Very much.'
(*Q: 'Is there anything you particularly like about looking after them?'*)

'I enjoy, as long as they're happy, that they should do roughly as they want. Everything really. I just enjoy having children, having a family.'

(Q: 'What are the best things about being a mother?)

'Having someone who really belongs to you. Your own parents belong to you. But your children are *part* of you. I suppose to be *responsible* for them. They give you something to work for. And they turn to you for everything they want. They need you. That's rather nice. To belong is the most important thing. That you're belonging to each other really.'

(Q: 'What are the worst things about being a mother?')

'Well, . . . tied to time. The other thing I think is the fact you don't go out as much. At least we don't, without the children. You don't go to the theatre very often, or dinner without the children. Not very often. A lot of our friends get baby-sitters but we don't want to, so our social life *apart* from the children – we go out a lot *with* them – but that does seem to change. But we've had a few years of doing it so I suppose one tends to settle a bit more. We don't miss these things. We *like* to go out as a family.'

(Lesley Dixon, middle class, daughter 7, son 11 months)

It is clear that her basic experience as a mother was thoroughly positive. She enjoyed everything about looking after children and found it difficult to single out anything in particular when saying she enjoyed it. Her sense of being needed by her children and of having a purpose in them was also a central theme. When asked about the worst aspect of motherhood she could, of course, give an answer but her answer was a dispassionate account of the restrictions children imposed on her which she said she did not feel strongly about: she experienced them as a change rather than as a loss. The worst aspects of motherhood, then, were not *felt* as particularly negative while the best aspects were *experienced* as very positive.

ALIENATED (WEAK MEANING AND PURPOSE AND IRRITATION WITH LOOKING AFTER CHILDREN)

In contrast to the women in the *fulfilled* group, the women in the *alienated* group felt essentially 'fed up'. They did not enjoy dealing with their children; they were frustrated with domesticity and the lifestyle of a housebound wife; and they resented being unable to pursue their interests outside maternity. This intense irritation coloured the whole of their experience. They recognized that their children were dependent on them and accepted their responsibilities as mothers, but they were inhibited by their strong feelings of irritation from feeling any sense of meaning and purpose as mothers, or any sense that child care was worth its frustrations and sacrifices. These themes are illustrated by Angela Bourne's comments:

(Q: 'Do you enjoy looking after your children?')
'I'm not a very domesticated person. I enjoy playing with them. I don't enjoy feeding them. I don't like cooking much. . . . I shouldn't ever have got married when you look at it like that. Because though I enjoy the end product, getting there is a bit of a drag. I hate the mornings and having to rush to get him off to nursery school, though it's doing him the world of good. There's been a terrific change in him. But getting him dressed and changing Emma's nappy! I *hate* nappies!! You get used to it because you have to but I really HATE nappies! *(said vehemently)*.'
(Q: 'Is there anything you particularly like about looking after them?')
'I just enjoy doing something I know will help them to learn. If they can *learn* something by what I do, I enjoy doing it *(said flatly)*.'
(Q: 'Is there anything you particularly dislike about looking after them?')
'The nappies, the bad temper. And this continual jealousy between Mark and Emma. He hits her and I find I get to screaming pitch at times. Whatever she's doing, he's there interfering. If I go off to do my housework, she'll start to cry and I'll have to come back to see what's wrong. Then I'm telling them off again. And it goes on and on, forever, without end. They don't take a blind bit of notice of me. Daddy comes home – they'll take notice. But I could scream at them till I'm blue in the face and they'll take no notice. It's a strain, it's a terrible strain with children this age. And there's no escape from it.'
(Q: 'What are the best things about being a mother?')
'Well, it's rewarding to see your children *(said flatly)*. And people come up to you and say "Oh, isn't he a lovely little boy", "Oh, isn't she sweet". This sort of thing. They're looking nice, clean.

That's rewarding. He's getting on well at nursery school. That's rewarding.'
(Q: 'What are the worst things about being a mother?')
'The nagging and everything else. The niggling and there's nothing wrong. They're just fed up and you've got to find something for them to do and you just run out of ideas. And you think, "*What* can I do next?". And they just keep on and on. She at the moment throws paddy. She lies on the floor and bangs with her fists and her legs and she says "I want such and such". . . . You read about baby battering but I've got a certain amount of sympathy for mothers who do batter their child. . . . You sacrifice a lot for your children. You sacrifice your freedom. We can't go away now. We can't do anything. If we go out for a meal even, it's a problem because Emma is still needing a high chair. And it's a bit of a drag on me having to feed her to a certain extent. We don't have a life of our own now. At this time, we're tied and I think this is what I miss really. This is what is driving me spare.'
(Angela Bourne, middle class, son 3½, daughter 1½)

Her basic experience was extremely negative. From the beginning she chose to talk about what she disliked and her account became progressively more negative as she got more involved in what she was saying. She could answer the questions on the enjoyable and best aspects of child care, partly because questions call for answers and partly because, like many women, she coped by trying to make motherhood rewarding. The difficulty she had in becoming involved in her account of her enjoyment, however, suggests that it was a relatively unimportant part of her overall experience of motherhood. What she claimed to 'particularly like' is very vague and suggests a socially desirable response. Any hint of a sense of personal significance in relation to her children is conspicuously lacking. On the whole, her positive comments are feeble and empty and her account is dominated by her feelings of irritation and frustration in dealing with her children.

SATISFIED (WEAK MEANING AND PURPOSE AND ENJOYMENT OF LOOKING AFTER CHILDREN)

Between the two extreme groups are two groups of women whose experience was not so consistently positive or negative. The first is

the *satisfied* group. The women in this group simply accepted that
as mothers they had responsibilities for the children which they
largely enjoyed fulfilling. This responsibility was not presented as
giving them particular meaning or purpose in life, but was seen as
arising from their social position as mothers which defined their
aims in bringing up children. The women in this group enjoyed
doing all that was involved in looking after their children, living out
the role in which they had previously imagined themselves. In this
sense they were happy as mothers. They were not in the *fulfilled*
group, however, because they seemed to find no deeper sense of
meaning and purpose in motherhood. Sharon Rogers conveys these
themes:

(Q: 'Do you enjoy looking after your children?')
'Yeah. I like it.'
*(Q: 'Is there anything you particularly like about looking after
them?')*
'I don't know. I like watching them play, watching them grow
up. They make me laugh, I don't know why. . . . I have a picture
of Lisa at her age. When Lisa was her age, they looked like twins.
I just like looking after them. I think if they weren't here in the
day I would be bored. There wouldn't be anything to do. I feel
happier when they're about. It does create work in a way, but I
don't mind.'
*(Q: 'Is there anything you particularly dislike about looking
after them?')*
'No. Not really. No.'
(Q: 'What are the best things about being a mother?')
'Looking after the children. I love it. . . . Doing things for them. I
enjoy getting them ready in the morning. They're all washed and
nice and clean and all their clothes are laying on the bed and they
look all nice. Not for long, though. . . . I enjoy getting them ready
to go out, going out with them.'
(Q: 'What are the worst things about being a mother?')
'I don't like it when they're ill. I worry when they're ill. It gets me
down.'
(Sharon Rogers, working class, daughters 5 and 1)

She was essentially positive about her life as a mother, though she
might be better described as passively accepting it. She seems to have
found great enjoyment in what she did with the children, but
she was notably *unreflective* about it. Indeed, she seemed to have

been somewhat bemused by the questions because, to her, it was obvious that looking after children was enjoyable. She accepted that it was and did not push beyond this level of enjoying child care.

Satisfied women are interesting because, although they enjoyed their lives as mothers at the time, they were at greatest risk of becoming *alienated*. Their enjoyment of motherhood seemed to be contingent on circumstances creating an enjoyable situation, and these circumstances were always changing, as children went through difficult stages, as more children brought more work and even as passing time turned their lives into routine. It is possible that, at different points in time, some women may move back and forth between the *alienated* and *satisfied* groups.

IN CONFLICT (STRONG MEANING AND PURPOSE AND IRRITATION WITH CHILD CARE)

The final group is the group *in conflict*. The women in this group felt a positive commitment to their children and a sense of meaning and purpose in bringing them up. At the same time, however, they did not enjoy child care and the lifestyle involved in looking after pre-school children and were frustrated at not being able to do a range of other things. Anne Wootton's comments are typical:

(*Q:* '*Do you enjoy looking after your children?*')
'Well, I do enjoy looking after them, so long as I feel physically well. If I'm not ill, or I haven't got a cold. Or I'm very tired. I generally enjoy looking after them but there are days when I don't (*said flatly*).'
(*Q:* '*Is there anything you particularly like about looking after them?*')
'I don't think so. I just generally . . . I'm not very good at playing with them. I can make suggestions for them to play. And I've got lots of toys, though we're very lucky they're quite imaginative children and love playing. But they can get on top of you at times, especially three in a small house.'
(*Q:* '*Is there anything you particularly dislike about looking after them?*')
'Yes. They're terribly *demanding*. I find them terribly demanding and egotistical. Children are only out for themselves. They very rarely think of you or how you feel, though Susie, the eldest, is a very thoughtful child.'

(Q: 'What are the best things about being a mother?')
'Oh, it's *terribly* rewarding. If you were to sit down and think about it, I don't think you could possibly do another job where you would be as important, as *vital* to somebody. Really, a mother's place is *vitally* important. You really are *needed* by the family. The home would collapse if you're not here. The husband can be very good with the children but I don't think anyone knows your children as well as you do. And no one is as *close* to the children, because you're with them all the time. . . . As far as I can remember, always, I wanted a family. I think mainly because I wanted to feel, instead of feeling so independent, I wanted to feel *part* of something. Belonging. Needed.'
(Q: 'What are the worst things about being a mother?')
'Sometimes I get very irritated. Sometimes I feel it's very fruitless. I get my days. I wouldn't say there was anything that stands out in my mind. It can be very demoralizing at times. But there again I think it's if you're stuck to the house. If you're very busy rushing around and don't get much time – half an hour in the house and I'm out to collect a child. The days I think are bad when I'm stuck at home and don't get out very much. And your life revolves around clearing up the house and looking after your children and that can be very demoralizing.'
    (Anne Wootton, middle class, daughters 5 and 2, son 3)

She was basically torn between finding child care very demanding and frustrating and finding it a source of personal meaning and significance. Her first answer was qualified and ambivalent but from there she went off on two clear and opposing lines. On the one hand, she did not particularly like any aspect of child care, even playing with the children, but rather found looking after children very frustrating and irritating. At the same time, she was very involved in the sense of meaning, purpose, and personal significance that the children gave her life. She felt just as strongly her sense of being needed by her family and of being close to her children as she did her irritation and frustration with looking after them. The two stood in opposition and neither made up for the other.

The women in this group are particularly interesting because they experienced inconsistent and even contradictory feelings in motherhood. They illustrate how a sense of meaning and purpose experienced in bringing up children does not necessarily make child care enjoyable or even balance out its frustrations. In fact, it is probably the opposite process which takes place: it is likely that the tension between the two dimensions of their experience motivated the women to reflect on motherhood more carefully and the contrast between them threw their sense of meaning and purpose into clearer relief. The women in the *fulfilled* group also felt a sense of meaning and purpose in relation to their children. But it may be that the women in the group *in conflict*, who felt a significant but not overwhelming frustration with child care, had a clearer or stronger sense of meaning and purpose than the *fulfilled* women. Though this is pure speculation, the women in the group *in conflict* did seem more articulate about their sense of being needed, wanted, and uniquely important to their children and at times did juxtapose their irritation and sense of meaning and purpose in this way.

Table 8(2) *Overall experience of motherhood and social class*

| Type of experience | Social class | | |
	working class no. (%)	middle class no. (%)	total no. (%)
fulfilled	10 (40)	9 (36)	19 (38)
satisfied	4 (16)	1 (4)	5 (10)
in conflict	2 (8)	8 (32)	10 (20)
alienated	9 (36)	7 (28)	16 (32)
total	25 (100)	25 (100)	50 (100)

$x^2 = 5.72 \, p > 0.05$

The number of women in each of the four categories is given in *Table 8(2)*. Over a third of the women are *fulfilled*, almost as many are *alienated*, while the *in conflict* and *satisfied* groups are quite small. There are similar numbers of working-class and middle-class women in the *fulfilled* group and only slightly more working-class than middle-class women in the *alienated* group. However, there are striking class differences in the composition of the two other groups. Four of the five women in the *satisfied* group are working-class women, while eight of the ten women in the group *in conflict* are middle-class women.

Orientation within the mother role

One possible explanation for these social-class differences may be the different orientations that the working-class and middle-class women had to the rewards of motherhood. As I shall describe in the rest of this chapter, the majority of working-class women *looked for* rewards in terms of their day-to-day enjoyment of child care, while most middle-class women did not. Thus, working-class women may have had a greater investment in making child care immediately enjoyable. For some of them, their enjoyment of looking after their children may even have been sufficient in itself, and if they could make motherhood rewarding in this way they may have looked no further. These would be *satisfied* women. Middle-class women, with their different orientation, however, were less likely to settle for rewards at the level of immediate enjoyment alone: only one middle-class woman was in the *satisfied* group.

A similar explanation can be given for the class composition of the group *in conflict*. Because they did not look for immediate enjoyment of child care, middle-class women may have more easily accepted some degree of frustration and irritation without it threatening their commitment to their children. Those who did not enjoy child care, then, may nonetheless have been able to sustain a rewarding sense of meaning and purpose in looking after their children. These were the women in the group *in conflict*. By contrast, working-class women, who looked to enjoy child care, may have felt a pervasive dissatisfaction when they did not do so and a resentment of their children for tying them into a frustrating role. In the light of this disappointment, it may have been difficult for them to maintain what sense of meaning and purpose they might have felt and they therefore felt completely alienated as mothers.

THE 'WORK' OF CHILD CARE

Oakley's research into women's satisfaction with housework suggests one way of investigating the orientations of the two class groups to motherhood (Oakley 1974a). In about a third of her sample, Oakley found a contradiction between the answer to the direct question 'Do you like housework?' and the pattern of housework satisfaction revealed by sensitive, in-depth interviewing. Working-class women in particular were likely to answer initially that they *did* enjoy housework when further questioning disclosed substantial dissatisfaction; in addition, two middle-class women said they did *not* enjoy housework when further questioning indicated that they did. Oakley also found that answers to the direct question were related to women's self-concept as expressed in a written statement and to the standards and routines they adopted in housework. She concludes that:

'These connections suggest that what a woman says about housework at the beginning of her interview (*i.e. in answer to a direct question*) does not only reflect on the mode of feeling-expression general in her class-specific linguistic code. A "like" or "don't mind" attitude seems symbolic of *a search for satisfaction in housework* (emphasis added); the declaration of "dislike" appears to indicate the recognition of dissatisfaction.'
(Oakley 1974a: 70)

In other words, Oakley suggests that a direct question taps a woman's orientation to her role, in the sense of her views of what is normal and appropriate with regard to that role.

In the present study, two direct questions were asked which tapped the women's orientation to the mother role: 'How do you feel about the actual work involved in looking after your children from day to day? Do you enjoy it?' and later, 'Would you consider looking after children if they were not your own? Would you enjoy looking after them?' The difference in orientation to child care can be seen in the different kinds of response which working-class and middle-class women gave to these questions *(see Table 8(3))*.

Table 8(3) *Attitude to work involved in child care and to looking after other children and social class*

Social class	Attitude to work involved in child care and to looking after other children			
	enjoy/consider no. (%)	enjoy/not consider or dislike/consider no. (%)	dislike/not consider no. (%)	total no. (%)
working class	17 (68)	0	8 (32)	25 (100)
middle class	6 (24)	1 (4)	18 (72)	25 (100)
total	23 (46)	1 (2)	26 (52)	50 (100)

$x^2 = 10.0 \ p < 0.01$

Most working-class women replied that they did enjoy the work of child care and that they would consider looking after other

Table 8(4)   *Attitude to work involved in child care and to looking after
other children, social class and immediate response to child
care*

Attitude to work involved in child care and looking after other children	Immediate response to child care				
	enjoyed		irritated		
	working class no. (%)	middle class no. (%)	working class no. (%)	middle class no. (%)	total no. (%)
enjoy/consider	12 (86)	4 (40)	5 (45)	2 (13)	23 (46)
dislike or not consider	2 (14)	6 (60)	6 (55)	13 (87)	27 (54)
total	14 (100)	10 (100)	11 (100)	15 (100)	50 (100)

$x^2 = 5.7$ $x^2 = 3.2$
$p < 0.01$ $p > 0.05$

children. This includes five women who, in their extensive discussion of their daily lives, expressed and reported a predominantly frustrating and irritating experience *(see Table 8(4))*. Their positive answers indicate an expectation that they ought to enjoy it and a normative orientation to enjoy it. Janet Hobson and Tammy Parsons are typical of the enthusiastic working-class women:

> *(Q: 'How do you feel about the actual work involved in looking after your children? Do you enjoy it?')*
> 'I think *I* do. I think if you like children and want children, I think you get the enjoyment out of doing it. My friend next door has two children and she didn't want any of them and she doesn't enjoy it.'
> *(Q: 'Would you consider looking after children if they weren't your own?)*
> 'Oh, yes, I could live with children all day. I'm a bit colour-prejudiced, though, and I don't think I'd look after a coloured child. But I would love to be a baby-minder.'
> (Janet Hobson, working class, daughter 5, son 2)
>
> *(Q: 'How do you feel about the work involved in looking after children?)*
> 'I don't mind it at all. I love it. I really enjoy it, because I enjoy being head of the household, keeping the house running. I like dressing them up and doing all their washing. I don't think it's work. Anyway, I take pride in doing it. I enjoy doing it.'
> (Tammy Parsons, working class, son 5, daughter 3)

Vera Watson made a point often mentioned by the working-class women:

(Q: 'Would you consider looking after children if they weren't your own?)
'Yes. I think I would. You have more patience with other people's children than you have with your own. I think it's – a child that knows you more knows how far he can push you, which another child doesn't. They don't try you on, but your own children try you on more. Other friends say that, too. You have more *patience* with other people's children.'
(Vera Watson, working class, son 6½, daughter 3½)

Although she did not enjoy looking after her own children, she would consider looking after other children because she felt she would have more patience with them.

Three working-class women were doing some childminding at the time of the interviews and five others had tried childminding at other times. Tracey Allen, for example, says:

'I did it once. It didn't work out. I did baby-minding after I packed up work. I looked after a little boy. It was wrong doing it because he was the same age as Michelle, and it was like having twins. I just couldn't take to him. I love children but I think he come from an unhappy home. He was such a quiet boy, he'd never play or anything. He just sat there all the time. I didn't enjoy it. I wasn't nasty to him, but I didn't love him. You can't love just anybody's child.'
(Q: 'Would you have enjoyed it with a different child?)
'Oh yes. If it was Mandy or another child. Yes, I would. I didn't mind looking after him, but it was just him. He was like a zombie. He didn't run about, he didn't laugh at all. He just wasn't the one for me. But I'd try again, with another child.'
(Tracey Allen, working class, daughters 4 and 11 months)

When she found she was bored staying home looking after her one child, she tried to relieve the tedium by getting another child to look after. She considered child care an appropriate area to *look* for enjoyment and since she did not get 'enough' from it, she tried to increase her rewards by expanding and elaborating on the work itself. It was the personality of the child minded that she blamed for her dissatisfaction with her particular experience, but she still thought of childminding in general as an activity which she would expect to enjoy. Six of these eight women did, in fact, enjoy looking after other children. Teresa Flanagan, for example, says:

> 'Oh, yes, I've done it and I enjoyed it. In Twickenham when we only had Elizabeth I used to look after a little boy who was just a year older than her. I used to look after him for just the day when his mother was working. And they used to get on super. He was a lovely little boy. We really got attached to him.'
>
> (Teresa Flanagan, working class, daughter 4, son 2)

In contrast to the working-class women, most middle-class women said that they disliked or were indifferent to the day-to-day work involved in looking after children and that they would not consider looking after children who were not their own (*see Table 8(3)*). This includes six women who expressed and reported a predominantly enjoyable experience in the rest of the interview (*see Table 8(4)*). Maureen Richards and Victoria Milton are typical of the middle-class women in their acceptance of day-to-day child care, but with little interest or expectation of enjoyment:

> (*Q: 'How do you feel about the work involved in looking after children?'*)
> 'I can't say that I *like* the work. I just do it because I have to do it. I don't think about it. It doesn't worry me. It's just like washing up the dishes after breakfast – you have to do it every day, so you do it. It's just part and parcel of having children.'
> (*Q: 'Would you consider looking after children who weren't your own?'*)
> 'Not particularly. I'm not particularly interested in it. I don't mind looking after friends' children but I wouldn't do it out of choice unless I was a teacher and could really feel I was teaching them something. Not just play with them or wash their nappies. You get enough of that with your own children. I wouldn't say I was the motherly type that way.'
> (Maureen Richards, middle class, daughter 3, son 11 months)
> (*Q: 'How do you feel about the actual work involved in looking after your children?'*)
> 'I think it's just a job that's got to be done.'
> (*Q: 'Do you find it enjoyable or satisfying?'*)
> 'No. But it's a means to an end. If you don't wash you've got dirty clothes. If you don't change him when he comes in wet, you've got to look after him when he catches cold.'

(Q: 'Would you consider looking after children who weren't your own?')
'No. Because I think every child is different. I don't mind looking after my friends' children or I wouldn't do it, but I think each child is so different that you've got to get to know the children first, so you can know how it's going to react.'
(Victoria Milton, middle class, daughter 3½, son 1½)

This view that it was important to know the children they looked after was voiced by several middle-class women. It is in direct contrast to the point made by the working-class women that they had more patience with children whom they did *not* know. Similarly, the main theme running through the working-class responses was in direct contrast to that in the middle-class responses:

'I can't work up much enthusiasm for other people's children. They're just children. Mine are *mine*, they're *special*. I couldn't be a foster mother. I couldn't cope with being a mother like that. I'm just not used to small children, apart from mine. I didn't have any contact with children before I had mine.'
(June Robertson, middle class, daughters 3½ and 2)

Like June Robertson, most middle-class women recognized the daily routines of child care as a fundamental responsibility, but concentrated their interests in a different area. For them, it was usually the fact that it was their own children whom they were bringing up that was important. Child care derived its meaning and significance from its contribution to the development of their own children, to whom they felt their commitment. The daily tasks of child care were simply accepted as necessary but not considered an important area in which to *look for* rewards. By contrast, among working-class women these daily tasks were looked on as an important source of enjoyment in motherhood.

PREVIOUS EXPERIENCE IN CHILD CARE

These differences in orientation can be traced back to differences between working-class and middle-class women in their experience with children during their own adolescence. As *Table 8(5)* shows, substantially more working-class than middle-class women had had experience in looking after young children when they themselves

Table 8(5) *Practical experience during adolescence of looking after children and social class*

Extent of practical experience		Social class		
		working class no. (%)	middle class no. (%)	total no. (%)
no experience		13 (52)	20 (80)	33 (66)
some experience looking after siblings	3 ⎫		2 ⎫	
looking after other kin	4 ⎬	12 (48)	1 ⎬ 5 (20)	17 (34)
looking after friends' or neighbours' children	5 ⎭		2 ⎭	
total		25 (100)	25 (100)	50 (100)

$x^2 = 4.37 \; p < 0.05$

were adolescents. Almost half of the working-class women had had some practical experience in looking after young children before they had their own, while only one-fifth of the middle-class women had had such experience. Furthermore, more working-class women had had a great deal of experience which usually had also entailed greater responsibility. Contrast the experience of Teresa Flanagan and Janet Hobson with that of Naomi Hildebrand and Angela Bourne:

'When I was fourteen I left school and my aunt was expecting her sixth baby and she was desperate for help so I was told I'd have to go and help her out. She had her sixth baby while I was there and her seventh baby while I was there. I was living with my aunt and her family and I did everything. She was lazy, she didn't do anything. I enjoyed it. I looked after the children, all the young ones. I enjoyed it. Mind you, now I think I might have been better staying on at school. But at the time I was glad to get away from it.'
(Q: *'Did you enjoy helping with the children?'*)
'Oh yes. At this stage I did. Because when I went there, they were all babies, three or four babies there together. I quite enjoyed it really.'
   (Teresa Flanagan, working class, daughter 4, son 2)

'From the time I was 13 or 14 I had younger children about me all the time. I had plenty of experience. My mother wasn't a well woman.'

(Q: 'Did you enjoy it?')

'Yes. Oh, yes. There were plenty of aunts willing to do it, but I suppose I just grew up liking looking after children. I used to have my younger brother, a few months old, in the pram, my brother, two, sitting on the side and the four-year-old on one hand and the dog on the other. I was about 12, 13. We used to go over to the park. I knew my husband then from all the school children and he can remember my brother from that age.'

(Janet Hobson, working class, daughter 5, son 2)

'I had no idea about babies before I had my own. I played it by ear. I'd never looked at a baby before, I wasn't interested in babies at all.'

(Naomi Hildebrand, middle class, daughters 4 and 1)

(Q: 'When you were a teenager, did you ever help to look after young children?')

'No. Not at all. I didn't even know how to pick up a baby. I had no idea at all.'

(Angela Bourne, middle class, son 3½, daughter 1½)

As for the five middle-class women who had had previous experience with children, their responsibility had been much more limited and less intense. Grace Collier is typical:

> 'There were four of us. I was the eldest. I had to help with the younger ones. We all had to help. Looking back, I had to help quite a lot with the younger ones.'
>
> *(Q: 'Did you enjoy helping with the younger ones?')*
>
> 'I think I kind of accepted it till I was 15 or 16. Then I didn't. I think there was probably just so much domestication with three younger ones. The house was always full of children. I think possibly I'd just had enough.'
>
> (Grace Collier, middle class, daughter 4, son 1½)

These comments highlight another difference between the working-class and middle-class women: of the five middle-class women who had had some contact with children in their teens, three had not particularly enjoyed that contact, while *all* of the twelve working-class women who had done so had enjoyed looking after children.

It seems likely that these differences in early experience contributed to their different orientations to motherhood when the women themselves had children. The working-class women who had previously taken care of other people's children may have learned to look toward those aspects of the mother role that they had rehearsed during that time. In caring for another person's children, the focus of interest is largely in child care itself, and the main rewards are the immediate pleasure and enjoyment in child care activities. Their early enjoyable experience in child care may therefore have taught the working-class women to orientate themselves to the activities of child care and to look for immediate rewards in carrying them out:

> 'Before I got married, I looked after my brother. My Mum had him quite late – I was 18 when she had him. So I always looked after him. He was only 4 when I got married. I always used to enjoy looking after him, so I always expected to have children myself. I knew I'd enjoy looking after them.'
> (Diana Hayes, working class, sons 10, 7½, and 3½, daughter 4½)

This orientation was less common among middle-class women. Their adolescence had not been channelled so narrowly and child care had not taken on the same connotations for them.

PART THREE
FATHERS AND HUSBANDS

· 9 ·
THE ORGANIZATION
OF CHILD CARE
IN THE FAMILY

While there has been much criticism of the view that marriages are now largely 'egalitarian' or 'symmetrical',[1] there appears to be some measure of agreement among sociologists that in recent years men have become more involved in domestic matters, especially in child care. As long ago as 1957 Bott stated that 'all research couples ... took it for granted that husband and wife should be jointly responsible for the welfare of their children' (Bott 1957: 71) and Young and Willmott that 'the sharing of responsibility between husband and wife is nowhere more obvious than over the children' (Young and Willmott 1962: 27). More recently, both Oakley (1974a) and Edgell (1980) found that although men rarely helped substantially with housework, they more often helped with child care. The implications of these studies are that men's involvement in child care has increased and that this increased help has relieved women of the burden of child care and enhanced their enjoyment of motherhood (Skolnick 1973).

In this chapter I shall look at the question of men's involvement in child care and at the common belief that this has increased and has made motherhood a more rewarding experience. The first part of the chapter describes the nature and extent of the men's participation in child care, the second part looks at how such involvement influenced a woman's experience as a mother, and the chapter closes with a consideration of factors which worked to restrict men's involvement in child care.

Husbands' help with their children

Virtually all the women in the study described their husbands as involved in their children on an emotional level: 80 per cent of the women said that their husbands were interested and involved in their children and 66 per cent that their husbands enjoyed their children as much or more than they did themselves. Similarly, all the women made it clear that the final responsibility for their children remained with them alone: however great their husband's help with their children, it remained help in carrying out what was ultimately the women's own responsibility.[2]

Within these common limits, however, the women in the sample described their husbands as giving three quite different patterns of practical help with the children.[3] At one extreme, a few women described their husbands as giving *extensive* help with all aspects of child care on a regular basis. One account of the previous evening gives an idea of the sort of help women in this group received:

'My husband came in about 6.15 and I was in the process of getting them into the bathroom, dressed, and ready for bed. He came up and helped to get them washed and dressed and into bed while I came down to get our meal. He read them a story and we ate about 7.00. Then I went out to work (*as a district nurse*). The toys were all over the place when I went out. When I came back they were all tidied up. He'd put the hoover around and swept the floor and he'd even got the ironing board out and done the pyjamas and things for the children. . . . I know people complain, most people get dreadful nights, but I'm all right. When they do cry during the night, my husband will get up without batting an eye. And I sleep through the whole thing.'
(Q: '*Do you ask him to do it or does he do it on his own?*')
'Oh on his own, he wouldn't think to – my husband has never called me to change, to clean, or to do anything for the children. He does it all himself (*when he is around*). I think he enjoys doing it. . . . I always have the energy to cope with them during the day. And in the evenings I flop and that's that. I fall asleep in the chair once I've had my meal. And at that point my husband falls in and copes with everything. *He* takes over the children. The same thing on the weekends. *He* takes over the children. . . . I find when Daddy's around they stick to him quite a lot and expect him to do far more than they expect me to do. I think probably my husband is almost always just sitting down but when they see

me I'm on my feet doing something. So they ask him, and let me get on with things.'
(Ruth Venables, middle class, daughter 5, sons 3 and 2)

When he was at home to do so, Jack Venables helped with everything that was to be done for the children and he helped spontaneously, out of a sense of his own duty towards them. His *extensive* involvement in the care of his children was in striking contrast to the *minimal* involvement of these two husbands:

'He isn't really interested in the domestic side of things. He's *never* changed or washed a nappy. For the first six months the baby woke up every night and he *never* got up. Not once. . . . He doesn't discuss things. He doesn't give advice. Because it's all left to us really. To the mother. We have to take them to school; we have to pick them up; we have to teach them to say please and thank you, because we're with them all day. We're the ones who have to keep on and on at them. We don't tell *each other* what to do. We've both got our own lives to lead.'
(Tracey Allen, working class, daughters 4 and 11 months)

'He sees them very little except in the mornings. And in the evenings maybe when John waits up to see him from time to time. He's ready for bed, but he waits. He'll read to them then but he won't bath them. On weekends he's around more than he is during the week. But he doesn't feed them or bath them. He will play with them *sometimes* or go and read to them in the evening and give a big hug and cuddles. But no, when it comes to bathing or nappies or meals. He might come and watch for a couple of minutes while *I* do it, but he's not usually home.'
(Rosemary Penrose, middle class, son 4½, daughter 2)

Men such as these took very little part in the care of their children. They helped occasionally and in very limited ways such as baby-sitting for short periods or playing with the children when they wanted to, but on the whole they left their wives to cope with the children alone.

Between these two extremes were a group of men whom the women described as helping in a number of ways but not to the same extent or with the same regularity as the men in the first group. In addition to playing with their children, they either helped irregularly with a range of minor tasks or engaged in some kind of joint child care activity with their wives. They discussed questions arising from bringing up children but did not have any independent ideas about it and generally left it to their wives to decide what should be done. One woman describes a typical pattern of help:

> 'I wouldn't say he does anything I would call *regular* work. Sometimes he helps. It depends if he's got any paper work to do. You can't *rely* on him doing anything from day to day. He'll wash up in the mornings. He'll mind the children while I go to the hairdresser Saturday morning, but nine times out of ten they're still in bed anyway. He'll bath them for me, he'll put them to bed, *sometimes*. But they've got to be done every day, these jobs, and he'll only do them when he feels like doing them. He does it as he *pleases* to do it. You can't ask him to do it. If I were to say "Would you do so and so" he wouldn't do it.'
> (Sarah Hepburn, middle class, daughter 6, son 2)

David Hepburn helped with the children when he wanted to but never felt an obligation to do so. This ability to choose what he did not only underlined his refusal to take it as a responsibility but also emphasized the charity nature of his help and all that goes with that notion.[4]

Help from this group of men was often in the form of back-up support. One woman, for example, describes her husband as helping her as *she* put the children to bed:

> 'He is helpful. He's always in the room at bedtime and we put the children to bed together. Particularly with David. David won't go to bed unless Daddy's in the room. It's Daddy who will read him a story or make up one.'
> (Nicola Savage, working class, son 4, daughter 1½)

As her account suggests, this sort of help was often based on playing with the children, which brought the men into the ritual aspects of routines:

> 'If I'm washing up and it's extra late I will take her into the bathroom and wash her down and then he'll go into the bedroom and get her nightdress and come in here. He'll help her get out of her clothes and into her nightdress. And while I'm still washing up he might play hide and seek or chase her round the room and then tuck her into bed.'
> (Karen Alexander, working class, daughters 3½ and 1)

Play also brought men into a more supervisory role, as Alice Gray's description of her husband's help shows:

'I think when he comes home, he should help as well. He plays with them and if they're naughty he might tell them off. When Sean plays up, I'm telling him off all day. When my husband comes home, it's his job. They listen to him much more. I suppose he hears me shouting all day so much he's used to me now.'

(Alice Gray, working class, sons 5 and 3)

Like other men who gave *moderate* help, Tony Gray helped his wife but not on a regular basis and largely in the context of playing with the children.

The number of men described as giving each pattern of help, given in Table 9(1), suggests that children are still almost exclusively the women's domain. In only nine families was there anything approximating to parenthood as a 'joint enterprise', while in almost half of the families the husband left the care of the children to his wife alone and in a third he did no more than support his wife with moderate help. There is little evidence from this study, therefore, to suggest that the sharing of child care between husband and wife is now widespread. Instead, what sociologists of the family such as Skolnick (1973) or Young and Willmott (1957, 1973) see as an increase in men's involvement in domestic matters may be little more than an increase in their interest in and enjoyment of their children. This is quite different from their sharing in responsibility for their children and does not necessarily presage any marked increase in their more practical help.

Table 9(1) *Husbands' help with child care and social class*

| Social class | Husband's help with child care | | | |
	extensive no. (%)	moderate no. (%)	minimal no. (%)	total no. (%)
working class	2 (8)	11 (44)	12 (48)	25 (100)
middle class	7 (28)	7 (28)	11 (44)	25 (100)
total	9 (18)	18 (36)	23 (46)	50 (100)

$x^2 = 3.62$ p$>$0.05

The finding that only a small proportion of men helped significantly with their children is in striking contrast to the findings of virtually all the other research which has looked at this question. *Table 9(2)* compares the findings of this study with those of ten others. All but the first two reported that the majority of fathers 'helped frequently' with their children over one year of age or were 'highly participant' in child care.

Table 9(2) *Comparison of research findings on husbands' help with child care*

	high help or equivalent (%)	medium help or equivalent (%)	low help or equivalent (%)
1. Boulton (1982) (pre-school)*	18	36	46
2. Oakley (1974a) (pre-school)	25	30	45
3. Oakley (1979) (5 months)	11	26	64
4. Newson and Newson (1965) (1 year)	54	27	21
5. Newson and Newson (1968) (4 years)	51	40	9
6. Gavron (1966)** (largely pre-school)	48	24	28
7. Richards, Dunn, and Antonis (1977)			
(30 weeks)	36	49	15
(60 weeks)	62	25	13
8. Komarovsky (1962)			
(infants)	36	33	31
(older children)	56	34	10
9. Graham and McKee (1980)*** (5 months)	46	50	4
10. Edgell (1980)****	(joint division of labour)	(intermediate division of labour)	(segregated division of labour)
(young)	25	58	17
(all ages)	44	39	16
11. Young and Willmott (1973)***** (unspecified ages)	(help with 'other tasks' including child care) 70		(no help) 16

    * age of children in the study
   ** adapted from Chapter 9 (combines working class and middle class)
  *** adapted from *Table E.3*; excludes 'not givens'
 **** adapted from *Table 4.4*, page 39
***** adapted from *Table 15*, page 115

There are two main reasons why these studies have reported a higher level of men's help with child care than would appear to be warranted. One lies in the methods of assessment used. Most studies obtained their information from general questions about how often the men did a selection of four or five specified tasks. The difficulties inherent in this sort of question mean that this method is unlikely to obtain an accurate picture. At a time when the ideal of the companionate marriage is widespread, it is to be expected that, when asked a general question, many women would present their relationship in such terms. Any such tendency would be facilitated by the use of ambiguous or relative terms like 'often' and 'sometimes' or 'high' and 'medium', which can be used in whatever way the respondent chooses. Moreover, the activities chosen to represent child care were often those in which men are most likely to be involved, such as playing with children, putting them to bed, and taking them out. Komarovsky, for example, considered amongst other things 'taking an interest in the children', 'playing with the children', and 'making toys for them' in rating husband's help with children. Other tasks which are, on the whole, less rewarding such as preparing meals, washing clothes, or tidying away toys were seldom asked about; the same applied to the more nebulous responsibilities such as getting the children ready for the husband to take out, supervising the children when friends are visiting, or the variety of residual tasks that occupy women. When it is looked at closely, then, the whole approach of asking 'who-does-what-how-often' is of questionable value. Child care is essentially about exercising responsibility for another person who is not fully responsible for herself and it entails seeing to all aspects of the child's security and well-being, her growth and development, at any and all times. It is of limited value to reduce child care to a set of independent tasks such as dressing the children, playing with them, correcting their behaviour, bathing them, and choosing their clothes (Edgell 1980: 123). This is simply a set of routine activities which, because of their very superficiality, can easily be done from time to time by anyone, including uninvolved fathers. It does not describe caring for children or 'mothering' which 'is not simply a set of behaviours, but participation in an inter-personal, diffuse, affective relationship' (Chodorow 1978: 33).

The second reason for the over-generous estimates of the husband's participation in child care is related to this last point. It arises from the apparent assumption that children are naturally the responsibility of the mother, an assumption which acts to exaggerate the value of *any* involvement in the children on the part of the husband and so to present his help as more extensive than it is. The Newsons, for example, begin their consideration of the 'father's place' with the statement that '*Obviously* the care of infants is a predominantly female occupation (emphasis added)' (Newson and Newson 1965: 133). Their acceptance of the woman's primary responsibility for children, and of the related norms for proper child care behaviour which this implies, led them to define 'high', 'moderate', and 'non-' participation in relation to expectations of very little participation. As a result, they classed as 'highly participant' men who helped with just three child-care tasks 'often' and three more 'sometimes'. Richards, Dunn, and Antonis (1977) used even lower standards, classing as 'highly participant' all those men who 'often' performed just two of feeding, changing, bathing, and taking out the children (in addition to playing with them) and as 'moderately participant' all those who performed even one of those tasks 'sometimes'. What is in practice very little in relation to what needs to be done and in relation to what a woman does is nonetheless defined as 'high participation' for men where the taken-for-granted expectation is that children are the woman's responsibility. With such low thresholds for 'high' and 'moderate' participation, it is hardly surprising that so many men were seen as helping substantially with child care.

Husbands' help with children and women's experience as mothers

IMMEDIATE RESPONSE TO LOOKING AFTER CHILDREN

The initial analysis of the data suggested that her husband's practical help with the children had a rather limited influence on a woman's immediate response to child care: *Table 9(3)* shows that, for the sample as a whole, there is little relationship between the two variables. Because these results were so surprising, I decided to look again at the relationship but to do so for the working-class and middle-class groups separately. A clearer and more interesting picture emerged from this analysis: *Table 9(4)* shows that for working-class women there was a strong positive relationship between her husband's help and a woman's enjoyment of child care and *Table 9(5)* that for middle-class women there was a weak negative relationship. Some of the reasons for these relationships, and for the clear class differences between them, can be seen in the ways their husbands' help with the children affected the women's daily lives and in the ways this differed between the social classes.

Table 9(3) *Husband's help with child care and woman's immediate response to child care*

| Immediate response to child care | Husband's help with child care | | |
	extensive or moderate no. (%)	minimal no. (%)	total no. (%)
enjoyed	15 (56)	9 (39)	24 (48)
irritated	12 (44)	14 (61)	26 (52)
total	27 (100)	23 (100)	50 (100)

$\gamma = 0.32$

Table 9(4) *For working-class women, husband's help with child care and woman's immediate response to child care*

| Immediate response to child care | Husband's help with child care | | |
	extensive or moderate no. (%)	minimal no. (%)	total no. (%)
enjoyed	10 (77)	4 (33)	14 (56)
irritated	3 (23)	8 (67)	11 (44)
total	13 (100)	12 (100)	25 (100)

$\gamma = 0.74$

Table 9(5) *For middle-class women, husband's help with child care and woman's immediate response to child care*

| Immediate response to child care | Husband's help with child care | | |
	extensive or moderate no. (%)	minimal no. (%)	total no. (%)
enjoyed	5 (36)	5 (45)	10 (40)
irritated	9 (64)	6 (55)	15 (60)
total	14 (100)	11 (100)	25 (100)

$\gamma = -0.20$

Among working-class women, the husband's help made a substantial difference to what was involved in looking after the children and, in this way, to a woman's enjoyment of it. First, and perhaps most important, in helping her with their children, her husband took some of the burden of work from her and eased the pressure of her diffuse responsibilities as a mother. By relieving her of the children's demands, he allowed her to get on with her housework undisturbed or to deal with one child without the other interfering. By reducing potential role conflict, his involvement allowed her greater flexibility in coping with all domestic responsibilities. By taking over some of the tasks of child care, he enabled her to get through her daily routines more quickly and easily and at times gave her a complete break from the children.

Because it reduced the volume and pressure of her work, her husband's help also enabled a woman to be more relaxed in looking after her children and so to focus more on the play or expressive aspects of their contact. By the same token, it meant she had more unscheduled time in which to play with her children and to enjoy their company, which, as I pointed out in Chapter 4, were important ways in which working-class women enjoyed their children.

Finally, her husband's help with the children turned child care into a shared activity between husband and wife, which was enjoyed for the companionship and support engendered in it. In working-class families, where verbal communication is said to be more limited and couples may find it more difficult to express themselves directly, the children may be an avenue of communication between husband and wife (Young and Willmott 1962; Komarovsky 1962; Klein 1965). Particularly when a woman's identification with her children is strong, her husband's involvement in them may be meant – and taken – as an expression of affection or appreciation for her. The opposite is also true: when a man has little to do with his children, they may be resented for reinforcing the barrier between her and her husband.

Among middle-class women, the situation was quite different. Her husband's help with the children, or the lack of it, had less of an effect on the nature of a middle-class woman's work and consequently less of an effect on the enjoyment or irritation she felt in looking after her children. There are several reasons why this was so. First, middle-class women had a number of material resources that working-class women did not have, which made their husbands' help relatively less important in shaping the content and conditions of day-to-day child care. In addition to having more money to spend on enjoying the children, many middle-class women had washing machines and tumble dryers, large enclosed gardens, large rooms with a great deal of storage space, a spare room or a playroom for the children to play in, access to a car during the day, and in some cases paid domestic help. These resources helped them to deal with the demands of pre-school children, to develop boundaries and routines for coping with their diffuse obligations, to avoid role conflict, and to have some measure of freedom from the home and children *regardless* of their husband's help. Under these conditions, extensive help from her husband may have been 'icing on the cake': it may have enhanced a woman's enjoyment of her children but it did not make the kind of striking difference that it made for a working-class woman. Similarly, while the lack of help from her husband may have been seen as disloyalty, the other resources available to her may have gone far enough towards lightening her workload so that the lack of help was not important. Certainly it was quite clear that middle-class women whose husbands did not help them were in a very different situation from their working-class counterparts.

Second, an essential frustration that the middle-class women described – their feelings of monopolization and loss of individuality in motherhood – was not substantially altered by their husbands' help, so long as it was limited to *help*. As I described in Chapter 6, many middle-class women spoke both of the difficulties they faced in trying to pursue interests outside the family and the feelings to which these difficulties gave rise: feelings that children were inhibiting their personal autonomy and that their identity as a mother was taking over their identity as an individual. These feelings are rooted in a woman's sole and final *responsibility* for her children which means she must put the children first and subordinate her own needs and interests to those of her children. So long as her husband's involvement in their children remained as help within the context of a woman's responsibility for them, it could have only a limited influence on her feelings of monopolization and loss of individuality. His help may have given his wife some time away from their children but it did not give her sufficient opportunity to develop and pursue her own interests, something which would be essential if she were to maintain a sense of individuality and identity not based on child care. Such 'freedom', however, is likely to be found only when the husband's help with the children approaches shared responsibility for them. This, in turn, is not likely to occur without a fundamental reorganization of society as a whole, so that social institutions are geared to cope with both men and women carrying several demanding responsibilities at the same time.

Third, the extent of a man's help with child care seemed in some instances to be more an *effect* of his wife's response to child care than a *cause* of it. That is, in the middle-class group, where the norm of sharing is generally believed to be well established, it appeared that some men accepted that they should adjust their help to what was appropriate for their family situation. In particular, the accounts of some middle-class women who were rated as frustrated with child care suggested that their husbands had responded to their frustration by increasing their help with the children. One woman, for example, recounts how her husband was sensitive to her feelings about full-time child care and tried to ease her irritation by helping as much as he could. He did so despite his own irritation with child care:

> 'Among my friends, he's the one who says "I don't know how you stand it all day, I really don't". Whereas most husbands hide the fact that it's a lot of work to have children. But I think that's because he's home one day a week, in the week, and he can see what it's like. . . . He's not here all day but when he is here, he's marvellous. When we were on this working rota, he even said I could go to work on the day he had off and he would have them all day. That's what made it possible. He did this for two weeks and when I got in both times he was nearly screaming. He'd had enough. He wasn't very pleased with the idea but he was willing to do it for me.'
> (Victoria Milton, middle class, daughter 3½, son 1½)

In contrast, the husbands of working-class women rated as frustrated with child care seemed to respond on the basis of their own irritation with the children by *not* helping more. Nola Hopkins's account is typical:

> 'He doesn't spend a terrible lot of time with them. They can get a bit irritating of an evening. Especially if he sits in the chair and watches the telly and they decide to play. He gets a bit irritated with them and that's that. He doesn't really have much to do

with them, because they irritate him so he leaves them to me.'
(Nola Hopkins, working class, daughters 9 and 3, son 6)

For middle-class women whose husbands responded to their
frustration with more help, however, the problem was not necessarily solved. That is, their help did not always make the crucial
difference to their response to child care for the reasons given
above: it did not alter the basic organization of child care and so
did not free them from their sense of loss of identity in motherhood.
As a result, there were probably some middle-class men who helped
a great deal *because* their wives were frustrated in child care but
who could not significantly alter this frustration by doing so. There
may also have been some middle-class women whose husbands did
not help at all *because* their wives enjoyed child care and did not
want to give it up.

SENSE OF MEANING AND PURPOSE IN MOTHERHOOD

With regard to the second dimension of their response to motherhood, *Table 9(6)* shows that, for the sample as a whole, there is a
moderately strong relationship between her husband's help with
child care and a woman's sense of meaning and purpose in
motherhood. This relationship remains relatively unchanged when
the working-class and middle-class groups are looked at separately.

Table 9(6) *Husband's help with child care and woman's sense of meaning
and purpose as a mother*

| Sense of meaning and purpose | Husband's help with child care | | |
	extensive or moderate no. (%)	minimal no. (%)	total no. (%)
strong	20 (74)	9 (39)	29 (58)
weak	7 (26)	14 (61)	21 (42)
total	27 (100)	23 (100)	50 (100)

$\gamma = 0.63$

For working-class women especially, her husband's help with the
children was important in allowing her the freedom and flexibility
to shift her attention from her child care activities and to reflect on
her life in relation to her commitment to her children. For women

whose husbands did not help them, the demands of child care were on the whole so great that they dominated their experience completely. These women were therefore too bogged down in day-to-day child care to have the time to reflect on their lives and too fundamentally irritated to be inclined to do so. In the working-class and middle-class groups alike, men who gave substantial help were also likely to be understanding and emotionally supportive of their wives. As I shall argue in the next chapter, a supportive husband was particularly important in the process of defining the goals and purposes they, as a couple, shared in the children, and in supporting a woman's view of herself as fulfilling these goals.

Factors affecting men's participation in child care

It is generally recognized that the basic factor influencing the extent of a man's help with child care is his commitment to paid employment: the demand that a man establish his worth through paid employment over-rides whatever ideology of sharing may exist in a family and ensures that he participates in the workforce rather than the family when both make demands on his time and energy. His participation in the workforce in turn means he is out of the house and away from the children for a substantial part of each day and so has little opportunity to look after them. In this study, those men who worked shifts, who had days off during the week, or who were teachers with long holidays helped more with their children than men who were home only at weekends: 8 of the 11 (73 per cent) in the former group were rated as giving extensive or moderate help, in contrast to 19 of the 39 (48 per cent) in the latter group. All of the men, however, were away from the children for long periods of time while they were at work which meant that all of them could do relatively little for their children. They were simply not available to deal with them most of the time:

> 'The thing is, *he's never here*. So he doesn't have to check them. He's only here Sundays and we just have a rough and tumble Sunday evening. He doesn't have much to do with them, not in that respect. He just isn't here.'
> (Candy Gibson, working class, daughters 6 and 3)

> 'Eighty per cent of the things they do they start when they're alone with me, so obviously it comes from me. I'm the one who's

with them all day. Of course I'm the one bringing them up in that sense.'

(Jane Crawford, middle class, twin daughters 2½)

Men's paid work, then, set the main parameters of their help with the children by severely curtailing the *opportunity* they had to help. While this was the most obvious and important way in which their jobs acted to limit their help, however, it was far from the only way. In a number of other, more subtle ways, paid employment also acted to curtail men's help even when they were at home and had the opportunity to help. Since these more subtle and pervasive influences are not well appreciated, there is value in considering them more closely here.

A man's primary commitment to paid employment reflects a basic sexual division of labour in society whereby men are responsible for paid work and women for domestic work. Within this social context, a total division of labour within the family was often seen as legitimate:

'He feels it's *my* job. The house and the children are *my* job. He's got *his* job. His job is to keep us alive with the money. The rest is *my* job.'

(Rosemary Penrose, middle class, son 4½, daughter 2)

The definition of domestic work as her responsibility may have reassured a woman that she had an important role and was making a contribution to the family equal to her husband's. This may well have been important to her self-esteem and as such may have been something she was not anxious to change. At the same time, however, it legitimated her husband's withdrawal from child care and made it difficult for her to ask him to help even when he was available to do so:

'He has a pretty heavy day anyway so when he gets home, he's tired, I don't like to ask him to help *me* then.'

(Angela Bourne, middle class, son 3½, daughter 1½)

'He works six days a week and I don't want him to spend his one day off working around the house. He'd rather go out or he likes the garden. I think his one day off should *be* a day off, not a day doing *my* work.'

(Victoria Milton, middle class, daughter 3½, son 1½)

The fact that paid work takes priority over domestic work gave further grounds for excusing men from helping with their children when such help was seen as interfering with their ability to do their own work. It was for this reason that men were generally not asked to get up at night for their children:

> 'I'm one of those who thinks, "He works hard all day. I don't. If I'm tired, I sit down. He can't". So I think it's *my* job. If I'm tired, I have a kip in the afternoon.'
> (Sandra Keating, working class, daughters 7 and 4)

Such views were widely held, but the situations to which they gave rise were nonetheless resented by some:

> 'I have to work the next day as well. Some husbands say "Well you can do what you want in the day. You can leave it and have a rest. You can sit and have a cup of tea if you're tired." I suppose it's right in a way but there might be something really demanding from the children.'
> (Sharon Rogers, working class, daughters 5 and 1)

While the sexual division of labour in society acts to exclude men from child care it also functions to provide an alternative pool of help among other women, particularly the women's own mothers and mothers-in-law (Young and Willmott 1957; Bott 1957; Rubin 1976). This resource of willing and able women, by its very efficiency in helping young mothers, can both reinforce the sexual division of labour and inhibit men from greater involvement in child care. One woman, for example, describes how her mother took over the children on Sundays, which was one of the few opportunities her husband had for looking after them:

> 'Sometimes he'll give him his dinner on weekends but usually he's working on the car or we're at my mother's and she wants to do it. We don't see them ever all day then, because she takes over. She's getting the benefit from grandchildren now.'
> (Debra Lennon, working class, sons 5 and 3)

Once this sort of pattern is established, a woman 'naturally' turns to her mother for help. Thus, Debra Lennon left her children with her mother, not her husband, when she took a Saturday job:

> 'They love their grandmother. They used to stay with her on Saturday the one time I got a job in Woolworths. I used to get up and leave early to get to the West End. I used to have to take

them first to my mother. By the time I got out of work it was 6.00. Then I had to go to my mother's to collect them and then come all the way back here. By the time I got in it was 7.30. It was too much.'

It was not a convenient arrangement but an obvious one.

In times of crisis such as illness or childbirth, women often looked to one another, rather than to their husbands, for someone to help. Teresa Flanagan, for example, describes an amazing network of women willing to look after her first child while she had her second:

'When I went into the hospital for John, my friend happened to be calling on me that evening. As soon as I felt pains, I rang Martin at work and wondered, "What am I going to do with Elizabeth". The woman upstairs said I could leave Elizabeth till my friend came. My friend took Elizabeth home with her and kept her until Martin picked her up and took her round to his aunt's place. She stayed with his aunt till I came home.'
(Teresa Flanagan, working class, daughter 4, son 2)

When suitable female relatives were available, child care remained a female activity and men were once again excused. The strong gender role expectations and the availability of enough people who were willing to keep the system working once again acted to inhibit men's help with children, even when they could do so.

The men's absence from the home for most of the children's waking hours, combined with the belief that child care is a woman's job, means that men rarely *learn how* to look after children. Even when they are at home and available to help, men have neither the knowledge nor the skills to make a *useful* contribution to child care. In these circumstances, their help was often not wanted:

(Q: *'Would you like him to help you more with the children?'*)
'No. Because I have my own way of doing things. And I found the two or three times he has helped, he makes such a big show of it, he makes more work. It was taking far too long and there were lots of other things I had to get on with.'
(Debra Lennon, working class, sons 5 and 3)

Men's incompetence in child care may have been further sustained by the belief that men were inherently incapable of doing women's work. Candy Gibson and Gillian Nichols felt there was no point in asking their husbands to help because, as men, they could not do it:

> 'He's only in on Sundays. And I usually bath and wash the kids' hair on Sundays. And that's the sort of thing a man can't do. You can't expect a man to do it. It's not in a man, to manage hair and things, like it is in a woman.'
>
> (Candy Gibson, working class, daughters 6 and 3)

> 'My husband could never change a nappy. Some men can do it, they are prepared to do it. But he was *never*. Not interested, not in the sense of really looking after them, feeding them and all that. He would make a right mess of it. Women have a better instinct. They know better. They know the difference between crying and crying. A man couldn't do it.'
>
> (Gillian Nichols, middle class, son 4, daughter 2)

It was because of this belief in their husbands' incompetence and their own instincts – or at least 'special skills' – that the women often accepted their husbands' lack of involvement in *babies*. Babies tended to be seen as making a special kind of demand and requiring a special mode of communication which only women could provide. Because they were involved in the rational world of business or industry all day, men were seen to find it difficult – or even impossible – to adjust in the evening to the intuitive and empathic ways of dealing with children. While women also found it difficult and frustrating initially (see Chapter 4), the fact that they were with the children constantly and had to deal with them meant that of necessity they had learned to do so. Nonetheless, they were still aware that looking after babies required a unique kind of skill and a particular knowledge which they did not expect their husbands to have. One woman, for example, describes her husband as finding the baby incomprehensible:

> 'He's not good with babies. He never changed Ann's nappy when she was in nappies. And he wouldn't dream of doing it for the baby. He's just not very good with babies. He's fine with Ann. But babies he's got no idea of at all. I left the baby once with him when I took Ann to a party. And he arrived *at* the party *with* the baby. If she cries, he has no idea. He says to me "Why is she crying?" I don't know why she's crying – she's just crying. He expects me to know the answer. . . . Ann he'd do anything for.

He can look after her very well. But not the baby. The baby is *all mine*.'

(Naomi Hildebrand, middle class, daughters 4 and 1)

The definition of child care as requiring special skills and abilities was important in bolstering the status of child care. It made a woman's self-image as a good mother rewarding and her day-to-day successes in coping with the children a satisfying achievement. As in most jobs, there may have been some attempt at mystification of child care, particularly among working-class women who looked for rewards in that area. To maintain her sense of special skill and expertise in her own and her husband's eyes, a woman may sometimes have co-operated in keeping him on the periphery of child care:

'He's as interested in them as I am but he still looks to me to take the lead. Like he says, if they're not well, "What do *you* think?" He seems to know that a mother always knows when a child is ill. Because I knew he was ill before the doctors did. My husband seems to realize if *I'm* worried about them, he'll worry about them. He's interested, but he leaves it to me because he feels *I* know best.'

(Jean Elliott, working class, sons 6, 4, and 2)

While it was rewarding at times, however, the emphasis on special skills and knowledge required in child care also meant that there was often little point in a woman asking her husband for help; without the necessary skills and knowledge there was not much he could do:

'As regards getting them dressed for me – he wouldn't even know where their clothes are. I've never sort of asked him. He'd say, "Where are they? What goes on first? How do you do it? You show me. You do it – you can do it quicker than me". In the end, it's not worth it.'

(Janet Hobson, working class, daughter 5, son 2)

Their husbands' ignorance in looking after the children helped to shield them since, under these circumstances, it was easier for the women to do everything themselves. The men could even offer to help in the full knowledge that their wives would be likely to decline:

'Sometimes he offers to do little things. But I think – by the time

I've told him where this and that is, and explained how to do it, I might as well have done it myself. I think this is why he offers. Because half the time he expects me to turn around and say, "Oh, never mind, I'll do it myself".'

(Dawn Straker, working class, son 4, daughter 1)

This of course made it appear that the women did not want their husbands' help and put them in an invidious position if they complained about their lack of help.

Not all men were unwilling to help with the children when they could. From the women's point of view, however, it was nonetheless often *impractical* for them to do so. Most of the women had developed a routine for their day in order to cope with the volume and the complexity of the tasks involved in looking after children and running a house (see Chapter 5). Because men were at work all day, this routine was unlikely to include them. As a result, on those occasions when they were at home the routine may have had the effect of excluding them from child care:

'My husband is *totally* out of my routine. I don't consider him at all in organizing my day. He leaves anywhere between 6.00 and 8.00 a.m. He's *never* here Monday to Friday and when he is home, he's still out of my routine. It's the only way – just carry on normally or you won't get it done.'

(Jessica Lloyd, middle class, son 3, daughter 1)

Like many women, she found it easier and less work to adhere to her own routine even on days when her husband was home. She did not look to him for help, not because in principle she did not want it but because in practice it would have disrupted her routine and ultimately caused more work. It is only when a man can be counted on to be there to take part in child care, as in the case of the eleven men who were home during the week, that it is sensible for a woman to develop a routine which includes her husband. And it is only when a man's help is part of the *routine* that his help is really substantial.

Because the father is away most of their waking hours, the children may become accustomed only to their mother's care. Thus, the children themselves may reinforce the pattern of child care in the family by insisting that the mother, not the father, look after them. Patricia Hawkins, for example, says that both she and her husband would have liked him to do more for the children, but the *children* would not let him:

'Because he can't put her to bed during the week, she's not keen on him doing it on weekends. We haven't insisted yet, but it's something where when they're at an age to both have a story, we get a routine that at weekends he does it and I don't.'
(Q: 'Would you like more help?')
'Yes. It's just that she's a child of routines. She likes to watch my husband wash and shave. That's part of the routine. I'm the one who puts her to bed and reads the story and does that part of the routine. When you've got a child that's already asleep, you tend to do it the quieter way.'
  (Patricia Hawkins, middle class, daughters 3 and 11 months)

Similarly, children often wanted their mother, not their father, when they woke up at night:

'He will get up if they wake in the night. But they don't want him, they want *me*, then, when they're upset. But he would go to them. One of their problems is that they're thirsty. And I can call him from their bedroom and say could you go down and get them a drink and he'll go down and bring one up. He'll put himself out for them quite a lot.'
  (Jane Crawford, middle class, twin daughters 2½)

The children wanted the familiar figure of their mother at a time when they were frightened or upset. Since their father was not available to comfort them during the day, he may not have established this sort of relationship with the children and so may have been less effective in this way at night. The women themselves felt ambivalent about these demands, on the one hand resenting the extra work and on the other hand enjoying the sense of being needed and wanted.

A final point concerns the meaning that may be given to men's help with child care in a society which defines it as a woman's job: a request for help may be seen as an admission of incompetence or failure, and an offer of help may be taken as implicit criticism. With such a connotation, it is not surprising that more women do not ask for help from their husbands. In working-class families in particular, the husband's help could be felt as threatening:

'He'll always wash them if they're dirty, if they've been in the garden. He can't stand dirty children, it's the way he was brought up. I was brought up the same, but I'm not as fussy. He'll always wash them if they're dirty. I snap down his throat – I say, "I was

going to do that in a minute". It's irritating. He'll always tell me.
Sometimes I get the impression he thinks I'm dirty.'
(Sharon Rogers, working class, daughters 5 and 1)

While Sharon Rogers accepted his help anyway, Debra Lennon
actively discouraged it:

(Q: 'Would you like more effective help?')
'No. Because I'd take it he was criticizing me, saying "Oh, this
should have been done a long time ago. Why didn't you do it. I
suppose I've got to do it myself".'
(Debra Lennon, working class, sons 5 and 3)

This comment suggests the ambivalence many women felt about
their husbands' involvement in child care. Like a number of
women, Debra Lennon was dissatisfied with her husband's lack of
help with the children and the burden this placed on her, but at the
same time she felt threatened when he did help her.

Among middle-class women, the threat was felt not only in the
help itself but in having to ask for it:

'I could possibly manage it better than him, but he would get up
in the night if I ask him. But I feel you shouldn't have to ask. And
you do resent it. But on the other hand, he does have to get up in
the morning and go to work and it's not really fair. But though
you feel that, you do *resent* it. He gets up for the dog.'
(Margaret Samuel, middle class, sons 4 and 2)

For Margaret Samuel, asking for help was a confirmation of her
dependence on her husband and her inability to manage on her
own. His voluntary help might have confirmed their joint responsibility for the children and might not have been so disturbing. But
having to ask for his help reinforced her sense that the children
were seen as her responsibility and that she simply could not cope
with them alone. She did not ask for help because she resented the
change in the relationship which this would imply.

Notes

1. For a discussion of the symmetrical family thesis, see Oakley 1974a;
   Meissner *et al.* 1975; Bell and Newby 1976; Edgell 1980; Leonard
   1980.
2. This is an important point and one noted in a number of other studies
   (Bott 1957; Oakley 1974a, 1979; Ericksen, Yancey, and Ericksen 1979;

Edgell 1980). Even when a woman works outside the home, the children are invariably her responsibility (Poloma and Garland 1970; Epstein 1971; Rapoport and Rapoport 1971; Bahr 1974).

3. Each woman was questioned about her husband's participation in a variety of aspects of child care, including physical care routines (e.g. putting to bed), occasional demands (e.g. getting up at night), play and leisure activities, discipline, education, and care not involving direct contact with the children (e.g. tidying up toys). For each activity that was mentioned in the interview she was asked whether her husband carried out that activity and what exactly he did; whether he usually did it and how often or under what circumstances he did it; and whether he did it on his own and without being asked. In addition, she was asked whether her husband had strong ideas of his own about bringing up children and whether they discussed the various problems which arose (e.g. how to deal with bedwetting or what school to choose).

4. This sort of discretionary help may give a man a false impression of what child care is like. By doing only one or two things for the children as he chooses, he takes the tasks out of their context and so avoids many of the central features of full-time child care. If child care seems enjoyable when he does it, without pressure and as he chooses, he may find it particularly difficult to sympathize with his wife's problems.

· 10 ·
MARRIAGE
AND MATERNITY

The previous chapter showed how her husband's practical help with child care influenced a woman's experience of caring for children. In this chapter I shall go on to examine the ways the more emotional relationship between a woman and her husband influenced, and was influenced by, her experience as a mother. Two questions are considered: first, how children had changed the relationship between a woman and her husband; second, how much sympathy and support she felt her husband gave her at the time of the interview. The first part of the chapter describes the nature of the relationship between the women and their husbands and the second part looks at how this relationship affected a woman's experience as a mother.

The marital relationship

CHANGE IN THE MARITAL RELATIONSHIP

The birth of children brings about substantial changes in the relationship between a wife and husband. Their roles are re-organized as the woman withdraws from the labour market to take over domestic responsibilities and her husband takes over as sole earner for the family. New relationships are created and emotional commitments are re-ordered: a woman's involvement in her children can mean an emotional withdrawal from the marital relationship (Rubin 1976; Oakley 1980; Graham and McKee 1980) or the children can 'make the marriage' (Busfield 1974; Graham 1977). One way of describing the nature of a woman's relationship with her husband, then, is in terms of the way she perceived that this relationship had been changed by the arrival of children.[1]

Table 10(1) shows that a third of the women felt that children improved their relationship with their husbands and a quarter that they created problems in the relationship.[2] It also shows interesting class differences that mirror Lopata's comment that for American women with little education 'parenthood roles add an important and meaningful bond to a relatively limited relationship bringing the husband and wife "closer together" through the creation of a common interest' while better educated women 'sometimes express a feeling of increased social distance between themselves and their mates' after the birth of their children (Lopata 1971: 199).

Table 10(1) *Perceived change in marital relationship and social class*

	Perceived change in marital relationship			
Social class	*improved* no. (%)	*no change* no. (%)	*created problems* no. (%)	*total* no. (%)
working class	12 (48)	12 (48)	1 (4)	25 (100)
middle class	4 (16)	11 (44)	10 (40)	25 (100)
total	16 (32)	23 (46)	11 (22)	50 (100)

$x^2 = 11.4 \, p > 0.01$

Middle-class women tended to see children as interfering in a sense of sharing and equality they had previously had (or at least expected) with their husbands. These qualities were ones that middle-class women valued and the fact that children were seen to threaten them made their diminution or loss the most noticeable consequence of having children. As a result, getting on for half the middle-class women felt that children created problems in their marriage.

Children were seen to threaten a sense of sharing and equality between husband and wife in a number of ways. First, they disrupted the activities that the couple had together and which formed an important part of their sharing and mutual interest:

'You'd like to sleep in together weekends and you can't because the children get you up. It *is* a bit disturbing. I would like some time when the children weren't around at all. . . . Before we got

married we were very, very close. We used to go for long walks and talk a lot. For hours and hours. This sort of thing you can't do with children. We've grown apart because of this. We're good friends but I wouldn't say we were all that close any more.'
(Maureen Richards, middle class, daughter 3, son 11 months)

Children made so many demands that the women often felt that they had little time left for their husbands:

'I think in many ways we may have grown apart because I'm so busy with the children and the housework and the cooking and the shopping and the preparing. And he with his work. So we haven't that much time to even talk to each other sometimes. Even in the morning over breakfast, I'm so busy seeing that the children are getting their breakfast and getting their coats on to go to school I haven't got time to talk to my husband. And if he *did* have something important to say to me he'd have a job getting two minutes peace and quiet to do so. And similarly in the evenings. One is tired. . . . I'm not saying we never talk. Of course we do. But I'm saying that it is less so than when we were just on our own. There's more activity. And I'm tired in a different way. I'm tired from the children and the home in the evening. Whereas when I went out to work I might have been tired but it was different being at home. I was glad to talk about what I was doing during the day and interested to hear what he'd been doing during the day. I didn't have anything else to occupy my mind. Now I have, constantly.'
(Susan Griffiths, middle class, sons 6½ and 1½)

Finally, children were seen to end any equality between a woman and her husband by imposing restrictions on her but not on her husband. As noted in the previous chapter, the final responsibility for the children was taken by the woman alone. This generally meant that she lost a great deal of her freedom and autonomy while her husband retained what freedom he had before the children were born. This *unequal* restriction was resented by a woman as also was the consequent disparity in lifestyle: his life remained interesting while hers became tedious and frustrating.

'I can still talk to him but sometimes I don't feel like talking. I just sulk. I think, "It's all right for him. He has an interesting day at the office. He comes home and his meal is ready for him. He sits down and I've got to get up and serve it and see to the children and do this and that". I resent it. His work becomes more interesting and mine becomes more drudgery. He can't understand this.'

(Margaret Samuel, middle class, sons 4 and 2)

In addition, women felt they became *dependent* on their husbands for help with the children and for possible breaks from them. This sense of dependence as well as the loss of status it implies were often resented even more than the restrictions:

'I think women are dominated by men. It isn't right. If my husband wants to go out for a drink or he's going out he just says, "Oh, I'm going out so and so". But if *I'm* going out, I have to *ask*. I don't think he'd appreciate it if I said "I'm going out to so and so and you've got to stay and mind the children". I've got to say "*Would it be all right* if I go out". I don't like it. He doesn't ask *me*. He's never refused to look after them if he isn't doing something himself. Otherwise, he'll say "No, I'm not looking after them". *I* couldn't do that. But *he* can!'

(Sarah Hepburn, middle class, daughter 6, son 2)

In the course of the pre-school years, this sense of lowered status could become a settled outcome. One woman, for example, describes the way her husband spoke to her almost as he would to a servant regarding her presumed responsibility for the children. Her own resentment is obvious:

'My husband gets very annoyed because he wants to go and do some gardening and James will insist on stepping on the spade when he does and things like this. He automatically says, "Claire, *do* something about this". He thinks I am the one who should stop what I'm doing and look to the children. If we go to my mother's, my mother looks after the children. Michael arrives and the children start pulling at his sleeve and he'll say, "Claire, see to them. I'm talking to your father". He doesn't think, "Oh, they're my children, I should stop them doing it". It's always, "Claire, will *you* stop them because *I* want to do something".'

(Claire Hughes, middle class, daughter 5½, son 2½)

On the whole, then, when they felt their relationship with their husbands had changed at all, middle-class women felt children made it difficult for them to share activities with their husbands and made them more dependent on them. Working-class women, on the other hand, did not expect sharing and equality to the same extent, nor were they likely to have had it before the children were born (Young and Willmott 1962; Komarovsky 1962; Klein 1965; Lopata 1971; Rubin 1976). The changes in the marital relationship which were clear to middle-class women were therefore much less so for working-class women.

Instead, working-class women often saw children as improving their marriages by clarifying their mutual rights and obligations. Children were seen as settling husband and wife into the defined, traditional male and female roles and so as providing a structure for the relationship which allowed them to relate easily and without conflict: 'Each partner becomes a specialist in certain tasks and sees the other in specialized roles' (Rainwater and Weinstein 1974: 68). Each knew and accepted what the other expected of him or her and what he or she could legitimately expect from the other. Alice Gray, for example, felt that her children had improved her marriage by settling her in to her proper role. As long as she worked, the conflict between her roles was too great and the insecurity felt by both herself and her husband about their respective rights and obligations too strong. The children eliminated these problems:

'My husband didn't like me working. When I was engaged we used to have talks and I said I'd carry on working. We used to have arguments that he didn't want me to work. Then when we got married by the time I got home it was gone 6.00 and we used to sit down to our meals so late. And I always seemed to be worn out travelling and everything. And I wanted children and he did at the time, so we went in for Mark. I stopped work and things have been better ever since.'
(Alice Gray, working class, sons 5 and 3)

They also provided a common interest which husband and wife shared. Alice Gray continues:

'I think it's brought us together, having children. Like when they're babies, we both put them to bed together. Or even saying, "Keep quiet because of the children". You realize you've got children.'

Another woman makes this point very poignantly:

'Naturally you don't go out so much with children. But you come closer together because you go through all different upheavals

together. Illnesses and things. We worry about his school, his not reading. It brings you together.'
(Vera Watson, working class, son 6½, daughter 3½)

The Watsons' closeness had come, not from a direct interest in one another, but indirectly through their mutual concern for the children. Many working-class couples lived in such different worlds that they may have found it difficult to take an interest in each other as individuals or to express affection directly to one another (Rainwater, Coleman, and Handel 1959; Kormarovsky 1962). Children, because they provided a common interest and a centre of concern and affection, therefore became a vehicle through which the couple could express positive feeling towards one another.

Finally, children were commonly seen as improving the marriage by providing a woman with an increased sense of security since her husband's vested interest in his children involved her as their mother. This sense of security at times developed despite apparent antithetical behaviour on her husband's part:

'We're just *happier* as a family. He goes out a lot on his own, but it doesn't worry me. Because I'm not the jealous type. Because I know he always comes back. He even says himself, he might flirt in a pub or at a party, but he likes to know he has a home and security here.'
(Tracey Allen, working class, daughters 4 and 11 months)

The fact that they had children had taken the strain and anxiety out of the relationship:

'The odd thing he's said in front of other people. He said to his mate he wouldn't go off the rails because he's got too much to lose, meaning me and the children.'
(Alice Gray, working class, sons 5 and 3)

Both she and her husband had a vested interest in the children and family and this was seen as holding them together.

In summary, about half the women felt that having children had changed their relationship with their husbands. Working-class women tended to see these changes as improving their relationship by clarifying and stabilizing their roles in the family. While children had not necessarily brought husband and wife closer together in terms of intimacy or confiding, they often tended to simplify practical arrangements and to provide an important common interest. By contrast, middle-class women much more often felt that the effects of children were to create problems in their relationship with their husbands by putting restrictions on them which were not placed on their husbands and by making it more difficult to share interests and activities with their husbands. These perceptions of the influence of children on their marriage may well have affected their feelings about looking after them. On the one hand, when children were resented because of the tensions they created in a marriage, it is likely that the resentment was expressed in irritation towards the children. On the other hand, when a woman enjoyed the warmth and security of her situation within a family, this pleasure, too, was probably expressed in warmth and enjoyment of the children.

HUSBAND'S EMOTIONAL SUPPORT

The way in which the women described the changes that children brought reflects their feelings about the salient aspects of their impact on their marriages. It does not follow, however, that because they saw the changes in these terms working-class relationships were better while middle-class relationships were full of problems. Couples could adjust to the changes that children brought or they could work at their relationship to mediate their effects. A second way of describing a woman's relationship with her husband, therefore, is in terms of the understanding and support she felt he was giving her at the time of the interview. From their accounts of their husbands' current support, three types of relationships were identified: those in which the husband was *understanding*, those in which he was *sympathetic*, and those in which he was *intolerant*.[3]

Those women who described their husbands as *understanding* said that they felt their husbands understood what was involved in looking after children full-time at home and recognized the difficulties they faced. The following comments are typical:

'He always says at weekends, "I don't know how you cope during the week, they're so demanding. I can appreciate how you feel". I suppose I'm lucky, he really is understanding. . . . He says it every weekend, but he forgets it during the week. But I suppose he's just as wound up in his own work. But then when he is

relaxing, he appreciates how difficult it is. He understands why I get so tied up.'
(Anne Wootton, middle class, daughters 5½ and 2, son 3)

Karen Alexander makes the point even more clearly. She felt her husband understood and supported her because he had had some experience of children himself:

'He often says, "It's a wonder you don't get thoroughly fed up with being stuck at home with the kids all day". Because his partner's wife – they work in his house – and he sees her and the children and he says to me "It's a wonder you don't get thoroughly fed up, the way kids carry on". He doesn't like to hear kids scream and carry on when he's working but on a Sunday when he's here he doesn't seem to mind.'
(Karen Alexander, working class, daughters 3½ and 1)

Women who described a *sympathetic* husband felt that he could not entirely understand what her life was like but he did his best to do so and gave her as much sympathy and support as he could within these limitations:

'He's very easy to talk to. We discuss everything. If I'm not sure of something, if David's done something and I'm not sure how to cope, we'll discuss it. It's always good if you're not sure. If you get someone else's opinion. He's very understanding.'
(Q: 'Does he understand what it is like to be a mother with young children?')
'No. I don't think so, I don't know. They probably don't realize that it can be very busy all day. Unless you do it yourself it's hard to realize. Your time's not your own. From the minute you get up, that's it. There's so much to do. Unless you do it yourself, I didn't know myself what was involved till I did it. I don't think you do, really.'
(Nicola Savage, working class, son 4, daughter 1½)

Nicola Savage was typical of the women in this group in feeling that there was a fundamental barrier between her husband and herself which limited the understanding and support he could give. Because he had not had the experience himself he could not really understand what she had to cope with and in this sense she was left feeling somewhat alone. Jane Crawford expresses a similar feeling. She appreciated the sympathy and support her husband gave her and found it invaluable:

'I think he thinks it's difficult. I think we both have reasonable confidence in each other. I feel he's capable of doing his job and he feels I'm capable of doing mine. There are going to be days when either of us feel we're not and we'll support each other through those.'

(Jane Crawford, middle class, twin daughters 2½)

She also recognized, however, that he could not really understand what it was like to be a mother:

'No, I don't think he does understand. Because I didn't before I was at home. I don't think he could, I don't think anyone could unless another Mum. Just as I could never understand what it's like to be a doctor. He's never had to do it. Occasionally he'll have them for half a day and he'll give them biscuits and walks for a special treat. I think he does his best. He is sympathetic. If he's got something on his mind he talks about it and if I've got something on my mind, I talk about it. We support each other that way. But no, he doesn't really understand what it's like. He can't.'

Both these women accounted for their husbands' lack of full understanding in terms of the structure of family roles. Their husbands were not in the position of a mother and so by definition could not understand what it was like. Their husbands' lack of understanding was not seen as a reflection on their personal sensitivity or desire to be understanding, and so was felt to be less significant than their *attempts* to understand and their willingness to be sympathetic and supportive as far as they could be.

Finally, those women who described their husbands as *intolerant* felt they were basically unsympathetic and had a mistaken view of their lives as mothers. In general, middle-class women felt their husbands had a *distorted* view of what it is like to be a mother, while working-class women described their husbands as holding firm views about their lives that were completely *contrary* to their own experience.

Although the middle-class women felt that their husbands did not understand their position, they made the point that their husbands thought they did. In contrast to those in the *sympathetic* group, these middle-class women saw their husbands' misunderstanding as a personal fault and resented them for it:

'He says he understands . . . but I'm sure he doesn't. He thinks he does. Before I had Sarah he used to have one day home a week and he'd look after Caroline while I went out to work. But it wasn't really difficult because the dinner used to be left ready to go on and everything. So all he had to do was make the beds and look after one child for the day. I don't call that being involved in being at home. But that's what he thinks it's all about. That's what he thinks *my* time is like, because he had it easy.'

(Colleen Johnston, middle class, daughters 6 and 3)

For these middle-class women, the sympathy their husbands offered was seen as ritualistic and patronizing and of no help at all:

(Q: 'Does your husband understand what it is like for you to be at home with young children all day?')
'He *thinks* he does. He says he does, but no, no. He doesn't, really. You can't tell him what it is like. He can't see it from your point of view. He can only see it from his point of view. He sees plenty of people. *He* can't be bored. So how can you? He has obviously come to the conclusion that mothers with small children who stay at home come to a point where they are simply bored out of their wits. Where they have to do *something*, never mind what. But he doesn't really *understand* it. He underestimates it a great deal because he doesn't know how it really is, being at home looking after children. It is difficult and it is also boring at the same time.'

(Gillian Nichols, middle class, son 4, daughter 2)

Gillian Nichols had convinced her husband that mothers get bored, but she saw that he had no sense of what this meant: he saw her life only from his own perspective. His gesture at offering sympathy and support was seen as no more than an empty ritual, resented all the more because he did not accept that he did not understand.

While these middle-class couples often maintained a pretence of sympathy, the working-class women in this group gave a more clear-cut picture of their husbands' lack of support and understanding. Most working-class women said that their husbands simply thought that looking after young children was easy, routine work with no difficulties, and were very impatient and unsympathetic with their problems:

'He thinks it's easy. He says it's boring. When he's home he says "Oh, is that all you do all day". He sees what it's like from his day off. He doesn't like it very much. He realizes it's not all roses,

but . . . If he came home and saw you sitting there he'd think "Oh, isn't this nice, being at home all day".'
(Tracey Allen, working class, daughters 4 and 11 months)

For two women this belief that child care was easy gave rise to what the women felt were unreasonable demands and expectations in their work as mothers. Sandra Keating, for example, says:

'He gets a little "Why haven't you done so and so? That was there yesterday. Why haven't you moved it?" He might pick things up like that. It's unreasonable. Sometimes I feel a bit hurt when he says "you haven't done so and so". But sometimes I haven't got round to it. He doesn't appreciate what's involved. He thinks it's all play – nothing to it.'
(Sandra Keating, working class, daughters 7 and 4)

Several other women added that their husbands believed that looking after children was inevitably and intrinsically enjoyable for women and were unsympathetic to their problems for this reason:

'No. It's the same old thing: "You wanted the children, you've got to put up with it. You should enjoy it". I don't think he realizes, I think he's just beginning to realize what it is to be stuck at home in the evening when you've only had the children all day. You haven't had an intelligent conversation all day. He's just beginning to realize now. He thinks, because you wanted the children, that's it. You're taken care of. You're happy all the time. Or you *should* be.'
(Janet Hobson, working class, daughter 5, son 2)

Table 10(2) *Husband's support and social class*

| Social class | Husband's support | | | |
	under-standing no. (%)	sympathetic no. (%)	intolerant no. (%)	total no. (%)
working class	8 (32)	7 (28)	10 (40)	25 (100)
middle class	12 (48)	8 (32)	5 (20)	25 (100)
total	20 (40)	15 (30)	15 (30)	50 (100)

$x^2 = 2.52 \ p > 0.05$

Table 10(2) gives the distribution of the women into the three categories. Getting on for half the husbands were considered *understanding*, about a third *sympathetic*, and a further third *intolerant*. Once again, however, there are interesting class differences: half of the middle-class husbands were *understanding* but only a third of the working-class husbands were; four in ten of the working-class husbands were considered *intolerant* but only half this proportion of the middle-class husbands. These findings are consistent with the traditional picture of working-class marriages as characterized by less communication, confiding, and support (Young and Willmott 1962; Rainwater, Coleman, and Handel 1959; Rainwater and Weinstein 1974; Komarovsky 1962; Klein 1965; Rubin 1976).

When *change in the marital relationship* with the arrival of children and current *support from husband* are considered together a picture emerges which clarifies the impact that children had had in the long term. *Table 10(3)* shows that the conflicts and resentments which some middle-class women felt may have disrupted their relationship but, on the whole, did not destroy the basic communication and mutual involvement of the marriages. A sense of sharing and understanding was expected as a fundamental characteristic of the marital relationship and it was worked at regardless of the children and the problems they created. While the children made this more difficult, half of the middle-class women were able to maintain an *understanding* relationship with their husbands and a further third a *sympathetic* one; each group included as many as a third of those who felt children created problems in their relationship.

Table 10(3) *For middle-class women, perceived change in marital relationship and husband's support*

| Husband's support | Perceived change in marital relationship | | | |
	improved no. (%)	no change no. (%)	created problems no. (%)	total no. (%)
understanding	4 (100)	5 (45)	3 (30)	12 (48)
sympathetic	0	5 (45)	3 (30)	8 (32)
intolerant	0	1 (9)	4 (40)	5 (20)
total	4 (100)	11 (99)	10 (100)	25 (100)

Among working-class women, on the other hand, the picture is quite different *(see Table 10(4))*. The stabilization of gender-specific roles that children precipitated restricted the men's understanding of the women's lives as mothers and limited the sympathy and understanding they could give. The improvement in the relationship which children brought was not primarily in terms of psychological or emotional closeness and support but in terms of the clarification of gender roles, which themselves separated and isolated husband and wife. For half of the working-class women who felt the children *improved* their relationship, their husbands were seen as well-meaning and *sympathetic* but nonetheless cut off from their lives. For a further two of the twelve, children had given rise to such stark role divisions that their husbands had totally unfounded views of the women's lives and were *intolerant* of their problems. For only a third of the working-class women who reported an *improved* relationship, then, had their common interest in the children provided grounds for a supportive *understanding* relationship.

Table 10(4) *For working-class women, perceived change in marital relationship and husband's support*

| Husband's support | Perceived change in marital relationship | | | |
	improved no. (%)	no change no. (%)	created problems no. (%)	total no. (%)
understanding	4 (33)	4 (33)	0	8 (32)
sympathetic	6 (50)	1 (8)	0	7 (28)
intolerant	2 (17)	7 (58)	1 (100)	10 (40)
total	12 (100)	12 (99)	1 (100)	25 (100)

The marital relationship and women's experience as mothers

Given the discussion so far, it is not surprising to find that the nature of a woman's experience as a mother is associated with the nature of her relationship with her husband. For the sample as a whole, the associations between the measure of her husband's emotional support and the two measures of a woman's experience of motherhood are quite strong *(see Tables 10(5) and 10(6))*. The associations are much the same when the working-class and middle-class women are distinguished: the only substantial difference is the particularly strong association for working-class women between their immediate response to child care and their husband's emotional support (gamma = 0.90).[4] Since the associations present such a similar picture for the two class groups, in what follows the two will be discussed together.

Table 10(5) *Husband's support and woman's immediate response to child care*

| Immediate response to child care | Husband's support | | | |
	under-standing no. (%)	sympathetic no. (%)	intolerant no. (%)	total no. (%)
enjoyed	15 (75)	6 (40)	3 (20)	24 (48)
irritated	5 (25)	9 (60)	12 (80)	26 (52)
total	20 (100)	15 (100)	15 (100)	50 (100)

$\gamma = 0.69$

Table 10(6) *Husband's support and woman's sense of meaning and purpose as a mother*

| Sense of meaning and purpose | Husband's support | | | |
	under-standing no. (%)	sympathetic no. (%)	intolerant no. (%)	total no. (%)
strong	17 (85)	10 (67)	2 (13)	29 (58)
weak	3 (15)	5 (33)	13 (87)	21 (42)
total	20 (100)	15 (100)	15 (100)	50 (100)

$\gamma = 0.81$

IMMEDIATE RESPONSE TO LOOKING AFTER CHILDREN

A supportive husband enhanced a woman's enjoyment of looking after her children through both his respect and appreciation for her efforts as a mother, and his recognition and acceptance of her inevitable feelings of frustration and irritation in child care. Since most women felt their children were too young to acknowledge the care they received, this appreciation from her husband was particularly important. His respect for her work gave some reward to child care and his regard for her as a mother confirmed her sense of accomplishment in it. Without such appreciation, child care may have seemed an empty, thankless task, and a woman may have felt exploited and taken for granted as a mother. A man who saw child care as an easy or 'cushy' job, for example, trivialized his wife's work and undermined her sense of self-esteem. His attitude denied her any sense of accomplishment and could lead to a sense of incompetence and failure when she was faced with difficulty from her 'undemanding' work. It also sharpened the contrast between the two of them, setting up her husband as superior in his demanding and paid employment and casting her as inferior in her easy and insubstantial domesticity.

In so far as his support involved recognizing the difficulties inherent in child care and accepting that frustration and irritation were appropriate responses to it, an understanding or sympathetic husband also helped a woman to see her frustration and irritation in child care as legitimate responses and so helped her to cope with them. His acceptance of and sympathy for these negative feelings helped her to accept that they were not unreasonable and did not reflect badly on her. When they were legitimated in this way, a certain amount of highly focused frustration and irritation could be disregarded as unimportant and kept from threatening her overall enjoyment of her children and child care. Pervasive feelings of monopolization and loss of individuality in motherhood could not be so easily dismissed, but they could at least be contained and prevented from engulfing the whole of a woman's experience. That is, feelings of monopolization and loss of individuality in motherhood could have bred such resentment of the children as would have destroyed her commitment to them and stripped motherhood of its sense of meaning and purpose. A husband who understood and sympathized with these feelings, however, helped a woman to express them and thereby to accept them for what they were. This, in turn, helped her to deal with her sense of monopolization and loss of individuality and prevented them from dominating the whole of her experience.

By contrast, an intolerant man's belief that, for women, child care is naturally enjoyable made any dissatisfaction on his wife's part particularly difficult to deal with. It implied that these feelings were the fault of her children or were due to her own inadequacies and failure as a mother. Rather than facing and coming to terms with her negative feelings, she was therefore more likely to feel guilty about them and to try and repress them. Such a way of dealing with them may simply have heightened her sense of frustration and irritation, increased her resentment of her children, and pushed these feelings to the centre of her experience.

SENSE OF MEANING AND PURPOSE IN MOTHERHOOD

The association between women's sense of meaning and purpose in motherhood and their husbands' emotional support is particularly interesting. Berger and Kellner have argued that marriage 'occupies a privileged status among the significant validating relationships for adults in our society' (Berger and Kellner 1970: 53). Marriage provides its partners with a sense of identity, 'stabilizing' or 'objectifying', through the relationship, their sense of themselves. This is a social process, achieved particularly by means of talk. In important ways, the meaning of parenthood in marriage has to be created and sustained through objectification.

The husbands in this study appeared to be major sources, for the women, of their view of themselves as mothers, and were important in the process of defining the goals and purposes they, as couples, shared in their children. By virtue of being less immediately and constantly involved in the tasks of child care, the men were less likely than the women to be swamped by the demands involved. Paradoxically, they could therefore often offer a more reflective perspective in conversations with their wives in the course of which wider goals and hopes might be brought to the fore. The discussions between *some* husbands and their wives helped to create and sustain women's sense of meaning and purpose in motherhood. As Berger and Kellner say, 'no experience is fully real unless and until it has been thus "talked through" ' (Berger and Kellner 1970: 61). Where women felt no sense of support from their husbands and where the couples did not jointly construct such views with regard to their children, the women were more vulnerable to being overwhelmed by the reality itself of unremitting child care tasks and to losing any sense of meaning therein. The view of the self as socially constructed seems consistent with and appropriate to the analysis of motherhood offered here in which meaning and purpose in motherhood are seen as precarious and sustained by social interaction.

Notes

1. The changes which are described here are largely the women's perceptions of the way their husbands had changed in relation to themselves. Several other studies (Breen 1975; Rubin 1976; Graham and McKee 1980; Oakley 1980), however, describe how *women* withdraw from their husbands when their children are born. For some

women, the intensity of their feelings for their children and the children's responsiveness to them may have a tremendous impact on them to the point where they become totally absorbed in their children to the exclusion of their husbands. Therefore, although they did not describe them directly, the women's own reactions to their husbands may be an important aspect of the change that children precipitate.

2. The way the women perceived their relationship to have been changed by their children was assessed on the basis of their answers to two questions: 'Many couples find that, when they have children, they have a feeling of "growing apart" from each other because the husband and wife live in separate worlds. Others find that having children brings them "closer together" because they share a common interest and concern. Have you found either of these situations in your own marriage?' and 'How do you think your relationship with your husband has changed since your children were born?'

3. The support the women felt they received from their husbands was assessed on the basis of their answers to two sets of questions: 'Is your husband sympathetic to you and your problems? Is he supportive? Do you discuss problems and difficulties with him? Is this helpful for you?' and later 'Does your husband understand what it is like to be a mother, looking after young children? What does he think of it?'

4. This may be due to the strong relationship for working-class women between *husband's support* and *husband's help*.

PART FOUR
A BROADER PERSPECTIVE

· 11 ·
SATISFACTION
WITH THEIR
LIVES AS MOTHERS

In the previous eight chapters I have described, and tried to account for, the enjoyment and sense of meaning and purpose which the fifty women in the study experienced in looking after their children. These were the main themes in their accounts of their experience and it was the nature of their experience of motherhood which was the main focus of the research. At the end of her interview, however, each woman was asked about the slightly different question of her satisfaction with her life as a mother.[1] The answers the women gave to these questions are of interest as an indication of the way they evaluated their lives as mothers in the context of the alternatives they felt were available to them.

Satisfaction with their lives as mothers

As I argued in Chapter 1, a woman's satisfaction with her life as a mother was not a response to motherhood but an indicator of her evaluation of it. This was apparent in the way the women spoke of themselves as satisfied or dissatisfied: whatever the degree of their satisfaction, it was clear that it was the result of a considered decision. Questions about their satisfaction were answered with little hesitation and well-rehearsed arguments were given to support the position they took. These arguments indicated that, in deciding on their degree of satisfaction, the women considered the variety of rewards and frustrations they anticipated in alternative ways of life. When they felt that the balance of rewards in their current situation was greater than it would be in other situations, they were satisfied with their lives as mothers. This did not mean that they necessarily found a particularly high level of reward in their lives as mothers, but simply that they saw the alternative ways of life as offering lower rewards. By the same token, they were dissatisfied when they felt that the balance of rewards they found in full-time motherhood was less than it would be in a different situation. Again, this did not mean that they necessarily found a low level of reward in their lives, so much as that they felt that the reward would be greater if their lives followed a different pattern.

Table 11(1) *Self-reported satisfaction with life as a mother and social class*

| Self-reported satisfaction | Social class | | |
	working class no. (%)	middle class no. (%)	total no. (%)
content	14 (56)	12 (48)	26 (52)
accepting	9 (36)	5 (20)	14 (28)
discontented	2 (8)	8 (32)	10 (20)
total	25 (100)	25 (100)	50 (100)

$x^2 = 4.88 \ p > 0.05$

As a result of their assessments, the women in the study took one of three positions *vis-à-vis* their lives as mothers: half were wholly *content* with their lives as they were, a fifth were wholly *discontented*, and a quarter were in between, *accepting* their current situation as the 'best' while acknowledging substantial dissatisfaction (*see Table 11(1)*). The women who were *content* with their lives as mothers felt that their current situation was preferable to any other. Bridget Mackie and Anne Fitzgerald saw their lives in this way:

(Q: 'Would you say you were satisfied or dissatisfied or neither in particular with your life as a mother?')
'I'm quite satisfied. I have odd days, but on the whole I'm satisfied. Because I don't think I'd like to do anything else. I am happy. There's nothing else I'd like to be doing at the moment.'
(Q: 'Is there anything you would like to be doing in addition to what you do as a mother?')
'No. I'm not really that sort of person. I have an active enough social life to satisfy my needs. I'm quite a home body really.'
(Q: 'Comparing the years you were nursing with your life now, would you say you were happier then or are you happier now?')

'It's difficult really. I enjoyed working. I enjoyed nursing when I did it then, and I enjoy my life now. It's hard to compare. It's different things. It's two separate lives, really.'
(Q: 'If you had the last ten years over again, what would you do differently?')
'Nothing really. I can't think of anything I'd like to rectify. I think I would have worked harder at school. I think I would like to have gone to university. That's why I encourage mine. My parents never encouraged me to work.'
(Bridget Mackie, middle class, daughters 7 and 2, son 6)

(Q: 'Would you say you were satisfied, dissatisfied, or neither in particular with your life as a mother?')
'Satisfied, yes, very satisfied. I'm quite happy with my lot.'
(Q: 'Is there anything you would like to be doing in addition to what you do as a mother?')
'I *do* quite a lot of things in addition to looking after the children. I do some piano teaching. I teach children in the choir at Church. I belong to the choir. I do a bit of maths coaching for friends' children – anything that comes along. I like to think that I'm not too tied down; that's why being a mother suits me. Having a few things but so I can have the unexpected that comes along. The *variety* I can have as a mother. The week is never the same.'
(Q: 'Comparing the time you taught with your life now, would you say you were happier then or are you happier now?')
'I think I enjoy married life more than single life. But I certainly enjoyed teaching before I got married. I seem to enjoy whatever I'm doing. I'm basically happier now I'm married because I'm not on my own. Once you're married with children, you set down roots.'
(Q: 'If you had the last ten years over again, what would you do differently?')
'I'd still work in the same place, still marry the same man, still live in the same place. Very little. Nothing important.'
(Anne Fitzgerald, middle class, sons 4 and 2)

Both these women found sufficient rewards in their lives and felt no major deprivations. In Bridget Mackie's case, this was because she had no significant interests outside her family and in Anne Fitzgerald's case because she could fulfil her interests within the context of her life as a mother.

Similarly, the women who were *accepting* of their lives as mothers felt that the balance of rewards over frustrations in their current situation was greater than it would be in other situations. They did not necessarily find a particularly high level of reward, however, and many commented on the frustrations they also felt as full-time mothers:

(Q: 'Would you say you were satisfied, dissatisfied, or neither in particular with your life as a mother?')
'I'm satisfied but I think you're never really satisfied. You always want more. I'd like a house. You're never really that satisfied. You get bored with things, fed up with it. But I think there'd be no point in living if you weren't.'
(Q: 'Is there anything you would rather be doing instead of being a mother?')
'No. Not really. I'm not longing to go back to work. . . . Some days I'm like everyone else. I get really bored. But there's no use getting depressed about it. You just got to get on with it.'
(Q: 'Is there anything you would like to be doing in addition to being a mother?')
'Yeah. I'd like to do just a little job, something different. Just a few hours. We've been looking for something to do outside the home. We tried typing envelopes but that didn't work out, so we're just looking and looking, every week. We don't really know what we're looking for. I wouldn't really want something where I had to say to her, "No, I'm sorry, go away. I'm too busy now".'
(Q: 'If you had the past ten years to do over again, what would you do differently?')
'I think I still would have married young, even if not to Doug. And I might have had more children. But when I look back, I'm pleased I've got two kiddies now. And I'd like another one.'
    (Tracey Allen, working class, daughters 4 and 11 months)

(Q: 'Would you say you were satisfied or dissatisfied or neither in particular with your life as a mother?')
'I think generally satisfied, because I am doing some things out-side the home and therefore I'm not too frustrated. Because I think I could do more than just be a mother and housewife. And I like to feel that eventually I will do something more outside the home.'
(Q: 'Is there anything you would rather be doing, apart from being a mother?')
'No. I don't think so. Because having had children I feel responsible for them and must carry the thing through, and I want to. But I feel as though I'd like to be using my brain more

than one does in just running the house. And I think maybe later I hope to do more.'
(Susan Griffiths, middle class, sons 6½ and 1½, daughter 4½)

Their attitude was one of acceptance of their situation as mothers and willingness to deal with their dissatisfaction by working within the basic framework of the mother role. They did not want to *change* their situation but to *add* something to it.

The women in both the *content* and *accepting* groups, then, assessed themselves as satisfied with their lives as mothers. The women in the *discontented* group, on the other hand, were explicitly dissatisfied with their lives and wanted fundamental changes in them:

(*Q: 'Are you satisfied or dissatisfied or neither in particular with your life as a mother?'*)
'I'm dissatisfied. I feel frustrated at having to stay at home with the children. I hope I don't show it to them. I think I might do occasionally. My nervous thing shows – I sometimes feel things are on top of me. I do feel dissatisfied because I've always been with other people – in the pub, in the telephone exchange. And I do tend to get depressed if I'm on my own for too long. I'm not a homely body. I'm just one of those people who *can't*!!'
(*Q: 'Is there anything you would rather be doing now?'*)
'Oh yes! I can't wait for my freedom to come round again. I don't know what I'll do. I'll have to be talking to and meeting people. . . . I think, really, looking back – if I had known what I know now I don't think I'd have had children. I'd have quite happily stayed at work. I loved working.'
(*Q: 'If you had the past ten years over again, what would you do differently?'*)
'I wouldn't have got married and had children.'
(Angela Bourne, middle class, son 3½, daughter 1½)

Most of the other women in the group were not so vehement in their wish to reject motherhood completely. Since the decision to have children is irrevocable and there is no chance of undoing maternity, regret and rejection of motherhood are pointless. The women themselves acknowledged these constraints but indicated that if they had the choice again they might not choose to have children:

'I wouldn't change anything now, but if I had my time again, I probably wouldn't have got married and had children. I probably

would still be single now, and perhaps got married at 30, 35. If I had got married over 30, I wouldn't have had children, because I don't believe in old parents.'
(Sarah Hepburn, middle class, daughter 6, son 2)

'Knowing what I know now, having two children and what it involves, whether or not I would have preferred *not* to have any children, I don't really know. That's not saying I don't *love* my children. I'm saying I wouldn't like my life to be exactly as it is, if I'd known ten years ago what I know now.'
(Colleen Johnston, middle class, daughters 6 and 3)

In more realistic terms, the *discontented* women accepted their children and their responsibilities towards them but nonetheless wanted fundamental changes in their situation:

(*Q:* '*Is there anything you would rather be doing?*')
'Yes, oh yes! I'd like to be doing a course leading to something. Doing something that's going to give me some material satisfaction. Not *material* – something where I can see something at the end of it. I know I can see them grow up and the rest but I wish I were doing something that was going to lead to something. I'm fed up with doing things that just have to be done. And done again and again. . . . Ideally, I would like to have someone come in and look after Peter and I will go out to work. That would be *super*. Up until the last six months I haven't wanted to. I thought, "I wanted the children so I'll have to stay at home and look after them". And I quite enjoyed it. I haven't yearned to go back to work until now. But at the moment he's getting older and I'm getting more and more annoyed with being here when I could be earning such a fortune and mixing with lots of people and how lovely it would be. I've got to the point where I'm really fed up!'
(Victoria Milton, middle class, daughter 3½, son 1½)

Like the other women in the *discontented* group, Victoria Milton felt that her life would be more rewarding if it followed a different pattern, and she wanted to change her situation accordingly.

In assessing their satisfaction, the women's primary consideration appeared to be the nature of their experience as mothers. *Table 11(2)* shows a strong relationship between their reported satisfaction with their lives as mothers and the ratings of their response to motherhood made by the interviewer. The association is strong for the working-class women (see *Table 11(3)*) and even stronger for the middle-class women (see *Table 11(4)*). There is, however, an interesting discrepancy for a number of women between their response to maternity as I rated it and their satisfaction with it as they reported it themselves. Almost half of the working-class women reported themselves as *more* satisfied with their situation as mothers than would have been predicted from the ratings of their response to motherhood (*see Table 11(3)*). This was most apparent among those rated as *alienated*: only one of the nine *alienated* working-class women reported that she was *discontented* with her life as a mother, while six *accepted* it and two even saw themselves as *content*. The middle-class women who were rated as *alienated*, on the other hand, reported a level of satisfaction more in keeping with my assessment of their experience: six of the seven *alienated* middle-class women reported that they were *discontented*. This tendency for working-class women to report themselves as satisfied while other measures of their experience indicate significant negative feelings has been noted before. Haavio-Mannila, for example, found that 'home-staying wives in the lower strata' reported high 'overall life satisfaction' but also the highest number of anxiety symptoms of any group in her sample of Finnish men and women. She speculated on a false consciousness among women and concluded that 'the stress inherent in women's underdog position gets its expression in anxiety not in open dissatisfaction with work, family, leisure and life' (Haavio-Mannila 1971: 597). For the working-class women in this study, the stress inherent in their situation as mothers seems to have been expressed in frustration and irritation towards children and child care rather than in open dissatisfaction with motherhood.

Table 11(2) *Experience of motherhood (interviewer-rated) and self-reported satisfaction with life as a mother*

Self-reported satisfaction	Experience of motherhood			
	fulfilled no. (%)	satisfied and in conflict no. (%)	alienated no. (%)	total no. (%)
content	18 (95)	6 (40)	2 (13)	26 (52)
accepting	1 (5)	6 (40)	7 (44)	14 (28)
discontented	0	3 (20)	7 (44)	10 (20)
total	19 (100)	15 (100)	16 (101)	50 (100)

$\gamma = 0.84$

Table 11(3) *For working-class women, experience of motherhood (interviewer-rated) and self-reported satisfaction with life as a mother*

| Self-reported satisfaction | Experience of motherhood | | | |
	fulfilled no. (%)	satisfied and in conflict no. (%)	alienated no. (%)	total no. (%)
content	9 (90)	3 (50)	2 (22)	14 (56)
accepting	1 (10)	2 (33)	6 (67)	9 (36)
discontented	0	1 (17)	1 (11)	2 (8)
total	10 (100)	6 (100)	9 (100)	25 (100)

$\gamma = 0.74$

Table 11(4) *For middle-class women, experience of motherhood (interviewer-rated) and self-reported satisfaction with life as a mother*

| Self-reported satisfaction | Experience of motherhood | | | |
	fulfilled no. (%)	satisfied and in conflict no. (%)	alienated no. (%)	total no. (%)
content	9 (100)	3 (33)	0	12 (48)
accepting	0	4 (44)	1 (14)	5 (20)
discontent	0	2 (22)	6 (86)	8 (32)
total	9 (100)	9 (100)	7 (100)	25 (100)

$\gamma = 0.98$

The difference between working-class and middle-class women in the match between interviewer-rated and self-reported satisfaction with maternity suggests that the women in the two classes may have dealt with their experience as mothers in different ways. Working-class women who were not *fulfilled* still tended to report themselves as satisfied with maternity and simply wanted something in addition to fill it out: they accepted maternity as appropriate or even necessary and did not want to change it. They did not blame maternity or try to use it to explain their dissatisfaction. Middle-class women, on the other hand, did tend to blame maternity for their sense of frustration and dissatisfaction. In this sense only, they were more dissatisfied with motherhood and felt a more pervasive resentment of their situation.

Education and employment experience

The most important differences between the working-class and middle-class groups which could account for the working-class women's more conservative appraisal of their situation were their different school and employment experiences before having children (see Tables 11(5) and 11(6)).[2] Virtually all the middle-class women stayed longer at school and on the whole held jobs of greater skill, responsibility, and prestige. The differences in experience implied by the crude classification of the jobs were confirmed in the women's descriptions of their work: working-class women generally described the work they had done as routine and boring while middle-class women generally described it as challenging and rewarding.

Table 11(5) *Education and social class*

| Education | Social class | | |
	working class no. (%)	middle class no. (%)	total no. (%)
no qualifications (left at school-leaving age)	24 (96)	2 (8)	26 (52)
1 O-level to 5 A-levels (or equivalents)*	1 (4)	13 (52)	14 (28)
degree level (BA, SRN, etc)	0	10 (40)	10 (20)
total	25 (100)	25 (100)	50 (100)

$x^2 = 38.88$ p<0.001

*includes three Pitman diplomas in secretarial studies

Table 11(6) *Occupation before having children and social class*

| Previous occupation | Social class | | |
	working class no. (%)	middle class no. (%)	total no. (%)
manual	8 (32)	0	0 (16)
routine non-manual	17 (68)	3 (12)	20 (40)
higher secretarial	0	8 (32)	8 (16)
professional and managerial	0	14 (56)	14 (28)
total	25 (100)	25 (100)	50 (100)

$x^2 = 39.80$ p<0.001

Table 11(6) gives a fourfold classification of occupations. The women in the *manual* group included four factory workers, a hairdresser, a nurse's aid, a cook, and a dressmaker. Tammy Parsons describes the typical work experience of the women in this group. She liked her work but saw it as essentially the means to the end she was enjoying now:

> 'I worked in a chocolate factory in Southend while my husband and I courted. We courted for three years. He lived in London and worked and I lived in Southend and worked. He visited for the weekend every other weekend. We both worked very hard; we both worked overtime and saved for a deposit on a flat in Croydon. I liked the work. We used to do all sorts of novelty things for children. It was hard work, thinking we didn't have much time together, but it was worth it. Now when we look back, we've got all this and a lot of people haven't got anything.'

The *routine non-manual* group comprised nine clerks, five telephonists, four typists, and two shop assistants. Helen Mowbray is typical:

> 'I did clerical work, typing. I've always done clerical work, nothing else. First in a warehouse; I started typing envelopes. Then I worked in an office up in London for a year. Then I got fed up with the journey. I got a local job then doing the ledgers. I was there till I was nineteen and then I got married and left because I wasn't earning a lot.'

So is Jean Elliott:

> 'I was a telephonist. I left the GPO when I was engaged. I had quite a few jobs. I was never one to stay in a job long. I'd get fed up so I'd move on to something new. I didn't really like working.'

The *higher secretarial* group was composed of four high-level secretaries, two personal assistants, a school laboratory technician, and a research assistant for a market research team (the latter two being included in this group on the grounds that it is the most appropriate in terms of level of skill, responsibility, and prestige). All of the women in this group had at least five O-levels or a Pitman diploma in secretarial studies in contrast to the women in the previous group who had no educational qualifications at all. The nature of their work was correspondingly more challenging and their experience of it more rewarding. Colleen Johnston is an example:

'When I first left school, I worked for an insurance firm as a shorthand typist. Then I got a job as a secretary to a factory manager. It certainly gave me a lot of experience. I stayed there two years and then decided to come to London. I went to work for a large charity then, and I stayed there till I left to have Caroline. My job was extremely interesting. I was meeting a lot of people. Not that you have a sense of *power*, but you had a sense of organizing other people. Influence. What you said went. You had a sense of achievement from a job well done. You take pride in what you're doing. It was out of the ordinary, out of the mundane.'

The *professional and managerial* group included seven teachers or lecturers, three SRNs, three civil servants of Executive Officer grade or above, and one freelance translator. Like the women in the higher secretarial group, they were very involved in their work and emphasized its rewarding nature. Ruth Venables is typical:

'I was a nurse, doing my training mostly before I had children. I love nursing. I love the district nursing that I do now. I did get quite a terrific satisfaction from nursing because I thought I was doing a worthwhile job. I enjoyed it. There are parts I enjoyed – I wouldn't say I enjoyed it all. I enjoyed it when patients were fit and well and shook your hand at the door. I had a tremendous sense of satisfaction when I nursed in a hospital, and I do have a terrific sense of satisfaction now.'

Jane Crawford describes a similar experience as a teacher:

(Q: 'Did you enjoy teaching?')
'Yes I did. Very much. I taught in a pretty ropy area of East London which is very eye-opening because I'd had a fairly sheltered life till then. It was very demanding and I got very involved with some of the children who had unfortunate backgrounds. I wanted to help them, though there wasn't much I could do. It was very rewarding. I'd rather do something like teach than work in an office. I felt I was doing something where I did get a response from the children. It was very satisfying.'

From this fourfold classification of occupations prior to having children two main groups of women can be distinguished: one group, the routine non-manual plus the manual workers, had jobs of relatively less skill, responsibility, and prestige; the other group, combining the professional and managerial and the higher secretarial occupations, had jobs of relatively high skill, responsibility, and prestige.[3] There was a slight tendency for women in the first group to report themselves more satisfied with maternity than those in the second group. When those women who were rated as *fulfilled* are excluded and only women for whom maternity was problematic (i.e. women rated *satisfied, in conflict,* or *alienated*) are considered, this trend is much clearer (*see Table 11(7)*). Among women who were frustrated and irritated or who lacked a strong sense of meaning as mothers, those who had routine non-manual occupations before having children tended to assess themselves as *content* with or *accepting* their situation as mothers despite the frustrations experienced. In contrast, women from professional and higher secretarial occupations were three times more likely to assess themselves as *discontented* with their situation when they experienced comparable frustrations. This difference is even clearer when only women rated *alienated* are considered (*see Table 11(8)*).

Table 11(7) *For women less than* fulfilled *as mothers (i.e.* satisfied, in conflict, *or* alienated*), occupation before having children and self-reported satisfaction with life as a mother*

	Previous occupation		
Self-reported satisfaction	*manual and routine non-manual no. (%)*	*professional and higher secretarial no. (%)*	*total no. (%)*
content	6 (33)	2 (15)	8 (26)
accepting	9 (50)	4 (31)	13 (42)
discontented	3 (17)	7 (54)	10 (32)
total	18 (100)	13 (100)	31 (100)

$\gamma = 0.56$

Table 11(8) *For* alienated *women, occupation before having children and self-reported satisfaction with life as a mother*

	Previous occupation		
Self-reported satisfaction	*manual and routine non-manual no. (%)*	*professional and higher secretarial no. (%)*	*total no. (%)*
content	2 (18)	0	2 (12)
accepting	7 (64)	0	7 (44)
discontented	2 (18)	5 (100)	7 (44)
total	11 (100)	5 (100)	16 (100)

$\gamma = 1.00$

These interesting differences between women from contrasting occupational backgrounds are similar to those reported by others concerned with the narrower issues of 'work commitment' among women (Sobol 1963, 1974). Haller and Rosenmayr found that, while blue-collar women worked after they had children for financial reasons, among middle-class women there occurred a 'change of the "traditional dream" attitude through motherhood experience, so that middle-class mothers show higher work commitment after having children' (Haller and Rosenmayr 1971: 516). Taking the increased desire to work (work commitment) as roughly equivalent to a desire to change their way of life as a mother (self-report of *discontent*), Haller's and Rosenmayr's findings support the suggestion made here that women with previous experience of skilled, responsible, and prestigious occupations are much more critical of their situation as mothers than women from less skilled, responsible, or prestigious occupations. Safilios-Rothschild (1971, 1973) reported evidence supporting the converse of this suggestion: that women who have had experience of dull, unskilled, and uncreative work are likely to assess themselves as content with maternity whatever their experience of it in more 'objective' terms. She reported an evaluation study of child-care allowances in Hungary which found that the lower the education of the working mother and the less meaningful the type of job she had, the greater the probability she would opt for a child-care allowance and full-time motherhood. Safilios-Rothschild concludes that 'these women are eager to give up their little meaningful work activity for something they hope might prove to be more rewarding and relevant in their lives: motherhood' (Safilios-Rothschild 1971: 490).

At this point it is important to point out that the women's experience of working prior to having children did not make maternity itself more or less rewarding for them. There was little relationship between work experience prior to having children and overall response to motherhood as assessed by the interviewer. The rewards and frustrations the women experienced as mothers were in response to their situation itself: their previous experience of working was important only in the way they *appraised* the rewards they found in motherhood.

There are a number of ways in which her education and previous work experience appeared to influence a woman's assessment of her life as a mother. First, they to a large extent shaped her expectations of the rewards she would get in her daily life. Women whose early work experience was more rewarding – the middle-class women in professional and managerial and in higher secretarial occupations – tended to develop expectations of greater rewards in their daily lives. Women whose early work experience was less rewarding – the predominantly working-class women in the routine non-manual and manual jobs – tended to develop lower expectations.[4] These differing expectations became, in effect, different standards for evaluating their lives as mothers. It is not surprising, then, that the working-class women were more satisfied than the middle-class women with a less than highly rewarding experience.

Second, her education and previous work experience set the limits on the alternatives to full-time motherhood available to a woman. Thus, those with better education and with training for more rewarding occupations saw the alternatives to their current situation as relatively more attractive. On this basis, they were more critical and assessed themselves as dissatisfied when they were less than *fulfilled* as mothers. In contrast, those without educational qualifications and with little hope of an intrinsically rewarding job saw their alternatives as relatively less attractive. On this basis, they were less critical and assessed themselves as satisfied as mothers despite the frustrations they experienced.

Finally, a woman's situation before having children influenced the opportunities she had to define specific interests or activities outside the family. Once again, women with better education and more skilled and responsible jobs were likely to have been in a better position to develop such interests and activities. While their loss with motherhood might have been felt as an acute deprivation, the reasons for the loss might also have been easily identified. These women, therefore, may have had a clearer idea of why they were frustrated and what sorts of changes might reduce their frustration. Because of this, they may have been more confident in critically evaluating their situation as mothers and more ready to want to change it. Women without educational qualifications and from less skilled and responsible jobs, on the other hand, were less likely to have had the opportunity to define interests or activities which were particularly rewarding for them. They had no known alternative to maternity and the unknown alternatives – simply because they were unknown – may have seemed less attractive and more threatening than their current situation. In these circumstances, they were likely to assess themselves as satisfied as mothers.

Summary

This chapter has looked at the women's own assessment of their satisfaction with their lives as mothers and has found that a number of them assessed themselves as more satisfied than would have been predicted from my ratings of their response to motherhood. Over three-quarters of the women reported that they were satisfied with their lives as mothers – that is, *content* or *accepting* – while only a third were rated as *fulfilled* and a further quarter as *satisfied* or *in conflict*. Since many studies which look at satisfaction with motherhood are of the type which call for a self-report of satisfaction, this finding is particularly important. It suggests that the results of these studies may be a product of the questions used: by looking only at their evaluation of their situation, such studies may fail to pick up a great deal of frustration and irritation which are nonetheless present and important aspects of the women's experience. Surveys which report high levels of satisfaction with motherhood should not be interpreted as indicating particularly high levels of rewarding experience in motherhood: their satisfaction may well reflect only the less attractive alternatives they face rather than any more rewarding experience as such. Studies based on self-reported satisfaction must therefore be interpreted with caution, recognizing what a complex construct satisfaction is.

The findings concerning reported satisfaction also highlight the importance of looking at women's experience as mothers within a broad social context. It was largely in relation to the kinds of employment they had had or felt they could get that the women evaluated their lives as mothers and their satisfaction is also a comment on the sorts of jobs available to women. So long as women are relegated to routine and repetitive jobs and a second-class status in the economic sphere it is not surprising that many will 'choose' to withdraw into or remain in the domestic sphere. Their appraisals of the relative rewards from their roles as mothers and from the jobs they would be likely to get on the whole seemed quite realistic. Until there are substantial improvements in the alternatives available to them, many women are likely to remain 'satisfied' as mothers despite the serious frustrations they feel in looking after their children.

Notes

1. Five satisfaction questions were asked during the interview:
   (i) Would you say you were generally satisfied or generally dissatisfied or neither in particular with your life as a mother?
   (ii) Is there anything you would *rather* be doing now?
   (iii) Is there anything you would like to be doing *in addition* to what you are doing now as a wife and a mother?
   (iv) Comparing the time you ——————— (occupation) with your life now as a mother, would you say you were happier then or happier now or neither in particular?
   (v) If you had the last ten years over again, what would you do differently?
2. Beliefs about the long-term rewards of motherhood were also important (Boulton 1982).
3. Recently, Murgatroyd (1982) has suggested a reclassification and regrouping of women's servicing occupations along similar lines.
4. Blauner makes a similar point with regard to industrial workers, though he puts it in terms of *needs* rather than *expectations*.
   'It is to some degree the work itself which a person secures that instils him with specific kinds of needs to be satisfied or frustrated in the work situation. A manual worker whose work does not involve such qualities, whose education has not awakened such aspirations, and whose opportunities do not include realistic alternatives, will not develop the need for intrinsically fulfilling work.'
   (Blauner 1964: 29–30)

· 12 ·
SUMMARY AND CONCLUDING DISCUSSION

Mothers in cross-cultural perspective

Like the majority of women with pre-school children in Britain, the fifty women in this study had exclusive responsibility for their children and responsibility for them all the time. As 'ordinary' mothers in our society, on the whole they saw this arrangement as 'natural' or at least 'usual'. Taken in historical or cross-cultural perspective, however, this manner of organizing child care – that is, giving the task entirely to the biological mother and making it, along with domestic duties, her only responsibility – appears as a peculiarity of Western industrial society. In almost all non-industrial societies women combine child care with important economic responsibilities and share responsibility for children with other women. While women and children are linked in these societies as they are in our own, both are a more important part of the wider social group.

The easy integration of productive work and child care in most non-industrial societies appears to be aided by two important features. First, in many societies the place of productive activity is not isolated from the general living area. Children go with their parents to the fields to gather or cultivate food or accompany them on hunts; when they return they play nearby as both men and women prepare food or ply their crafts in open courtyards or around the domestic hearth (Blurton Jones 1974b). In these circumstances mothers, and indeed all adults in the society, are in a position to carry out productive work and keep an eye on their children at the same time. Second, in many societies women work alongside their mothers and sisters or other women of the group, producing food, clothes, or other items. Since they are all together with their children they can share, at least to some extent, the care of their children, and minimize the conflict between their responsibilities.

These features of their situation – the variety of their responsibilities, including vital productive work, and the sharing of work activities, including child care – are important to the quality of the relationship of women with their children and, by implication, to their experience as mothers. This is well illustrated in the cross-cultural study of mothers of six cultures (Minturn and Lambert 1964), which compares child rearing in communities in Mexico, the Philippines, Okinawa, India, Kenya, and New England (USA). Looking at variation both among the communities and within each community, Minturn and Lambert found consistent differences in *maternal warmth* and *maternal instability* according to the conditions under which the women looked after their children.[1] Two sets of findings are particularly interesting.

The first is that 'mothers who are primarily responsible for the care of their children are variable in their expressions of warmth and do not gear their hostility to the behaviour of the children' (Minturn and Lambert 1964: 116). That is, women who have excessive responsibility for their children and who are forced to spend long periods of time caring for them without help and without a break are likely to be irritable and emotionally unstable in their dealings with them.[2] At the same time, the extent of their responsibilities for productive work does not seem to be related to maternal instability: in contrast to the common belief that conflict between responsibilities can increase friction between mothers and children, a woman's involvement in economically productive work does not create further strains in their relationship. This is because 'few tasks are as harassing as caring for small children and the increased responsibility of other duties is compensated for by the respite from child care' (Minturn and Lambert 1964: 91).

In relation to these findings, the 'six culture' study also highlights the fact that it is unusual for a mother to spend the majority of her time caring for her children and to have no responsibilities besides child care. *Table 12(1)* shows that in all the societies except the African and American, the majority of women spend less than half their time looking after their children and have a high proportion of

Table 12(1) *Caretaking-of-child scales (children aged 3–6 years)* *

Society	proportion of time mother cares for child: less than half (% of families)	proportion of caretaking done by mother: low (% of families)	proportion of time caretaking done by another: never (% of families)
USA	0	9	75
Africa	13	0	50
Mexico	58	58	25
Okinawa	50	50	67
India	75	55	44
Philippines	75	63	17

* adapted from Minturn and Lambert (1964), *Table 5.4*, page 109

child care done by another. Mothers in the Mexican and Philippine communities go to market regularly to sell produce but live near sisters-in-law and mothers-in-law who help with the children. In Mexico, where children rarely go to school, older children are also used to care for younger children. Okinawan mothers spend several hours away every day cutting firewood to sell, during which time a grandmother or older child takes over the children. In the Indian extended family a grandmother directs her daughters-in-law in both child care and spinning or carding cotton and a father may take his son to work with him. Mothers in all of these societies spend a relatively low proportion of their time in caring for children. African mothers spend more time in charge of children than mothers of the other four groups and also have extensive economic tasks (cultivating the gardens and tending the fields allotted to them by their husbands). However, their child care responsibilities largely involve overseeing children who are old enough to be able to help with the agricultural work, as these older children both help with the chores and take immediate charge of the younger children.

It is only the New England mothers, then, who are primarily responsible for children of all ages and who spend the majority of their time engaged solely in their care. Since they are confined to their homes and perform no economically productive work, they can afford to give their children individual attention and to tailor their responses to the situation at hand. However, their exclusive and often trying responsibility for them acts to counter the warmth that would be expected between mothers and children under such conditions. As a result, 'their behaviour vacillates between self-conscious warmth and sympathy and impatience born of the fatigue of being constantly "on duty" and the frustration of personal desires' (Minturn and Lambert 1964: 89).

The second set of findings of particular interest to us is that mothers who have another adult (especially a grandmother) living with the family are warmer towards their children and more stable emotionally. Another adult both reduces the isolation of a mother in the nuclear family, giving her companionship and emotional support, and relieves her of her child care chores: these, in turn, allow a mother to express more warmth to her children than she could were she their sole caretaker.

In relation to these findings, the cross-cultural comparisons again draw attention to the fact that the American and African communities are unusual in their form. 'Stem' families (families with one or more grandparent living with them) and a large living unit are common in all other communities. In the Mexican community, for example, the ideal living unit is a compound consisting of a cluster of separate dwelling units surrounding a common courtyard. Each family, whether nuclear or stem, typically maintains separate cooking, eating, and sleeping facilities but shares the courtyards and engages in common activities with the other families. The women, children, and grandparents spend most of their time together within the compound while the men are away in the fields. Similarly, the basic living unit in the Philippine community is the *sitio*, a housing cluster containing five to seven patrilocal households grouped together around common family yards through which the major footpaths pass. The yard is both the playground for the children and the place where a large part of the daily work is done. Around the yard are railed porches from which the women 'can gossip with their sisters-in-law, watch the children at play, check on some of the chores, chat with their husbands if they are not in fields and get news from each passerby' (Minturn and Lambert 1964: 20). In the Indian community, the extended family, consisting of grandparents, aunts, uncles, and cousins as well as parents and siblings, is by far the most common type of family. Once married, women are secluded within their houses, which are separate from the men's houses. The women's houses are built close together, however, each around its own courtyard. Here the women of the household spend most of their time together under the supervision of their mother-in-law, spinning, carding cotton, preparing grain for storage, cooking their food, and supervising their children at play.

About half of the households in the Okinawa community are 'stem' families consisting of parents, children, and the surviving paternal grandparents. Each household occupies a simple house built on the main road or on one of the side streets running off it. While these single dwelling units afford a great deal of privacy, the sliding doors or panels in the large living rooms of each house are generally kept open during the day and residents can watch those passing and be watched from outside. Children play in the yards of these houses or in the streets throughout their part of the village and are benignly watched by the adults of the community, most of whom can trace kinship relations with them.

In contrast to the large households of the preceding four communities, the basic household unit in the African community consists of a married woman and her pre-adolescent children. However, each household is part of a polygynous extended family homestead, consisting of the man who is head of the homestead, his wives and unmarried children, and his married sons and their wives and children. Each married woman has a house of her own, separated from those of her co-wives by at least one field in order to limit jealousy and dissension among them. Young children live with their mother in her house, helping her to produce and prepare food for the household, while their father moves about within the homestead, apportioning his time among the households of his several wives. For the most part, then, the mother is the only adult in the household, although in the fields there is a good deal of neighbourly interaction among the women as they work together. Mothers have sole responsibility for their children, despite the fact that they are overburdened with an agricultural and domestic workload which limits the attention they can give them. 'In consequence, they delegate a good deal of caretaking and training to older children in the homestead and they reduce their maternal role to what they consider its bare essentials' (Whiting 1963: 161).

The circumstances in which the women in this study looked after their children were very different from those of these five other societies. Like that of the New England women, their situation included many features which Minturn and Lambert found created tension and emotional instability in their relationships with their children. They alone were responsible for their children and they spent much of their time engaged exclusively in child care with little help from anyone else and with few breaks from it. Only a quarter of them had a job outside their homes and even among these women their jobs were largely casual and peripheral to their domestic responsibilities. For the most part, they were confined to their homes with no recognized and valued role for the community as a whole. As a consequence, they lacked the variety of responsibilities which could give them a break from the strain of child care, add interest to their lives, and enable them to maintain an involvement in the wider community. They lived in privatized nuclear families physically separated from both other family members and other women and children. Only one woman lived within walking distance of her mother and only a third of the women saw their mothers even once a week. While virtually all saw friends or neighbours every day, this contact was on the whole brief, limited, and outside any formal or enduring context. They therefore had no one with whom to share the burden of child care, who could take the strain of responsibility as well as make the work manageable, and who could provide companionship and support in a difficult and demanding job.

This description of the social conditions in which the fifty women in the sample looked after their children forms the context in which the main findings of this study should be interpreted and in terms of which they clearly make sense. These findings can be summarized and discussed briefly under the headings of the three aims of the research.

Summary

WOMEN'S EXPERIENCE AS MOTHERS

Getting on for two-thirds of the women experienced a sense of meaning and purpose in their lives as mothers. They felt their children needed and wanted them and they invested their personal hopes and dreams in their children. Their children therefore gave them a purpose to which they were deeply committed and in pursuing this purpose they experienced their lives as meaningful and worthwhile. At the same time, however, half of the women also found child care a predominantly frustrating and irritating experience. This included one-third of the women who felt a sense of meaning and purpose in looking after their children as well as other women for whom feelings of frustration and irritation completely dominated their experience. These women conveyed that they found pre-school children difficult and demanding to deal with over extended periods of time; that they felt overburdened by their boundless obligations towards their children; that they found their children disruptive of their otherwise enjoyable activities; and that they felt guilt and anxiety as a consequence of the conflict between their responsibilities as mothers and as housewives. They also complained of the lack of the interesting and stimulating company of those not involved in child care and of the fact that their children tied them to their homes and the domestic sphere. With the two themes taken together, four types of experience of motherhood were distinguished in the women's accounts: a third of the women were *fulfilled*, a third *alienated*, a quarter *in conflict*, and a tenth *satisfied*.

While the emphasis in this book has inevitably been on describing the negative aspects of motherhood, we should not overlook the fact that a significant minority of the women were rated as *fulfilled* as mothers. Since all the women in the sample enjoyed basically good social conditions, it was expected that a number of them would find motherhood predominantly rewarding. The way in which women in our society are brought up instils in them both the desire to have children and the relational needs and capacities to look after them (Chodorow 1978). When they can eventually live out these inclinations, without significant financial or social difficulties, some may well enjoy doing so. This is likely to be the case particularly when factors in their personal circumstances can to some extent modify the social circumstances which make child care seem a frustrating and irritating activity. A large house and domestic conveniences, for example, can lighten the burden of child care and give a woman the time and space for her interests apart from the children; a car and telephone can also help her maintain these interests as well as reduce her sense of isolation at home. The help of a mother or an au pair can further relieve her of some of the burden of responsibility and give her time on her own; this sort of assistance can also enable her to be more fully integrated into the larger society by allowing her to take on a paid job. Alternatively, an active and supportive neighbourhood group can give her both practical help and a sense of belonging to a valued community. A sympathetic and understanding husband can appreciate her otherwise unrecognized work and, by sharing her commitment to their children, can help her experience her life as meaningful and her efforts and sacrifices as worthwhile.

SOCIAL CLASS DIFFERENCES

Differences between working-class and middle-class women were found in a number of their attitudes and approaches to motherhood. The clearest differences were found in relation to their attitude towards their children as 'company', their approach towards playing with their children, the way in which they evaluated their children (though not in the extent of their consequent pride in their children), their enjoyment of a community of mothers, the level at which they located and 'explained' their frustrations in child care, and their orientation towards the work of child care. Working-class women on the whole conveyed a more 'traditional' orientation to motherhood, looking for rewards from their roles as mothers and expecting to find pleasure in looking after their children. When they did not, they emphasized the practical difficulties they encountered in carrying out their role and looked to improved material conditions for their solution. Middle-class women, though they gave priority to their domestic roles, were on the whole less likely to expect rewards from child care itself and were more able to deal with the specific frustrations they felt as mothers. In talking about these frustrations, they emphasized the more basic difficulties that arose from the way child care is institutionalized in our society, describing a sense of monopolization and loss of individuality in motherhood. These social class differences may be related to differences in current material resources for coping with children (within the context of overall good social conditions) and to early differences in socialization experience in relation to social roles generally (Goldthorpe *et al.* 1969) and to gender roles in particular. In regard to this latter point, working-class women were more likely to have had experience during their adolescence in looking after young children, and to have had greater responsibilities in doing so.

A further point of contrast between working-class and middle-class women was in their satisfaction with their lives as mothers. Middle-class women, with comparatively better opportunities outside the domestic sphere, tended to be more critical in assessing their satisfaction with their lives as mothers than working-class women, whose prospects in the economic sphere appeared to be comparatively less attractive. These differences became stronger, however, when the women's *own* occupation before having children was substituted for their husband's occupation as a basis for classifying the women. This finding highlights one of the shortcomings in the conventional method of analysing women's experience according to their husband's occupation. In so far as husband's occupation does not correlate well with women's own occupation (Oakley 1981b: 284), grouping women according to husband's occupation may tend to confuse rather than to clarify our understanding of women's experience and to obscure more meaningful lines of division among them.

Since one of the concerns of this study was to look at the differences between working-class and middle-class women, throughout the book I have contrasted the two social class groups and pointed to the differences between them. These differences, however, exist within the context of other more fundamental similarities between them. There were no *statistically significant* differences between working-class and middle-class women in relation to the two main measures of the quality of their experience as mothers. Similar proportions of working-class and middle-class women were assessed as feeling frustrated and irritated in looking after their children and similar proportions as finding a sense of meaning and purpose in motherhood, though a slightly larger proportion of working-class women were assessed as enjoying child care and a somewhat larger proportion of middle-class women as feeling a sense of meaning and purpose as mothers. These differences might well have been substantially larger had working-class women in markedly adverse social conditions been included in the sample. The reason for excluding such women was to allow a clearer examination of the effect of other features in the way the care of children is organized in our society (though the fact that a significant proportion of women with young children live around or below the poverty line is itself not unrelated to the way child care is organized in our society). The absence of marked class differences between women in overall good social circumstances suggests that the obligations inherent in the mother role – exclusive responsibility for their children, responsibility for them all the time – largely over-ride class differences in attitudes and approaches to motherhood and are the main influences on women's experience as mothers. This again calls into question the value of dividing women along social class lines in that it draws attention away from similiarities in their experience that derive from their common position as mothers of young children. For working-class and middle-class women alike, their sole and final responsibility for their children meant that their daily lives were centred on, and dominated by, their children. While they accepted their responsibility, and tried to perform it to the best of their ability, they often felt it a heavy responsibility from which there was little break or relief. As a result, they felt physically and psychologically tied to their children and required to organize their other activities around this central responsibility. Similarly, the fact that child care was their only major occupation meant that they were limited in the activities they were involved in and the sorts of people they met in the course of their day. There was at times little variety in their activities and little change or respite from their domestic duties. Because they had given up the paid jobs they had had before their children were born, they were outside the mainstream of society and socially and economically dependent on their husbands. Finally, the segregation of their work into individual households left them socially and psychologically isolated – cut off from help, from one another, and from the outside world. For similar proportions of working-class and middle-class women, these features of their situation gave rise to feelings of frustration and irritation in motherhood that predominated over what pleasure they found in caring for their children.

HUSBAND'S PRACTICAL HELP AND EMOTIONAL SUPPORT

The active involvement in their children on the part of their husbands was an important factor in modulating the frustration and irritation that the women felt. For a working-class woman in particular, her husband's practical help with the children relieved her of some of the burden of child care and so allowed her more enjoyment from them than would otherwise have been possible. For working-class and middle-class women alike, their husbands' emotional support greatly helped in creating and sustaining a sense of meaning and purpose in their lives as mothers. In the absence of any other kin in the household, then, it may be her husband who is central to a woman's experience of motherhood as rewarding.

Does the solution of the problem of women's distress as mothers therefore lie in encouraging men to help more with their children? Substantial help from her husband is certainly important to a woman, but there are two major limitations on the value of encouraging such help alone. First, a man's help with their children can have only a limited impact on the feelings of monopolization and loss of individuality experienced by a third of the women in the sample. Such feelings arise from a woman's sole and final responsibility for her children, responsibility which requires her to subordinate her own interests and to put the children first. Her husband's help with the children, unless it is so extensive as to equate with *sharing responsibility* for them, cannot alter this basic obligation nor enable her to develop and express her individuality further. To deal with this kind of frustration, a more fundamental reorganization of society would be required, which would integrate women and children into the mainstream of society. Such a change would entail ensuring that women as well as men had a role in productive work vital to society and that men as well as women shared in responsibility for their children.

Nevertheless, their husbands' help with their children was of great value to a number of the women and it seems likely that there would be much to be gained from encouraging men in other families to increase their help. The difficulties entailed in doing so discussed in Chapter 9, however, highlight the second limitation of this strategy: in our society as it is at present, it is simply not within a man's power to increase substantially his help with the children. The many apparently minor reasons why men do not help a great deal suggest that the fundamental sexual division of labour in society, whereby men are responsible for outside employment and earning an income and women for domestic labour and looking after the family, sets the basic constraints on the division of labour in the home. The major restriction on a man's involvement in child care, and therefore to a large extent on his understanding of his wife's world, is his obligation to his job. Not only does this mean he cannot help with the children during the hours he is at work, it also means he is limited in the help he can give when he is at home: the children want him less than the more familiar figure of their mother; he lacks the requisite skills and knowledge to do the job; he disrupts routines; his offers of help give rise to feelings of criticism and intrusion or to generous but realistic sympathy for his need to rest before going to work and so on. The fundamental organization of society, then, limits the extent to which, on a wide scale, men can be effectively encouraged to help more with their children. The implication of these observations is clear and in line with the conclusions of other research (Eichler 1975; Edgell 1980): an increase in men's help with the children may be essential to relieving the strains and enhancing the rewards of motherhood but such a change can be founded only on a prior change in the sexual division of labour in society as a whole.

Concluding remarks

This book has presented a description of fifty women's experience of motherhood. As such it is a contribution to our understanding of the details of family life, and in particular to our understanding of the experience of women in the family. It has highlighted the distress to which women are vulnerable by virtue of their role as mother and has discussed the role of the husband and the marital relationship in regard to this distress. In this way it has contributed to our understanding of one particular social problem. Finally, it has examined the pervasive influence on women's experience of social factors to which others (e.g. Firestone 1970; Mitchell 1971; Blumenfeld and Mann 1980) have drawn our attention.

In recent years, feminist sociologists such as Oakley (1974a, 1974b), Gardiner (1976), and Seecombe (1980) have made much progress in looking at women's role within the family from the perspective of *labour*. This perspective allows the use of standard sociological concepts and the concept of *domestic labour* has been particularly valuable in drawing attention to the fact that housework and child care are 'work' and may be experienced as tiring, boring, oppressive, or alienating in the way that any work may. This present research, however, has highlighted the difficulties and shortcomings inherent in the labour perspective when it is applied to the arena of personal relationships within the family. As Stacey (1981) has pointed out, the vocabulary of concepts and categories created to describe wage labour in the public domain does not provide an adequate framework to throw light on all aspects of women's experience in the private domain. The lack of suitable concepts for making sense of the women's accounts was a problem that plagued this research from the time it was realized that *satisfaction* was an inadequate concept with which to approach women's experience as mothers. A further contribution of this study, therefore, has been the rethinking of concepts for describing women's experience as mothers. Much emphasis has been placed on developing the concepts of *immediate response* and *sense of meaning and purpose* in motherhood and they represent an advance on the indiscriminate use of concepts derived from the public sphere for describing experience in the private sphere.

With the conceptual framework presented here and the rethinking of sociological concepts which Stacey suggests, further research into the area of women's experience as mothers, and their experience of family relationships in general, should prove more productive. Clearly there is a need to investigate further a range of issues highlighted in this study, among other categories of mothers and using other methods of research. An approach which involved direct observations of women and their children in a range of contexts and over a longer period of time, for example, would be valuable in testing some of the ideas presented here which are based on interpretations of interview material. Research on women who have combined motherhood with rewarding careers, on women with school-aged children, and on women in less materially advantaged circumstances would all extend and elaborate on observations presented in this research. Does the opportunity to express one's individuality in a career, for example, enhance one's enjoyment of motherhood as this study would predict? Do poorer social conditions make it difficult to find any rewards in motherhood? Can a strong sense of meaning and purpose in relation to her children sustain a woman through a crisis and protect her from a depressive breakdown?

Another area which requires further exploration is that of the influence of social networks on the women's experience as mothers. Although it was not explored in depth, there was evidence in this study to suggest that financial assistance, practical help, advice, and companionship from parents and friends could significantly alter a woman's experience. Many working-class women in particular felt very close to their mothers once they had children and stressed the value of being able to share their worries and pleasures with someone who understood them and was emotionally involved in them. Once they were independent and 'properly settled' they felt there was less tension in their relationship with their mothers and more friendship between them: each felt the other was a confidante and a major source of emotional support. To what extent, then, can help and support from a woman's mother compensate for a lack of help and support from her husband? To what extent does her help and support *preclude* the husband from giving them? Visits from their own mothers were in the main happily anticipated as a break from the isolation and boredom of the home and as an opportunity to maintain contact with the outside world. In addition, their own mothers were often the first source of advice and reassurance in child care, particularly about illnesses, and the only trusted baby-sitter for the children. How, then, do women without mothers in the locality cope? Do they rely more on the provision of the health and social services (health visitors, clinics, one o'clock clubs)? Are they more lonely and irritable? Or are they simply less domestic and child-oriented?

Friends and neighbours may be another source of help and support, through formal organizations such as baby-sitting circles or school rotas, or more casually on an individual basis. What are the various patterns of self-help among young mothers? Do they differ by social class? How do they help? While virtually all the women in the study saw friends or neighbours every day, whether it was on the way to school, at the shops, or in their own homes, reactions to this contact varied considerably. For some, the community of young mothers provided them with friends with whom to share their daily activities as well as to venture into others (e.g. Keep Fit or a day trip to Brighton) and a sense of belonging to a supportive group. Their 'special friend' became a regular visitor, who sympathized with their frustrations and understood their point of view. Others, however, felt cut off from the wider world despite their many friends because their friendships were dominated by their children. They complained of feeling bored and boring with these friends and longed to meet others independent of the mother role. What are the implications of this boredom for the traditional organizations geared to housebound women? How can their felt needs best be met? On the other hand, what are the costs of deep involvement in the community of mothers?

Finally, motherhood is not simply a matter of academic interest but a matter of growing public concern and debate. Those involved in the health and employment of women, in children's welfare, and in a variety of other social concerns have called for changes in official policy regarding the position of women with children and have proposed a variety of programmes for legislation. As I pointed out in Chapter 1, however, each group has its own views on what is right and natural for women and each argues for its own legislation.

On the one hand, there are those such as Pringle (1974), Leach (1979) and Kitzinger (1978) who see full-time motherhood as the best for both children and mothers and who therefore propose measures to make it easier for women to stay at home with their children. Leach, for example, believes 'that many women need only social approval and support to enable them to settle happily to full-time caring for their children' (Leach 1979: 104). Among the measures proposed are (i) earning-related allowances for women caring for their own children at home; (ii) self-help groups along the lines of the one o'clock clubs; (iii) community and housing facilities catering to the needs of women with children; (iv) drop-in centres for expert advice; (v) part-time jobs which will not interfere with the needs of children; and (vi) education to improve society's attitudes towards children and child care. While these changes are likely to be valuable in helping women cope with some of the practical difficulties they face in looking after their children, they are also likely to give rise to new problems. For example, by increasing their dependence on their husbands for help, advice, and contact with the world at large, these measures might well increase women's resentment of their husbands and their own secondary positions both in the family and in the wider society. By reinforcing the division between men's and women's worlds they might leave women more isolated, unsupported, and vulnerable within the family. By pushing women back into the family and domestic sphere (and providing no acceptable excuse such as money to leave it) they might increase the number of women who felt monopolized in motherhood. The affluent middle-class women in this study, who by and large already enjoyed many of the advantages that Leach and others want to give all women, did not necessarily enjoy child care as a result. They often simply felt stresses and frustrations in a different way from the less well-off working-class women. The problems which women face as mothers may not disappear as their resources increase: they may simply change. Making it easier for women to stay home with their children may increase the pressure on them to do so, but it will not necessarily make it more attractive or rewarding for them. Many women may still feel that the mother role cannot fulfil the whole of their personalities and may continue to suffer from the domination of children in their lives.

In contrast to these proposals are those of people such as Gavron (1966), Bernard (1972, 1974, 1975), Safilios-Rothschild (1971, 1973), and the Rapoports (1971) who see full-time motherhood as imposing restrictions on the development and self-realization of women as individuals and as sustaining their 'second-class status' in society. Safilios-Rothschild (1973), for example, has argued that the need to curtail non-family interests and to spend all her energy, emotions, and time in the continuous care of her children is bad for a woman, her children, and her marriage; and Rapoport, Rapoport, and Strelitz (1977) have suggested that for many women their expectations of fulfilment in caring for their families have not been met because women have needs which cannot be met in motherhood and child care makes demands which cannot be met by a mother alone. They therefore argue for measures which will make it easier for women to participate in the labour force on an equal standing with men and to be re-integrated 'in all their many roles with the central activities of society' (Gavron 1966: 146). Among the measures proposed to achieve this are (i) changes in the education of girls to prepare them for *both* family and employee roles; (ii) a recognition of fathers as 'sharers of the active parenting required' and domestic work-sharing on a principle of equity; (iii) provision of supervised play areas in public buildings to enable women to take their children with them as they lead active 'public' lives themselves; (iv) the provision of an adequate number of good child care centres open all hours of the day and night for children of all ages whether healthy or ill, and a change in attitude towards non-parental child care so that it is considered as good as (or better than) a mother's care; and, on a more ambitious level, (v) restructuring of the workplace, encouraging more part-time jobs, flexible working arrangements, and job sharing, and pressure on the government to assign greater priority to the needs of families. These changes would give rise to new patterns of parenting and new patterns of outside activities for both husband and wife which might well overcome some of the basic difficulties described by the women in this study. By breaking up the time a woman spends alone with her children, they might raise her tolerance to her children's demands. By increasing the involvement of others in child care, they might reduce the strain, pressure, and conflict she feels as well as increase the companionship and emotional support she gets from others, particularly her husband. And perhaps most importantly, by allowing her to develop and pursue her own interests and activities, such changes might enable her to maintain a sense of individuality and personal identity not based on child care. It has to be recognized, however, that some women would not see their interests as served by the kind of social arrangements implied by these policies. A third of the women in this study were rated as *fulfilled* mothers and it is likely that many of them would experience it as a significant loss if they were to give up full-time motherhood. Some were particularly nurturant and felt that child care and domesticity best suited their interests, skills, and personality. Some also felt their commitment to their children both arose from and sustained their intense involvement in their children: they felt uniquely needed and wanted by their children and were jealous of the depth and exclusiveness of their relationship. In addition, as many of them implied, the jobs available to them, were they to work, were unskilled, uncreative, marginal to the enterprise, poorly paid, outside the promotion structure, and generally less attractive than full-time motherhood.

The need for new policies relating to the position of women with young children is clear. Research reporting the mental and physical distress associated with women's role as mothers was reviewed in Chapter 1; others have highlighted the problems of child abuse and violence in the family (Gil 1973; Kempe and Kempe 1978). What is also clear, however, is the need for social policy decisions to be informed by an adequately complex picture of women's experience as mothers.

Notes

1. *Maternal warmth* measures the 'relative warmth or hostility of the mother's behaviour towards her children' (Minturn and Lambert 1969: 68). *Maternal instability* measures the extent to which the mother is 'subject to wide, frequent and unpredictable shifts in mood' (Minturn and Lambert 1969: 82).
2. From their study of thirty-six mother-infant pairs, Schaffer and Emerson concluded that 'Satisfaction of physical needs does not appear to be a necessary precondition to the development of attachment, the latter taking place independently and without any obvious regard to the experiences that the child encounters in physical care situations' (Schaffer and Emerson 1964: 67). This conclusion when taken with those of Minturn and Lambert suggests that exclusive responsibility for children and responsibility for them all the time (that is, the obligations of the mother role in our society) are not only *not* essential to a warm and rewarding mother-child relationship but, on the contrary, are likely to engender irritability and emotional instability in it.

REFERENCES

Acker, J. (1973) Women and social stratification: a case of intellectual sexism. In Huber (ed.) *Changing Women in Changing Society*. London: University of Chicago Press.

Ainsworth, M. D. S. (1969) Object relations, dependency and attachment: a theoretical review of the infant-mother relationship. *Child Development* 40: 969–1025.

Ainsworth, M., Bell, S. M., and Stayton, D. J. (1974) Infant-mother attachment and social development: 'socialization' as a product of reciprocal responsiveness to signals. In Richards (ed.) *The Integration of a Child into a Social World*. London: Cambridge University Press.

Antony, E. J. and Benedeck, T. (eds) (1970) *Parenthood: Its Psychology and Psychopathology*. Boston: Little, Brown, and Co.

Aries, P. (1965) *Centuries of Childhood*. New York: Vintage Books.

Bacon, L. (1974) Early motherhood, accelerated role transition and social pathologies. *Social Forces* 52: 333–42.

Badinter, E. (1981) *The Myth of Motherhood: An Historical View of the Maternal Instinct*. London: Souvenir Press.

Bahr, S. J. (1974) Effects on power and division of labour in the family. In Hoffman and Nye (eds) *Working Mothers*. London: Jossey-Bass.

Balint, A. (1949) Love for the mother and mother love. *International Journal of Psychoanalysis* 30: 251–59. Reprinted in M. Balint (1965) *Primary Love and Psychoanalytic Technique*. London: Tavistock.

Battista, J. and Almond, R. (1973) The development of meaning in life. *Psychiatry* **36**: 409–27.

Baum, F. and Cope, D. R. (1980) Some characteristics of intentionally childless wives in Britain. *Journal of Biosocial Science* **12**: 287–99.

Bell, C. and Newby, H. (1976) Husbands and wives: the dynamics of the deferential dialectic. In Barker and Allen (eds) *Dependence and Exploitation in Work and Marriage*. London: Longman.

Bell, R. Q. (1974) Contributions of human infants to caregiving and social interaction. In Lewis and Rosenblum (eds) *The Effects of the Infant on its Caregiver*. New York: John Wiley.

Benedeck, T. (1959) Parenthood as a developmental phase. *Journal of American Psychoanalytic Association* **7**: 389–417.

—— (1970a) The family as a psychologic field. In Anthony and Benedeck (eds) *Parenthood*. Boston: Little, Brown, and Co.

—— (1970b) The psychology of pregnancy. In Anthony and Benedeck (eds) *Parenthood*. Boston: Little, Brown, and Co.

—— (1970c) Motherhood and nurturing. In Anthony and Benedeck (eds) *Parenthood*. Boston: Little, Brown, and Co.

—— (1970d) Parenthood during the life cycle. In Anthony and Benedeck (eds) *Parenthood*. Boston: Little, Brown, and Co.

Berger, P. L. and Kellner, H. (1964) Marriage and the construction of reality. *Diogenes* **46**: 1–25. Reprinted in Dreitzel (ed.) (1970) *Recent Sociology No. 2*. New York: Macmillan.

Bernard, J. (1975) *Women, Wives, Mothers: Values and Options*. Chicago: Aldine.

—— (1975) *The Future of Parenthood*. London: Calder and Boyars.

—— (1976) *The Future of Marriage*. Harmondsworth: Penguin.

Bibring, G., Dwyer, T., Huntington, D. S., and Valenstein, A. (1961) A study of the psychological process in pregnancy and of the earliest mother-child relationship. *Psychoanalytic Study of the Child* **16**: 9–72.

Blake, J. (1974) Coercive pronatalism and American population policy. In Peck and Senderowitz (eds) *Pronatalism*. New York: Crowell.

—— (1979) Is zero preferred? American attitudes towards childlessness in the 1970s. *Journal of Marriage and the Family* **41**: 245–55.

Blauner, R. (1964) *Alienation and Freedom: The Factory Worker and His Industry*. London: University of Chicago Press.

Blood, R. and Wolfe, D. (1960) *Husbands and Wives.* Glencoe: Free Press.

Blumenfeld, E. and Mann, S. (1980) Domestic labour and the reproduction of labour power: towards an analysis of women, the family and class. In Fox (ed.) *Hidden in the Household.* Toronto: Women's Press.

Blurton Jones, N. G. (1972) Characteristics of ethological studies of human behaviour. In Blurton Jones (ed.) *Ethological Studies of Child Behaviour.* London: Cambridge University Press.

—— (1974a) Ethology and early socialization. In Richards (ed.) *The Integration of a Child into a Social World.* London: Cambridge University Press.

—— (1974b) Biological perspectives on parenthood. In *The Family in Society: Dimension of Parenthood.* London: HMSO.

Bott, E. (1957) *Family and Social Network.* London: Tavistock.

Boulton, M. G. (1982) 'Women's Experience of Motherhood: A Study of Women with Preschool Children.' Unpublished Ph.D. thesis, University of London.

Bowlby, J. (1957) An ethological approach to research in child development. *British Journal of Medical Psychology* 30: 230–40.

—— (1958a) Psychoanalysis and Child Care. Reprinted in Bowlby *The Making and Breaking of Affectional Bonds.* London: Tavistock, 1979.

—— (1958b) The nature of the child's tie to his mother. *International Journal of Psychoanalysis,* Volume 39. Reprinted in Bowlby *Attachment and Loss: Vol. 1, Attachment.* London: Hogarth Press, 1974.

—— (1969) *Attachment and Loss: Vol. 1. Attachment.* London: The Hogarth Press.

—— (1973) Affectional bonds: their nature and origin. In Weiss (ed.) *Loneliness: the Experience of Emotional and Social Isolation.* London: MIT Press.

Brazelton, T. B., Koslowski, B., and Main, M. (1974) The origins of reciprocity: the early mother-infant interaction. In Lewis and Rosenblum (eds) *The Effect of the Infant on its Caregiver.* New York: Wiley.

Breen, D. (1975) *The Birth of a First Child.* London: Tavistock.

Brody, S. (1956) *Patterns of Mothering.* New York: International Universities Press.

Brown, G. W. and Harris, T. (1978) *The Social Origins of Depression.* London: Tavistock.

Brown, G. W. and Rutter, M. (1966) The measurement of family activities and relationships: a methodological study. *Human Relations* 19: 241–63.

Brown, G. W., Ni Bhrolchain, M., and Harris, T. (1975) Social class and psychiatric disturbance among women in an urban population. *Sociology* 9: 225–54.

Burr, W. R. (1970) Satisfactions of various aspects of marriage over the life cycle. *Journal of Marriage and the Family* 32: 29–37.

Busfield, J. (1974) Ideologies and reproduction. In Richards (ed.) *The Integration of a Child into a Social World*. London: Cambridge University Press.

Busfield, J. and Paddon, M. (1977) *Thinking About Children: Sociology and Fertility in Post-War England*. London: Cambridge University Press.

Cartwright, A. and Jefferys, M. (1958) Married women who work: their own and their children's health. *British Journal of Preventive and Social Medicine* 12: 159–71.

Chadwick, B. A. Albrecht, S. L., and Kunz, P. R. (1976) Marital and family role satisfaction. *Journal of Marriage and the Family* 38: 431–40.

Chertok, L. (1969) *Motherhood and Personality: Psychosomatic Aspects of Childbirth*. London: Tavistock.

Chodorow, N. (1978) *The Reproduction of Mothering: Psychoanalysis and the Sociology of Gender*. London: University of California Press.

Coleman, R. W., Kris, E., and Provence, S. (1953) Studies of variations in early parental attitudes. *Psychoanalytic Study of the Child* 8: 20–47.

Comer, L. (1974) *Wedlocked Women*. Leeds: Feminist Books.

Cooperstock, R. (1978) Sex differences in psychotropic drug use. *Social Science and Medicine* 128: 179–86.

Cooperstock, R. and Lennard, H. L. (1978) Role Strains and Tranquilizer Use. Paper presented at BSA Medical Sociology Study Group Conference, York.

Dally, A. (1978) *Mothers: Their Power and Influence*. London: Weidenfeld and Nicolson.

——(1982) *Inventing Motherhood*. London: Burnett Books.

Dalton, K. (1971) Prospective study into puerperal depression. *British Journal of Psychiatry* 118: 689–92.

Davies, J. M. (1981) Problems in the care of the newborn. *The Practitioner* 225: 289–94.

Delphy, C. (1981) Women in stratification studies. In Roberts (ed.) *Doing Feminist Research*. London: Routledge and Kegan Paul.

Deutsch, H. (1945) *The Psychology of Women*, Vol. 2. New York: Grune and Stratton.

—— (1950) The psychology of woman in relation to the function of reproduction. In Fliess (ed.) *The Psychoanalytic Reader: An Anthology of Essential Papers with Critical Introductions*. London: Hogarth Press.

Devore, I. and Konner, M. (1974) Infancy in hunter-gatherer life: an ethological perspective. In White (ed.) *Ethology and Psychiatry*. Toronto: University of Toronto Press.

Dyer, E. D. (1963) Parenthood as crisis: a restudy. *Marriage and Family Living* 25: 196–201.

Edgell, S. (1980) *Middle-Class Couples: A Study of Segregation, Domination and Inequality in Marriage*. London: George Allen and Unwin.

Edmonds, V. H. (1967) Marital conventionalization: definition and measurement. *Journal of Marriage and the Family* 29: 681–88.

Edmonds, V. H., Withers, G., and Dibatista, B. (1972) Adjustment, conservatism, and marital conventionalization. *Journal of Marriage and the Family* 34: 96–103.

Eichler, M. (1975) The egalitarian family in Canada. In Wakil (ed.) *Marriage, Family and Society: Canadian Perspectives*. Toronto: Butterworth.

—— (1980) *The Double Standard: A Feminist Critique of Feminist Social Science*. London: Croom Helm.

Epstein, C. F. (1971) Law partners and marital partners. *Human Relations* 24: 585–602.

Ericksen, J., Yancey, W., and Ericksen, E. (1979) The division of family roles. *Journal of Marriage and the Family* 41: 301–13.

Erikson, E. H. (1959) Identity and the life cycle. *Psychological Issues* 1: 18–171.

—— (1964) Inner and outer space: reflections on womanhood. *Daedalus* 93: 582–606.

Feld, S. (1963) Feelings of adjustment. In Nye and Hoffman (eds) *The Employed Mother in America*. Chicago: Rand McNally.

Feldman, H. (1971) The effects of children on the family. In Michel (ed.) *Family Issues of Employed Women in Europe and America*. Leiden: Brill.

Firestone, S. (1970) *The Dialectic of Sex: The Case for Feminist Revolution*. London: Paladin.

Fletcher, R. (1962) *The Family and Marriage*. Harmondsworth: Penguin.

Fonda, N. and Moss, P. (1976) *Mothers in Employment*. Uxbridge: Brunel University Management Programme and Thomas Coram Research Unit, Institute of Education, University of London.

Fraiberg, S. (1974) Blind infants and their mothers: an examination of the sign system. In Lewis and Rosenblum (eds) *The Effects of the Infant on its Caregiver*. New York: Wiley.

—— (1977) *Insights from the Blind*. London: Souvenir Press.

Fransella, F. and Frost, K. (1977) *On Being a Woman*. London: Tavistock.

Franzwa, H. H. (1974) Pronatalism in women's magazine fiction. In Peck and Senderowitz (eds) *Pronatalism*. New York: Crowell.

Freedman, D. G. (1974) *Human Infancy: An Evolutionary Perspective*. London: Wiley.

Friedan, B. (1963) *The Feminine Mystique*. New York: Norton.

Friedl, E. (1975) *Women and Men: An Anthropologist's View*. New York: Holt, Rinehart, and Winston.

Fromm, E. (1975) *The Sane Society*. London: Routledge and Kegan Paul.

Gardiner, J. (1976) Political economy of domestic labour in capitalist society. In Barker and Allen (eds) *Dependence and Exploitation in Work and Marriage*. London: Longman.

Gavron, H. (1966) *The Captive Wife: Conflicts of Housebound Mothers*. Harmondsworth: Penguin.

General Household Survey Unit (1978) The changing circumstances of women 1971–76. *Population Trends* 13: 17–22.

Gibson, C. (1980) Childlessness and marital instability: a re-examination of the evidence. *Journal of Biosocial Science* 12: 121–32.

Giddens, A. (1973) *The Class Structure of the Advanced Societies*. London: Hutchinson.

Gil, D. G. (1973) Violence against children. In Dreitzel (ed.) *Childhood and Socialization*. Recent Sociology No. 5. New York: Macmillan.

Ginsberg, S. (1976) Women, work and conflict. In Fonda and Moss (eds) *Mothers in Employment*. Uxbridge: Brunel University and London University.

Glenn, N. D. and Weaver, C. (1978) A multivariate, multisurvey study of marital happiness. *Journal of Marriage and the Family* 40: 269–82.

Goldthorpe, J., Lockwood, D., Bechhofer, F., and Platt, J. (1969) *The Affluent Worker in the Class Structure*. London: Cambridge University Press.

Gordon, B. (1978) The vulnerable mother and her child. In Kitzinger and Davis (eds) *The Place of Birth*. Oxford: Oxford University Press.

Gove, W. R. (1978) Sex differences in mental illness among adult men and women: an evaluation of four questions raised regarding the evidence on the higher rates of women. *Social Science and Medicine* **12B**: 187–98.

Gove, W. R. and Hughes, M. (1979) Possible causes of the apparent sex differences in physical health: an empirical investigation. *American Sociological Review* **44**: 126–46.

Gove, W. R. and Tudor, J. F. (1973) Adult sex roles and mental illness. In Huber (ed.) *Changing Women in a Changing Society*. London: University of Chicago Press.

Graham, H. (1977) Women's attitudes to conception and pregnancy. In Chester and Peel (eds) *Equalities and Inequalities in Family Life*. London: Academic Press.

Graham, H. and McKee, L. (1980) *The First Months of Motherhood* (7 vols). London: Health Education Council.

Grimm, E. (1967) Psychological and social factors in pregnancy, delivery and outcome. In Richardson and Guttmacher (eds) *Childbearing – Its Social and Psychological Aspects*. Baltimore: Williams and Wilkins.

Haavio-Mannila, E. (1971) Satisfaction with family, work, leisure and life among men and women. *Human Relations* **24**: 585–602.

Haller, M. and Rosenmayr, L. (1971) The pluridimensionality of work commitment. *Human Relations* **24**: 501–18.

Hansen, E. W. (1966) The development of maternal and infant behaviour in Rhesus monkeys. *Behaviour* **27**: 107–49.

Harlow, H., Harlow, M. K., and Hansen, E. W. (1963) The maternal affectional system of Rhesus monkeys. In Rheingold (ed.) *Maternal Behaviour in Mammals*. London: John Wiley and Sons.

Hart, N. (1976) *When Marriage Ends: A Study in Status Passage*. London: Tavistock.

Hicks, M. W. and Platt, M. (1970) Marital happiness and stability. *Journal of Marriage and the Family* **32**: 553–74.

Hobbs, D. (1965) Parenthood as crisis: a third study. *Marriage and Family Living* **27**: 367–72.

—— (1968) Transition to parenthood: a replication and an extension. *Journal of Marriage and the Family* 30: 413–17.

Hobbs, D. E. and Cole, S. P. (1976) Transition to parenthood: a decade replication. *Journal of Marriage and the Family* 38: 723–31.

Hoffman, L. (1963) The decision to work. In Nye and Hoffman (eds) *The Employed Mother in America*. Chicago: Rand McNally

—— (1974) Psychological factors. In Hoffman and Nye (eds) *Working Mothers*. New York: Jossey-Bass.

Hoffman, L. and Nye, F. I. (eds) (1974) *Working Mothers*. New York: Jossey-Bass.

Hollingworth, L. S. (1916) Social devices impelling women to bear and rear children. *American Journal of Sociology*. Reprinted in Peck and Senderowitz (eds) *Pronatalism*. New York: Crowell, 1974.

Houseknecht, S. (1979) Childlessness and marital adjustment. *Journal of Marriage and the Family* 41: 278–84.

Hudson, W. and Murphy, G. (1980) The non-linear relationship between marital satisfaction and stages of the family life cycle: an artefact of type I errors? *Journal of Marriage and the Family* 42: 263–67.

Hurley, J. R. and Palonen, D. P. (1967) Marital satisfaction and child density among university student parents. *Journal of Marriage and the Family* 29: 483–84.

Jephcott, P., Seear, N., and Smith, J. (1962) *Married Women Working*. London: George Allen and Unwin.

Kamerman, S. B. (1977) Public policy and the family. A new strategy for women as wives and mothers. In Chapman and Gates (eds) *Women into Wives: The Legal and Economic Impact of Marriage*. London: Sage Publications.

Kaufman, C. (1970) Biologic considerations of parenthood. In Anthony and Benedeck (eds) *Parenthood*. Boston: Little, Brown, and Co.

Kempe, R. S. and Kempe, C. H. (1978) *Child Abuse*. Glasgow: Fontana/Open Books.

Kitzinger, S. (1978) *Women as Mothers*. Glasgow: Fontana.

Klaus, K. H. and Kennell, J. H. (1976) *Maternal-Infant Bonding*. St Louis: Mosby.

Klein, J. (1965) *Samples from English Cultures*. London: Routledge and Kegan Paul.

Klein, V. (1965) *Britain's Married Women Workers*. London: Routledge and Kegan Paul.

Klinger, E. (1977) *Meaning and Void: Inner Experiences and the Incentives in People's Lives.* Minneapolis: University of Minnesota Press.

Kohn, M. (1959) Social class and parental values. *American Journal of Sociology* **64**: 337–51.

—— (1963) Social class and parent-child relationships. *American Journal of Sociology* **68**: 471–80.

Komarovsky, M. (1962) *Blue Collar Marriage.* New York: Random House.

Konner, M. J. (1972) Aspects of the developmental ethology of a foraging people. In Blurton Jones (ed) *Ethological Studies of Child Behaviour.* London: Cambridge University Press.

Lampl-de Groot, J. (1927) Zur Entwicklung des Oedipus Komplexes der Frau. *Internationale Zeitzchrift für Psychoanalyse* **XIII**: 269. Translated (1928) as The evolution of the Oedipus complex in women, in *International Journal of Psycho-analysis* **IX**: 322. Reprinted in Fliess (ed.) (1950) *The Psycho-Analytic Reader.* London: Hogarth Press.

Lasch, C. (1977) *Haven in a Heartless World: The Family Besieged.* New York: Basic Books.

Laws, J. L. (1971) A Feminist review of the marital adjustment literature: the rape of the Locke. *Journal of Marriage and the Family* **33**: 483–516.

Leach, P. (1979) *Who Cares: A New Deal for Mothers and their Small Children.* Harmondsworth: Penguin Books.

LeMasters, E. E. (1957) Parenthood as crisis. *Marriage and Family Living* **19**: 352–55.

—— (1974) *Parents in Modern America.* London: Irwin-Dorsey International.

Leonard, D. (1980) *Sex and Generation: A Study of Courtship and Weddings.* London: Tavistock.

Lopata, H. Z. (1971) *Occupation Housewife.* London: Oxford University Press.

—— (1973) Loneliness: forms and components. In Weiss (ed.) *Loneliness: The Experience of Emotional and Social Isolation.* London: The MIT Press.

Lott, B. (1973) Who wants the children? *American Psychologist* July 1973: 573–82. Reprinted in Skolnick and Skolnick (eds) *Intimacy, Family and Society.* Boston: Little, Brown, and Co., 1974.

Luckey, E. G. and Bain, J. E. (1970) Children: A factor in marital satisfaction. *Journal of Marriage and the Family* **32**: 43–4.

Luxton, M. (1980) *More Than a Labour of Love*. Toronto: Women's Press.

McCall, G. J. and Simmons, J. L. (1966) *Identities and Interaction*. New York: The Free Press.

MacFarlane, J. A., Smith, D. M., and Garron, D. H. (1978) The relationship between mother and neonate. In Kitzinger and Davis (eds) *The Place of Birth*. London: Oxford University Press.

MacIntyre, S. (1976) Who wants babies: the social construction of instincts. In Barker and Allen (eds) *Sexual Divisions and Society: Process and Change*. London: Tavistock.

—— (1977) *Single and Pregnant*. London: Croom Helm.

Mackie, L. and Pattullo, P. (1977) *Women at Work*. London: Tavistock.

Maslow, A. (1954) *Motivation and Personality*. New York: Harper.

Matthieu, N. C. (1979) Biological paternity, social maternity: on abortion and infanticide as unrecognized indicators of the cultural character of maternity. In Harris (ed.) *The Sociology of the Family*. Keele: Sociological Review Monograph.

Mead, M. (1972) *Sex and Temperament in Three Primitive Societies*. New York: Dell, Laurel edition.

Meissner, M., Humphreys, E. W., Meis, S. M., and Scheu, W. J. (1975) No exit for wives: sexual division of labour. *The Canadian Review of Sociology and Anthropology* 12: 424–39.

Meyerowitz, J. R. and Feldman, H. (1966) Transition to parenthood. *Psychiatric Research Reports* 20: 78–94.

Miller, B. C. (1975) Child density, marital satisfaction and conventionalization: a research note. *Journal of Marriage and the Family* 37: 345–47.

Miller, J. B. (1978) *Towards a New Psychology of Women*. Harmondsworth: Penguin.

Minturn, L. and Lambert, W. L. (1964) *Mothers of Six Cultures: Antecedents of Child Rearing*. New York: Wiley.

Mitchell, J. (1971) *Women's Estate*. Harmondsworth: Pelican.

Moss, P. (1976) The current situation. In Fonda and Moss (eds) *Mothers in Employment*. Uxbridge: Brunel University and Institute of Education, London University.

Moss, P. and Plewis, I. (1977) Mental distress in mothers of preschool children in Inner London. *Psychological Medicine* 7: 641–52.

Moyo, E. (n.d.) *Big Mother and Little Mother in Matabeleland*. History Workshop Pamphlets, No. 3.

Murgatroyd, L. (1982) Gender and occupational stratification. *Sociological Review* 30: 574–602.

Nathanson, C. A. (1975) Illness and the feminine role: a theoretical review. *Social Science and Medicine* 9: 57–62.

Newson, J. and Newson, E. (1965) *Patterns of Infant Care in an Urban Commnity*. Harmondsworth: Penguin.

—— (1968) *Four Years Old in an Urban Community*. Harmondsworth: Penguin.

—— (1974) Cultural aspects of childrearing in the English-speaking world. In M. Richards (ed.) *The Integration of the Child into a Social World*. London: Cambridge University Press.

Nye, F. I. (1963) Adjustment to children. In Nye and Hoffman (eds) *The Employed Mother in America*. Chicago: Rand McNally.

Nye, F. I. and Hoffman, L. W. (1963) *The Employed Mother in America*. Chicago: Rand McNally.

Oakley, A. (1972) *Sex, Gender and Society*. London: Temple Smith.

—— (1974a) *The Sociology of Housework*. Oxford: Martin Robertson.

—— (1974b) *Housewife*. Harmondsworth: Penguin.

—— (1979) *Becoming a Mother*. Oxford: Martin Robertson.

—— (1980) *Women Confined: Towards a Sociology of Childbirth*. Oxford: Martin Robertson.

—— (1981a) Interviewing women: a contradiction in terms. In Roberts (ed.) *Doing Feminist Research*. London: Routledge and Kegan Paul.

—— (1981b) *Subject: Women*. Oxford: Martin Robertson.

O'Connor, P. (1982) Supportive relationships: their nature and their association with psychiatric state. Paper presented at the British Sociological Association Conference, Manchester, April 1982.

Office of Population Censuses and Surveys (1970) *Classification of Occupations 1970*. London: HMSO.

Pahl, J. M. and Pahl, R. E. (1971) *Managers and their Wives*. Harmondsworth: Penguin.

Parkin, F. (1979) *Marxism and Class Theory: a Bourgeois Critique*. London: Tavistock.

Payne, J. (1978) Talking about children: an examination of accounts about reproduction and family life. *Journal of Biosocial Science* 10: 367–74.

Peck, E. (1974) Television's romance with reproduction. In Peck and Senderowitz (eds) *Pronatalism*. New York: Crowell.

Pohlman, E. (1969) *The Psychology of Birth Planning*. Cambridge, Mass. Schenkman.

Poloma, M. (1972) Role conflict and the married professional woman. In Safilios-Rothschild (ed.) *Towards a Sociology of Women*. Lexington, Mass.: Xerox College Publishing.

Poloma, M. and Garland, T. N. (1970) The myth of the egalitarian family: family roles and the professionally employed wife. Paper presented at the 65th annual meeting of the American Sociological Association, September 1970. Reprinted in Theodore (ed.) (1971) *The Professional Woman*. Cambridge, Mass.: Schenkman.

Poster, M. (1978) *Critical Theory of the Family*. London: Pluto Press.

Prendergast, S. and Prout, A. (1979) What will I do? . . . teenage girls and the construction of motherhood. Paper presented to the Tenth BSA Medical Sociology Conference, York.

Pringle, M. K. (1974) *The Needs of Children: A Personal Perspective*. London: Hutchinson.

Radl, S. (1974) *Mother's Day is Over*. London: Abelard-Schuman.

Rainwater, L. assisted by Weinstein, K. (1974) *And the Poor Get Children*. New York: Franklin Watts.

Rainwater, L., Coleman, R., and Handel, G. (1959) *Workingman's Wife*. New York: Oceana.

Rapoport, R. and Rapoport, R. (1971) *Dual Career Families*. Harmondsworth: Penguin.

Rapoport, R., Rapoport, R., and Strelitz, Z. (1977) *Fathers, Mothers and Others*. London: Routledge and Kegan Paul.

Renne, K. S. (1970) Correlates of dissatisfaction in marriage. *Journal of Marriage and the Family* 32: 54–67.

Rheingold, H. L. (1963) *Maternal Behaviour in Mammals*. London: Wiley.

Rich, A. (1977) *Of Woman Born: Motherhood as Experience and Institution*. London: Virago.

Richards, M. P. M. (ed.) (1974) *The Integration of a Child into a Social World*. London: Cambridge University Press.

Richards, M. P. M. and Bernal, J. F. (1972) An observational study of mother-infant interaction. In Blurton Jones (ed.) *Ethological Studies of Child Behaviour*. London: Cambridge University Press.

Richards, M. P. M., Dunn, J. F., and Antonis, B. (1977) Caretaking in the first year of life: the role of fathers' and mothers' social isolation. *Child Care, Health and Development* 3: 23–36.

Richardson, S. A., Dohrenwend, B. S., and Klein, D. (1965) *Interviewing: its Forms and Findings*. New York: Basic Books.

Richman, N. (1974) the effects of housing on pre-school children and their mothers. *Developmental Medicine and Child Neurology* 16: 53–8.

—— (1976) Depression in mothers of pre-school children. *Journal of Child Psychology and Psychiatry and Allied Discipline*. 17: 75–8.

—— (1978) Depression in mothers of young children. *Journal of the Royal Society of Medicine* 71: 489–93.

Robson, K. S. (1967) The role of eye-to-eye contact in maternal-infant attachment. *Journal of Child Psychology and Psychiatry* 8: 13–25.

Rollin, B. (1970) Motherhood: myth or need. *Look* 22 September 1970. Reprinted in Peck and Senderowitz (eds) (1974) *Pronatalism*. New York: Crowell.

Rollins, B. C. and Cannon, K. L. (1974) Marital satisfaction over the family life cycle: a re-evaluation. *Journal of Marriage and the Family* 36: 271–82.

Rollins, B. C. and Feldman, H. (1970) Marital satisfaction over the family life cycle. *Journal of Marriage and the Family* 32: 20–8. Reprinted in Laswell and Laswell (eds) (1973) *Love, Marriage, Family: A Developmental Approach*. Brighton: Scott, Foresman, and Co.

Rossi, A. (1968) Transition to parenthood. *Journal of Marriage and the Family* 30: 26–39.

—— (1977) A biosocial perspective on parenting. *Daedalus* 106(2): 1–31.

Rubin, L. B. (1976) *Worlds of Pain: Life in the Working Class Family*. New York: Basic Books.

Russell, C. (1974) Transition to parenthood. *Journal of Marriage and the Family* 36: 294–302.

Rutter, M. and Brown, G. W. (1966) The reliability and validity of measures of family life and relationships in families containing a psychiatric patient. *Social Psychiatry* 1: 38–53.

Ryder, R. (1973) Longitudinal data relating marriage satisfaction and having a child. *Journal of Marriage and the Family* 35: 604–6.

Sackett, G. P. and Ruppenthal, G. C. (1974) Some factors influencing the attraction of adult female macaque monkeys to neonates. In Lewis and Rosenblum (eds) *The Effect of the Infant on its Caregiver*. New York: Wiley.

Safilios-Rothschild. C. (1971) Towards the conceptualization and measurement of work commitment. *Human Relations* 24: 489–94.

—— (1973) The parents' need for child care. In Roby (ed.) *Child Care – Who Cares*. New York: Basic Books.

Sayers, J. (1982) *Biological Politics*. London: Tavistock.

Schaffer, H. R. (1971) *The Growth of Sociability*. Harmondsworth: Penguin.

—— (1977a) *Mothering*. Glasgow: Fontana/Open Books.

—— (ed.) (1977b) *Studies in Mother-Infant Interaction*. London: Academic Press.

Schaffer, H. R. and Emerson, P. E. (1964) The development of social attachments in infancy. *Monographs of Social Research in Child Development* 29: serial No. 94.

Schram, R. W. (1979) Marital satisfaction over the family life cycle: a critique and proposal. *Journal of Marriage and the Family* 41: 7–14.

Sears, R. R., Maccoby, E., and Levin, H. (1957) *Patterns of Child Rearing*. Evanston: Row, Peterson.

Seecombe, W. (1980) Domestic Labour and the Working-Class Household. In Fox (ed.) *Hidden in the Household*. Toronto: Women's Press.

Shorter, E. (1975) *The Making of the Modern Family*. Glasgow: William Collins, 1976.

Skolnick, A. (1973) *The Intimate Environment: Exploring Marriage and the Family*. Boston: Little, Brown, and Co.

Sobol, M. (1963) Commitment to work. In Nye and Hoffman (eds) *The Employed Mother in America*. Chicago: Rand McNally.

—— (1974) Commitment to work. In Hoffman and Nye (eds) *Working Mothers*. New York: Josey-Bass.

Spanier, G., Lewis, R., and Cole, C. (1975) Marital Adjustment over the family life-cycle: the issue of curvilinearity. *Journal of Marriage and the Family* 37: 263–75.

Stacey, M. (1981) The Division of Labour Revisited or Overcoming the Two Adams. In Abrams, Deem, Finch, and Rock (eds) *Practice and Progress: British Sociology 1950–1980*. London: George Allen and Unwin.

Steiner, M. (1979) Psychobiology of mental disorders associated with childbearing: an overview. *Acta Psychiat. Scand* 60: 448–64.

Stern, D. N. (1974) Mother and infant at play: the dyadic interaction involving facial, vocal, and gaze behaviours. In Lewis and Rosenblum (eds) *The Effect of the Infant on its Caregiver.* New York: Wiley.

—— (1977) *The First Relationship: Infant and Mother.* Glasgow: Fontana/Open Books.

Stone, L. (1979) *The Family, Sex and Marrriage in England, 1500–1800.* Harmondsworth: Penguin.

Thompson, B. and Finlayson, A. (1963) Married women who work in early motherhood. *British Journal of Sociology* 14: 150–68.

Thornton, A. (1977) Children and marital stability. *Journal of Marriage and the Family* 39: 531–40.

Tiger, L. and Shepher, J. (1977) *Women in the Kibbutz.* Harmondsworth: Penguin (Peregrine).

Tomkins, S. S. (1965) The biopsychosociality of the family. In Coale, Fallens, Levy, Schneider, and Tomkins *Aspects of the Analysis of Family Structure.* Princeton: Princeton University Press.

Townsend, P. (1979) *Poverty in the United Kingdom.* London: Allen Lane.

Townsend, P. and Davidson, N. (1982) *Inequalities in Health: the Black Report.* Harmondsworth: Penguin.

Trause, M. A., Klaus, M., and Kennell, J. (1976) Maternal behaviour in mammals. In Klaus and Kennell (eds) *Maternal – Infant Bonding.* St Louis: Mosby.

Turnbull, C. (1974) *The Mountain People.* London: Pan Books.

Turner, C. (1969) *Family and Kinship in Modern Britain: An Introduction.* London: Routledge and Kegan Paul.

Valman, H. B. (1980) Mother-infant bonding. *British Medical Journal* 280: 308–10.

Veevers, J. (1973a) the child-free alternative: rejection of the motherhood mystique. In Stephenson (ed.) *Women in Canada.* Toronto: New Press.

—— (1973b) Voluntary childless wives: an exploratory study. *Sociology and Social Research: an International Journal.* Reprinted in Peck and Senderowitz (eds) *Pronatalism.* New York: Crowell, 1974.

—— (1973c) The social meanings of parenthood. *Psychiatry* **36**: 291–310.

Veroff, J. and Feld, S. (1970) *Marriage and Work in America*. New York: Van Nostrand.

von Mering, F. H. (1955) Professional and non-professional women as mothers. *The Journal of Social Psychology* **42**: 21–34. Reprinted in Theodore (ed.) *The Professional Woman*. Cambridge, Mass.: Schenkman, 1971.

Walters, J. and Stinnett, N. (1971) Parent-child relationships: a decade review of research. *Journal of Marriage and the Family* **33**: 70–111.

Weiss, R. (1969) The fund of sociability. *Transaction* **7**: 36–43.

—— (1973) *Loneliness: The Experience of Emotional and Social Isolation*. London: MIT Press.

Weiss, R. S. and Samelson, N. M. (1958) Social roles of American women: their contribution to a sense of usefulness and importance. *Marriage and Family Living* **20**: 358–66.

Whiting, B. B. (ed.) (1963) *Six Cultures: Studies of Child Rearing*. New York: Wiley.

Willmott, P. and Young, M. (1971) *Family and Class in a London Suburb*. London: Mentor.

Winnicott, D. W. (1956) Primary maternal pre-occupation. In Winnicott (1975) *Through Paediatrics to Psychoanalysis*. London: Hogarth Press.

—— (1960) The theory of the parent-infant relationship. *International Journal of Psychoanalysis* **41**: 585–95.

—— (1970) The mother-infant experience of mutuality. In Anthony and Benedeck (eds) *Parenthood*. Boston: Little, Brown, and Co.

—— (1975) *Through Paediatrics to Psychoanalysis*. London: The Hogarth Press.

Woodward, D. and Chisholm, L. (1981) The expert's view? The sociological analysis of graduates' occupational and domestic roles. In Roberts (ed.) *Doing Feminist Research*. London: Routledge and Kegan Paul.

Wortis, R. (1971) The acceptance of the concept of the maternal role by behavioural scientists: its effects on women. *American Journal of Orthopsychiatry* **41**: 733–46.

Young, M. and Willmott, P. (1962) *Family and Kinship in East London*. Harmondsworth: Penguin.

—— (1973) *The Symmetrical Family: A Study of Work and Leisure in the London Region*. London: Routledge and Kegan Paul.

Yudkin, S. and Holme, A. (1963) *Working Mothers and their Children*. London: Michael Joseph.

Zaretsky, E. (1976) *Capitalism, the Family and Personal Life*. London: Pluto Press.

NAME INDEX

SUBJECT INDEX

Names in italics are those given to individual women interviewed during the study whose comments are quoted in the text